"Profound! It is rare to find a book that ⸬
and examples, and the critical knowled
your life. Interesting and inspiring, Dav
**Dr Marshall Goldsmith**, the ⸬
Coach and *The New York Times* bestselling author of *The Earned Life*,
*Triggers*, and *What Got You Here Won't Get You There*

"David is a true eclectic, a curious skeptic, and coaching's most prolific writer. This book is a fitting testament to all that he has given to the field of coaching."
**Dr David Drake**, *The Moment Institute*

"This book is a feast to be savoured. It is David's fine interweaving of insight, humour, instruction, calculation, percipience, confidence and humility that make this book a triumph. If I had to choose only one source of knowledge to give to a coach, new or seasoned, this would be it. Thank you, David, for bringing your compelling and articulate self to every sentence, and to our lives."
**Nancy Kline,** President, Time To Think; Author,
*The Promise That Changes Everything* and *Time To Think*

"A conversation with David is always fun, enjoyable and spiced with learning, and this book is a rich David Clutterbuck conversation. David draws on all his rich gleanings from 75 years of learning, teaching, researching and practising, always keen to challenge himself and others and go to the next learning edge. To get the best from this rich conversation, I recommend having a good red wine and boundless curiosity with you, as well as responding with the learning and questions that it invokes for you."
**Professor Peter Hawkins**, Co-Dean with David of the
Global Team Coaching Institute, and chair of Renewal Associates

"It is a risk writing a book reviewing a career. The temptation to nostalgia or self promotion is great but even more so the rehashing of old ideas. David Clutterbuck is well aware of the risks and set out not to declare his achievements but rather to look at the journey he and indeed the fields of coaching and mentoring have taken. They are very much tied together since he is pre-eminent in shaping both disciplines. What might a reader of this book gain apart from a curiosity about the man and his work? An overview of major ideas influencing the field will certainly be one area. More important perhaps is the way ideas have been changing and the key place of learning his own and the practices in the field. David is a continuous learner in the best sense and is open to challenge and change – if the evidence so indicates. In 75 years he has written 75 books. I cannot claim to have read them all but those I have were influential in shaping thinking. Beyond this his contribution with others to creating the European Mentoring Centre and later the European Mentoring and Coaching Council has been of major significance in building a professional approach to coaching and mentoring. Do you need to know David's work to benefit from reading? No. Will you gain from it? Yes. It is a short trip through our history as well as an account of a personal journey. Definitely a good read and one that appropriately marks David's career and contribution for which we are grateful."
**Professor David A. Lane**, Director,
Professional Development Foundation, Middlesex University

# Coaching and Mentoring

This book represents both a milestone and a celebration. It brings together in one place all the theories and models that have emerged from the work of David Clutterbuck, one of the last surviving, first pioneers of coaching and mentoring, who has significantly helped to shape the field; and is published as his 75th book at the age of 75.

Many of the models and approaches familiar to coaches and mentors are based on David's prolific research, writing, and practice, from Systemic Talent Management, through Team Coaching from a Complex, Adaptive Systems perspective, Personal Reflective Space, to the Diversity Awareness Ladder. In bringing more than 60 of these innovations into one volume, the book provides an invaluable contribution to the practice of coaching, and puts the evolution of coaching theory into context, tracing its development over time. This book is a one-stop-shop for coach practitioners and students to get up to speed and understand these foundational models.

This book will appeal to coaches and HR professionals across the world, at all levels.

**David Clutterbuck** is one of the original pioneers of coaching and mentoring and co-founder of the European Mentoring & Coaching Council, EMCC Master Practitioner, author of more than 70 books and visiting professor at four universities. David is practice lead for Clutterbuck Coaching and Mentoring International Limited – a global network of researcher-trainer-consultants specialising in coaching and mentoring across 100+ countries.

# Coaching and Mentoring

A Journey Through the Models, Theories, Frameworks and Narratives of David Clutterbuck

**David Clutterbuck**

Routledge
Taylor & Francis Group

LONDON AND NEW YORK

Designed cover image: Getty Images / olaser

Illustrations by Lisa Cooper

First published 2023
by Routledge
4 Park Square, Milton Park, Abingdon, Oxon OX14 4RN

and by Routledge
605 Third Avenue, New York, NY 10158

*Routledge is an imprint of the Taylor & Francis Group, an informa business*

*British Library Cataloguing-in-Publication Data*
A catalogue record for this book is available from the British Library

*Library of Congress Cataloging-in-Publication Data*
Names: Clutterbuck, David, author.
Title: Coaching and mentoring: a journey through the models, theories,
frameworks and narratives of David Clutterbuck/David Clutterbuck.
Description: Abingdon, Oxon; New York, NY: Routledge, 2023. |
Includes bibliographical references and index. |
Identifiers: LCCN 2022032298 (print) | LCCN 2022032299 (ebook) |
ISBN 9781032346595 (hbk) | ISBN 9781032348223 (pbk) |
ISBN 9781003323990 (ebk)
Subjects: LCSH: Executive coaching. | Mentoring.
Classification: LCC HD30.4 .C587 2023 (print) | LCC HD30.4 (ebook) |
DDC 658.4/07124–dc23/eng/20220711
LC record available at https://lccn.loc.gov/2022032298
LC ebook record available at https://lccn.loc.gov/2022032299

ISBN: 978-1-032-34659-5 (hbk)
ISBN: 978-1-032-34822-3 (pbk)
ISBN: 978-1-003-32399-0 (ebk)

DOI: 10.4324/9781003323990

Typeset in Bembo
by Deanta Global Publishing Services, Chennai, India

If you don't look back at yourself and think, "Wow, how stupid I was a year ago," then you must not have learned much in the last year.

Bridgewater founder Ray Dalio, quoted in Adam Grant's *Think Again*

Dedication

I count myself fortunate to have the support of so many good friends and colleagues around the world, who have challenged my thinking, been my mentors, and collaborated with me on hundreds of projects. If I listed all those to whom I feel gratitude, it would cover several pages. So, I confine the mentions here to those, who are no longer with us: my first mentor, Wilf Tallis, my role model Peter Drucker, my great friend and co-writer, David Megginson, and the energetic Sir John Whitmore and Eric Parsloe, who both helped shape the field of coaching. To all those, who are still here, I would like to say thank you and remind them that I am looking forward to working with them in another quarter century of creative stimulation in coaching, mentoring, leadership, and beyond!

# Contents

# Author's note

Much of the text in this book is extracted from the hundreds of articles and blogs I have created over the decades. The copyright of these rests with the original publication. Many of these articles and blogs as well as the via the online Coaching and Mentoring Resource can be accessed via my website http://www.clutterbuck-cmi.com/

# Concepts and models

## Chapter 1

Levels of listening
Power of BDQs (bloody difficult questions)
Matrix of questioning perspectives
The nature of dialogue
Influence of context on how people communicate,
Communication style
Questions to enhance the quality of meetings
The structure of learning conversations, the
Seven conversations of leadership, the
Four conversations of systemic talent management,
How communications create value in organisations

## Chapter 2

Listening modes
Powerful questions
Four questioning perspectives
Debate, discussion and dialogue
The influence of context on how people communicate
Communication style
Structure of learning conversations
Questions to enhance the quality of meetings
Seven dialogues of leadership
Four conversations of systemic talent management
How communications create value in organisations
How words create ideas

## Chapter 3

Seven questions for social action
Ten balances of leadership

## Chapter 6

Seven steps of traditional coaching
Situational model of line manager coaching
Questioning cycle for coaching
Styles of line manager coaching
The coaching energy field
Stages of development of a coaching culture
The coaching culture quality model
Coaching culture diagnostic
Coaching and mentoring strategy
Building coaching cultures inside teams
Coach assessment and development centres
The role of the coaching and mentoring programme manager

## Chapter 7

Methods of helping to learn
Coach maturity
Goal commitment
How goals emerge
Goal evolution
Seven conversations of coaching
A systemic view of supervision

## Chapter 8

Six types of learning team
Drivers and barriers to team learning
Key processes for team learning
Developmental roles for team learning
Where high performing teams focus
PERILL – a complex, adaptive systems model of team function and dysfunction
The team development plan
Teams of teams
New team formation
BEAU teams – Business *Evolving* As Usual

## Chapter 9

Ethical mentoring
Democratisation of coaching
Decolonisation of coaching
Raising client awareness of ethical issues
Partnering with Artificial Intelligence

# Figures

# Introduction

Reaching 75 years is a minor but personal significant achievement. Reaching 75 books – as an author, co-author, or editor – is perhaps more notable. (Especially when the number doesn't include my children's stories!) Six months before the big day, I realised what an opportunity this milestone was to review the learning I have acquired over five decades and bring together in one collection some of the concepts, models, and frameworks I have developed with dozens of generous and stimulating colleagues over those years. Directly and indirectly, I have been privileged to touch the lives of hundreds of thousands of people around the world, sharing with them new ways of thinking that they can apply to the betterment of themselves and others. However, few, if any, will have been exposed to the breadth of these ideas. This book is an attempt to remedy that omission.

My first question to myself, on coming up with the idea for this book, was "Is this just an old man's vanity?" I have a deep-seated and long-lived aversion to self-promotion, to the extent that I eschew engagement with top guru lists. It's only occasionally that I remember to take any of my books to conferences and workshops. To answer my question, I reflected upon three further questions:

- What will others find useful learning?
- What can I learn from the compilation?
- What would Wilf say?

Wilf, I should explain, was my first mentor. He was small and wrinkled – the closest person I have ever seen to Yoda – and my English teacher. A descendant of the composer Thomas Tallis, he was the archetypal eclecticist. Our lessons would invariably diverge into an unfathomable well of interesting facts and ideas from algebra, architecture, astronomy – and that was just the A's. I learned two very valuable lessons from Wilf. One was that every subject was fascinating, if you approached it with open eyes and curiosity. The other was that creativity and innovation come about by blending ideas from different, often unrelated disciplines.

DOI: 10.4324/9781003323990-1

From a first degree in English Language and Literature (with a minor in Old Norse) an early career in journalism was probably inevitable. Becoming a *science* journalist was not and I owe that move to the eclectic spirit that Wilf had instilled in me. My role on the journal *New Scientist* (of which I am still a subscriber more than 50 years later) was to make developments in science and technology in one area understandable and accessible to scientists in another. Joining the dots between disciplines became a habit.

After three years I moved from science into management science, working for McGraw-Hill on a now-defunct journal *International Management*. I soon learned that academics in management and social sciences also had difficulty in connecting their narrow research to bigger themes and other bodies of knowledge. Once again, it was my role to make their work accessible to the wider world. Ten years later, I left to set up my first formal business venture, in employee communication, in parallel with being an independent management journalist. My first week out on my own I worried how I would make a living. The second week, I realised I was going to do alright. The third week I hired the first of a series of young assistants, almost all of whom I mentored to become successful journalists in their own right.

At that point I had written just one book, on corporate social responsibility. Several more followed rapidly, but most significantly, *Everyone needs a mentor*, published in 1985. Now soon to be in its sixth edition, this was the first book on developmental mentoring and appeared at the same time as a book by the American academic, Kathy Kram, whose research had stimulated my interest in mentoring. Kathy's depiction of mentoring was very US-centric, mixing the concepts of sponsorship and mentoring (which we now know to be broadly incompatible). I didn't know it at the time, but mentoring and its newly born sibling coaching had got me by the short and curlies and was never going to let go.

The transition from journalist to academic (or as I prefer "pracademic" – both practitioner and academic) was gradual but inexorable. The employee communication business, ultimately sold to the employees in a management buyout, stimulated a stream of studies in areas such as the actual contribution of employee communication departments (unrelated to what they judged their performance on!) and communication styles.

Research into mentoring brought me into contact with an academic who was to become my greatest friend, collaborator, and critic, David Megginson. Together, we formed the European Mentoring Centre, in 1991, with the first conference at Sheffield Hallam University the following year. This organisation evolved into the European Mentoring and Coaching Council, as the world of coaching became too big to be ignored.

Along the way, I found myself drawn into the world of corporate governance, co-writing one of the first books on being a non-executive director, advising the Czech government on privatisation and leading new director programmes for the UK National School of Government. Inevitably, this too led to multiple research projects and the development of frameworks for Board effectiveness.

I also brought together the worlds of marketing and human resources, exploring how HR could be more effective through authentically marketing itself within the organisation. Then, around the turn of the century, my attention switched to four intertwined themes, all of which still preoccupy me today: coaching culture, coach maturity, systemic talent management, and team coaching. Along the way, I developed an interest in how artificial intelligence could enhance (or threaten) coaching and more recently, the potential for coaching in virtual reality.

## Stretching boundaries: a new challenge every year

People sometimes mistake me for an adrenaline junkie. I've jumped off the side of a helicopter with a parachute (tied firmly to an instructor), canoed down crocodile-infested rivers, skied off the side of a mountain with a parachute (and another instructor) on my back, tried by hand at caving, and – scariest of all – learned to be a stand-up comedian. Truth is, I'm not actually very good at any of these things, though stand-up and improv have been useful in my role as a public speaker. I get to be good enough. I also get very scared, but I do things anyway. And I do them because I learn about myself, the world around me, and the people within it. I am curious about my fear and how understanding it can help me be more effective in helping others. And it is exhilarating to know that I have grown just a little bit more.

I recall vividly standing on a ledge on a mountain in the Canadian Rockies. The name of the mountain was Mount Clutterbuck[1] and it had only been climbed once before, a few years ago. It seemed a fitting way to celebrate my 60th birthday. We had reached this point after days of trekking through the wilderness in a conservation area that required special permission to enter. Setting out from our base camp early in the morning, we had ascended a glacier and then gradually made our way up the side of a gaunt pinnacle. At the point I had stopped, there was nothing in front but a drop of hundreds of metres. One of our two guides had ascended to the top, just 50 metres away. Behind me on the ledge was my son, Daniel and behind him the second of our guides. I could not see how I was going to gain the purchase I needed to ascend. In the end, I told myself: "The guide will keep me safe. I have travelled so far to get to this point. I'm not giving up now." I don't know how I found the holds that took me to the top. I just know that I was in a determined, focused blur for what seemed like no time, before that welcome hand reached out to haul me over the last edge.

I set myself at least one new challenge each year. Most of them don't require me to overcome fear. Covid put a damper on several things I had intended to do, but I found outlets to be stretched in more placid activities, such as expanding my repertoire as a cook or trying my hand at glass engraving. Every new area of learning I embrace gives me new perspectives that I can integrate into what I do and who I am.

I now realise that that process of integration is what distinguishes two forms of eclecticism. One form, which we see frequently in the world of coaching, is the jackdaw approach – constantly acquiring new shiny somethings to adorn the nest. The other form of eclecticism seeks to find the connections between acquisitions of knowledge and experience. So, when I picture my small group standing on the top of our Canadian peak, with no other humans for perhaps 50 miles in any direction, I connect that with having the courage to question my deepest assumptions, looking down on them from a viewpoint that says: "Wouldn't it be exciting if I were wrong?"

The eclectic approach can be daunting (where is the horizon?) but has stood me in good stead. I always have at least three research projects on the go at the same time. Creating models and frameworks is important partly to help me and my colleagues understand the phenomena we are observing; but equally important in making them accessible to others.

The models and frameworks presented in this book are chosen either because they have had the most impact, or because I particularly like them, or because I think they may stimulate new thinking in the readers. Whether you read from cover to cover, pick out the cherries, or dip in from time to time, I recommend you keep in mind the value of an eclectic approach. Having lots of disconnected bits of knowledge is only marginally useful. It's how you make the connections that count. Look for the connections between the ideas in this book and your existing knowledge bank. And, if you discover connections between ideas in this book that haven't occurred to me, let me know – I will be grateful!

David Clutterbuck 2022

## Note

1 That was the name given to it by the Canadian Government 100 years ago, but it undoubtedly already had a name from the indigenous peoples.

# 1 The importance of evidence-based approaches

My role as a management journalist gave me access to the world's leading thinkers and innovators in management. My role model and for a time mentor was the legendary Peter Drucker. One of my favourite quotes from him was along the lines of *When I was a journalist, I thought journalism was just badly done academic research. Now I am an academic, I realise that research is often just badly done journalism.* It's a lesson I took to heart as my own career took a similar shape.

One day, Peter jokingly told a small group of us in Oxford, with a twinkle in his eye, *Being an authority has its advantages. Sometimes I'm stuck for a statistic. If I make one up, no-one will question it!* From this was born an experiment. At a *Financial Times* conference on total quality and customer care, I was giving a presentation to an audience of several hundred. In the middle of my session, I slipped in the comment that "Research shows that it always costs at least five times more to gain a new customer than to keep an existing one." When it came to questions, I expected at least someone to query the statement. No-one did and that statistic can now be found in 98.34% of all textbooks on customer care. (Just kidding – but you would be surprised at how many students fall for the follow-on false statistic!) A few years ago, I corresponded with the Nobel Prize winner Daniel Kahneman about the psychology of this. His explanation was that if something fits with what we expect and is said by someone with a level of authority, the human brain is conditioned not to query it.

As a management journalist, I stumbled across many intriguing ideas. One was what we now know as 360-degree feedback, which originated in a heavy engineering factory in St Petersburg, then Leningrad. Designed by the Communist trade union as a means of keeping line managers from getting above themselves, I did some of the first experiments with the concept in the West. I deeply underestimated the impact of giving the top team of a large financial services company feedback they would never have received before. Yet, when they recovered from the shock, the executives all wanted to repeat the exercise a year later.

One of the lessons learned was not to fall into the trap of using 360 as a policing mechanism. Unfortunately, 360 is a classic example of a good idea distorted by consultants out to make a buck, without carrying out research to

DOI: 10.4324/9781003323990-2

*Table 1.1* My learning journey

| My Learning Journey | | |
| --- | --- | --- |
| Science is fact | Science is the best understanding of the evidence we have now – but "facts" will change as we continue to learn | Science and philosophy are intricately linked and constantly influence each other |
| Seeking the evidence for and against a hypothesis | Seeking a hypothesis from the evidence | Assuming that everything we think we know from the evidence is "a temporary truth" |
| Research creates clarity | Research is often contextual – change the context and everything changes with it | Research is an adventure where the outcomes include changes in the researcher |

understand the tool in its context. Hence, most 360 instruments we see today break all the rules of evidenced good practice:

- They use the same questionnaires for everyone, regardless of context or job role
- Feedback givers are imposed
- They use the results to try to force the employee to focus their development on broad competences that may or may not be relevant to the requirements of their role
- They substitute for co-learning conversations rather than enhance them

In an effective 360-degree feedback process:

- The feedback receiver is in control of the process and selects (with agreement from stakeholders) the few key areas they want feedback on
- They are supported in crafting the questions they want to ask (feedback givers can be useful here)
- They select people to give feedback, whose opinion they will respect and value (paradoxically, they are *more* likely to include people they don't count as friends)
- Feedback givers have a subsequent responsibility to support the receiver in making changes – for example, by giving subsequent in-the-moment feedback

I spent a while a decade or so ago working for a large US consultancy. I was asked to fill in a 360 on people I rarely met. The questionnaire was full of vague statements, such as "Lives the company values." When I asked exactly what those values were, no-one could tell me …

I learned early on to take a deeply sceptical look at all consultancy models. What is the actual evidence? I learned too that academics can also be lured by consultancy fees to distort their own research findings.

There are two phenomena that give rise to dodgy consultancy models. One happens when consultants draw on limited, personal experience and then cherry-pick from the evidence-based literature to create an air of scientific validity. (It always reminds me of advertisements for hair shampoo that use scientific language that sounds credible but means nothing to the consumer.) An example of this is Patrick Lencioni's dysfunctions of a team. It's a good read, full of practical advice and tools. All of the factors in the model reflect evidence from research into team effectiveness. But the literature as a whole refers to many other factors and one of the most important of all – external influences – does not appear anywhere in the Lencioni model. The claims of cause and effect don't stand up, not least because this is a linear model trying to describe a complex, adaptive system.

The other phenomenon is where a good piece of research is distorted and used in a context for which it was never intended. An example of this is Tuckman's model of forming, storming, norming, and performing. Originally a desk study of the evolution of groups of patients in therapy for conditions such as depression, it had little relevance to teams. A large-scale study for the US government found that only 2% of new project teams actually followed the pattern described. The dynamics of teams and groups are not the same and we now realise that trying to follow this model may actually slow down the development of teaming.

What we have in both of these examples is a reflection of the phenomenon in my customer care experiment. If it sounds plausible and is presented with authority, it's likely to be accepted.

I also find it helpful to distinguish between science and philosophy. Science helps us recognise the patterns and rules that underpin how our worlds work. Philosophy helps us connect our understanding of the world with our own and other people's values. The Enneagram is a product of philosophy. It has no science behind it and in fact to try to give it a scientific underpinning would miss the point. Both science and philosophy give us languages and perspectives to explore an issue and grow in insight. It's being able to integrate the two perspectives that gives the most profound learning. We shouldn't be too surprised at this – after all, PhD stands for Doctor of Philosophy.

Having companies of my own to run provided lots of opportunities to experiment. We were the first organisation (to my knowledge) in the world to encourage everyone to create their own job titles. The reasoning was that they knew how they added value far better than I or my fellow directors. Within each department, the employees agreed on their collective job title and any individual titles that reflected job specialisations. One person in the company was not allowed to do this, however – me! With some trepidation, I awaited the title they had crafted for me – knowing as Chairman, I could turn it down, but being aware of the impact that would have on their motivation. They

RECOGNISE AN ISSUE NEEDS ATTENTION — GATHER DATA — IDENTIFY PATTERNS — EXTRACT MEANING — IDENTIFY POTENTIAL FOR CHANGE — CREATE IMPETUS FOR CHANGE

*Figure 1.1* Everyday research in the workplace.

chose Grand Master of Chaos, to reflect my role as a positive disruptor and innovator. I wore the title with pride!

For the past 25 years or so, I have had a foot in both academia and practice. Hence my neologism, *pracademic*. Particularly in coaching and mentoring, there are growing numbers of practitioners who take an evidence-based approach and are engaged in developing the evidence base for good practice; and academics, who are also highly experienced practitioners. I would like to have contributed more to the development of research methods in my fields of interest, but I can only claim to have championed the use of multi-method studies (for example, qualitative and quantitative, longitudinal and dyadic, as in my own PhD) and the value of academic-practitioner partnerships.

Given, however, that this is a book about models, frameworks, and concepts, I do have one model (See Figure 1.1) that addresses the research method. It relates to evidence-based decision-making and problem-solving in the workplace. The difficulties and wasted effort (and sometimes catastrophes) that arise from instinctive jumps from problem to solution are explored in depth in Daniel Kahneman's heavyweight book *Noise*.[1] There are several well-founded and generally effective tools and processes for decision-making, but these can only work if the data is accurate, relevant, and in context.

In this model, the starting point is *recognising that an issue needs attention*. It could be the result of feedback, or something going wrong, or a sensed opportunity. Things often go wrong here when, for example:

- The issue is seen as discrete and self-contained, when it is part of a bigger issue or cluster of connected issues
- It is posed as a statement rather than a question (e.g., Not: "We have to fix this for our customers," but "what do our customers need us to do about this?")
- The individual or team moves straight to solutions that have worked before, without considering what has changed or is different

The second step is *gathering data*. Among the many things that can go wrong here are:

- Administering questionnaires without checking how people from different backgrounds or cultures will interpret the questions
- Lumping together groups of people who may have very different perspectives
- Missing out significant but less obvious stakeholders who may have a different perspective

Once you have data, you can start to analyse it. Whether you use quantitative data analysis or qualitative, thematic analysis, it's the *patterns* that emerge that make the data useful. One of the big dangers here is that we tend to notice more easily and attach more weight to patterns we expect, compared to those we don't expect, or which challenge our existing narrative about the issue. One of the big lessons for me over the years has been, wherever possible, to involve survey participants in reviewing the data. They often spot patterns that I was blind to. That's one of the downsides of being a subject matter expert![2]

Another common error is to move straight from pattern identification to solutions. To be sure you are addressing the right issues, it's essential to go back to step one and reconnect with the purpose of the investigation. Only then should we move to the next stage of *extracting meaning*. Here we look at the implications, for ourselves and for stakeholders. We can also bring in contexts such as time horizons. Is this something that needs a quick fix? Or a much longer-term, deeper issue that requires continuous monitoring?

Only then should we come to *identify potential for change*. Based on the data, what changes are possible and practical? What conversations need to happen with stakeholders to ensure the changes will be accepted?

Finally, we need to create *impetus for change*. Paradoxically, we have to start thinking about this step right at the beginning. After all, what's the point of investing all that effort, if we are not going to do anything as a result of the research results? I recall interviewing a senior marketing executive in a Global 500 top company about how they got inside the minds of their customers. He took me into a side office with cupboards full of files and reports. "We add about a dozen every month," he said. "How many lead to significant change?", I asked. "About one in 20," he replied. No prizes for guessing what his need for coaching was!

I am, I admit, hopelessly addicted to surveys. They are invaluable in providing context for books and articles, identifying trends and creating a starting point for crafting research questions for deeper, more intensive research. I coined the term QUAD Research (Quick and Dirty) to describe the initial scoping surveys that provide a brief helicopter view of an unexplored or underexplored topic area. These don't involve any analysis; they just give an indication of themes and perspectives to be explored. Yet they are an invaluable first step.

As a dedicated iconoclast, I also enjoy being the kid in the crowd who points out that the king has no clothes. In all my areas of interest – leadership, human resources, coaching, and mentoring particularly – I am deeply unimpressed by the weight of academic literature and much more interested in the quality. As we will explore in Chapter 4, most academic literature on mentoring is of marginal value, because it is a house or cards built on the shaky foundations of conflating very different roles and viewing the topic through one specific cultural lens.

I'm not sure at what point I realised that every scientific "fact" is a statement in time, based on the data we have now, which could be overturned by different experiments at a later time. This book is to a considerable extent an account of my adjustments in thinking to take account of new evidence – and at the same time of the evolution of understanding in the professions of coaching, mentoring, and leadership. I have found being ahead of thinking in these professions to be fun. I recall, for example, presenting to HR audiences the conclusions of my study into the efficacy of HR standard approaches to talent management and succession. When I explained that much of this practice was part of the problem rather than part of the solution, quite a few people walked out. Yet just two or three years later, the data having spoken for themselves, these controversial concepts became part of the normal narrative.

There is a price to pay for being an iconoclast, of course. You have to be prepared for other people to challenge your own ideas, often robustly. I've been privileged to have multiple colleagues, who do that for me frequently. I hope they continue to do so!

### Notes

1  Kahnemann, D, Sibony, O and Sunstein, CR, (2021), *Noise: A Flaw in Human Judgement.*
2  My definition of an expert is "someone whose great knowledge gets in the way of their learning."

# 2 Communications

Right from about the age of ten, I knew I was going to be a writer. I recall being fascinated by Agatha Christie novels and trying (very badly) to emulate her style. Not surprisingly, I took arts topics rather than science at school and was set on a path towards studying English Language and Literature at university by my first mentor, Wilf Tallis. I didn't know it at the time, but I was fortunate to be in the hands of one of the finest mentors a young man could wish. A consummate eclectic, Wilf's lessons meandered into multiple areas of science, architecture, history, astrophysics, and other esoteric subjects.

I learned in those lessons the power of words to inspire, to make someone think, to release creativity, and make connections between different bodies of knowledge. I was hooked!

A degree in English Language and Literature (with a minor in Old Norse) led me naturally into … science. I became the first non-scientist writer on *New Scientist*, with a remit to make technology from one field intelligible to scientists from another. I learned quickly that, frequently, scientists needed a translator – someone, who could turn their esoteric jargon into language that was meaningful and relevant to people in other specialisms. After three years, I moved into management journalism, where I found that management scientists had the same problem.

Over time, I recognised that most problems in organisations were communications issues. Missed communication, bungled communication, inauthentic communication – these failings lay at the heart of every failure of leadership.

In 1982, after ten years with McGraw-Hill, I and a colleague from the same company set up one of the first employee communication boutiques. With a lot of boot-strapping, it grew to nearly 50 people, before the collapse of the sector in the late 1990s caused everyone to hunker down for survival. As the only substantial boutique company in the sector to survive, I had the luxury of being able to learn how to make myself obsolete – to the extent that I felt in the way every time I came to the office. One management buyout later, I started to disengage from active involvement in employee communication. On the way, however, we had engaged in a wide range of original research in the field, created the Association for Strategic Planning in Communication, and strengthened my belief in the power of the right conversation at the right

DOI: 10.4324/9781003323990-3

*Table 2.1* My learning journey

| My learning journey | | |
| --- | --- | --- |
| Listening is an innate skill | Listening is a rare skill | Listening is a state of attentiveness that bridges internal and external awareness |
| The key to good communication is being articulate | The key to good communication is enabling others to be articulate | The key to good communication is achieving multiple layers of dialogue |
| Clarity comes from structure and logic | Clarity is contextual and influenced by culture | Clarity is a chimera – we work with constantly evolving approximations |

time. Indeed, one of my definitions of leadership is the ability to have the right conversation when it will have the greatest positive impact.

This chapter looks at some of my key learning from this period and beyond. In particular, it explores the complexity of **listening**, the power of **BDQs (bloody difficult questions)**, the **matrix of questioning perspectives**, the nature of **dialogue**, the **influence of context on how people communicate, communication style, questions to enhance the quality of meetings**, the structure of **learning conversations**, the **seven conversations of leadership**, the **four conversations of systemic talent management, how communications create value in organisations** and **how words create ideas**.

## The complexity of listening

Ask a group of people how they rate themselves as good listeners and most will describe themselves as above average. In my observation, introverts tend to rate themselves lower as listeners than do extroverts, but are generally better listeners. To make it more complex, just because someone isn't saying anything doesn't mean they are listening – their attention may be far away. It's also extraordinary how defensive we become, when someone else accuses us of not listening – "Oh yes, I am. It's you who aren't listening to me!"

There are at least five levels of listening. The first is *listening while waiting to speak*. While this shows respect for the other person, the listener's thinking processes are focused primarily on determining what they are going to say, when their turn to speak arrives. In early-stage coaching and mentoring, it's common to divert attention to the question you are going to ask next, for fear of silence when the other person stops talking. With maturity, the coach or mentor learns to relish the silence as an opportunity to help the client reflect more deeply. The second is *listening to disagree*. You may be paying more attention to what the other person is saying, but only to find the fault in their logic or assumptions. Academics can be very accomplished at this. At both these levels, the listener is more concerned with their own ego than with the needs of the client.

A third form of listening is *listening to understand*. Here your attention is much more deeply on what the other person is saying, although your mind is still in parallel trying to extract meaning and significance from their words – making sense in your terms. A fourth level is *listening to help the client understand*, where the coach's focus of attentiveness shifts from themselves to the client and how they make sense of what they are saying. And finally, the fifth level involves *listening without intent* – relaxing into the moment, being hyper-aware of words, tone, body language, atmosphere, and other intangible elements of the conversation. Here, meaning emerges of its own accord and the coach can truly be said to be listening fully. Sometimes this highest level of listening involves no conversation at all – the two people may communicate in and through silence. In the words of the song – "You say it best, when you say nothing at all."

In my work with coaches and mentors, I learned that people have a "centre of gravity" – a level that they naturally gravitate towards. For most people, it lies with listening to understand. For mature coaches and mentors, it lies in listening to help the client understand. The good news is that it is relatively easy to shift your centre of gravity, by listening to yourself listening, developing your curiosity about what is happening for and in the other person, until a new habit is formed.

An axiom I have found useful in developing listening skills in myself and others is: *The moment you think you understand is when you need to listen twice as hard … .*

It is one of the most deceptive moments in coaching or mentoring. You have listened to the other person's story, trying to understand the situation. Eventually, there comes a moment, when it all seems to fall into place. We relax our listening and start thinking about what we can do to help them manage the issue they have raised.

But wait. All we have done at this point is make sense of the situation in the context of *our own* experience and the patterns we recognise from our own mental associations. Yet what really matters at this point is the sense the client is making – or wants to make – of his or her narrative. When we prioritise our own sense-making, we devalue theirs. So, the moment we think we understand is when we need to concentrate even harder on helping them articulate the patterns and insights that they see. To do that, we need to park our own insights, labelling them in our minds as "interesting, but premature."

What tends to happen, especially with coaches, who have a strong need to bring the client to a solution, is that we delude ourselves into thinking we are being non-directive, when in reality, the questions we ask are based on our own interpretations and sense-making. So, we lead the client into solutions that seem rational and relevant to us. The trust that exists between coach-mentor and client is such that the client abandons their own exploration of the issue and their own attempts at sense-making, deferring to what they perceive as our greater wisdom.

So, how can we overcome this instinctive tendency? Some practical ways include:

- *When our instincts tell us to say more, say less.* We don't have to share our own thoughts right away. Indeed, it is better to let our subconscious develop further links and associations that enrich the picture we have allowed to emerge
- *Be curious about how they are making sense of what they are saying.* Use questions, such as:
  - Who or what matters and is not in the picture?
  - What patterns are emerging for you?
  - What do you notice about yourself in giving this account?
  - What's the most liberating thought you could have right now?
  - What's unique in the way you are experiencing this situation?
  - What would be different in how you explain this, if you were being totally honest with yourself?

    (Notice that these questions contain nothing that relates to your own understanding of the situation.)
- *Use tools, such as getting them to draw the situation, which will capture their dominant metaphors.* Encourage them to take different positions in viewing each of the players (people or things) in their metaphor. If you also find that the drawing reinforces your own sense-making of the issue, *be curious.* Ask yourself, "What is it about me and my experience that draws me to see this pattern?"

Having gone through these steps, you may well find that your initial interpretation of the issue and its context was quite accurate and very similar to the perspective the client has worked their way towards. But this is now *their* discovery, not yours, and likely to have a much higher impact on them as a result.

Finally, in your subsequent reflections on the coaching session, consider:

- What did I learn about the client?
- What did I learn about myself?

### The power of Bloody Difficult Questions

I collect powerful questions – ones that make people stop and think at a level they would not normally reach. What makes them powerful is their immediate relevance, their unexpectedness, and the quality of empathetic challenge they carry. I have published some of the hundreds of such questions that I have developed and acquired over the years as the books *Powerful Questions for Coaches and Mentors* and *Powerful Questions for Team Coaches*. Analysing the questions in my collection revealed a pattern that can be highly useful for reflecting upon and improving how we generate and ask questions. While impactful questions typically emerge intuitively, that intuition can be refined and enhanced through subconscious recognition of patterns.

The characteristics of powerful questions that emerged from the analysis spell the acronym PRAIRIE. This translates to:

- *Personal.* Even if the question is an "off the peg" one, rather than tailor-made, it *feels* like it was specially chosen or crafted for this person at this time. Most of the time, it will include the word "you." The instinctive response of the person on the receiving end is that someone took the trouble to create this question especially for me
- *Resonant.* It has an emotional impact. The receiver experiences it at both a rational and an emotional level
- *Acute and incisive.* It gets right to the point. It's a thrust of a stiletto, not a swipe with a hatchet!
- *Reverberant.* It can't be answered more than superficially in the moment. It grows on you and keeps coming back for a deeper answer. It is relatively common, I have found, for coaching or mentoring clients to get back in contact to say "That question you asked me years ago – I've been thinking about it on and off for ages. Now finally, I think I have an answer." Significant changes in life or career can often be traced back to a powerful question
- *Innocent.* It has none of the questioner's agenda in it – no hidden vested interest. It is offered without strings or hidden intent
- *Explicit.* It is very simply expressed, even when it connects two or more ideas that were not linked before

Here are some powerful questions that aren't in either of the two published collections above. Think about your clients or people you work with. When might asking any of these questions be just what the other person needs?

- How lonely is it being you?
- What do you want to influence and how? (This relates particularly to what you have to let go of as you go up the leadership pipeline – such as controlling and achieving. The higher you go, the more you let go of each of these …)
- What are you doing that prevents other people from being totally honest with you?
- How could the person you are today become your future self's best friend?
- What is it you want to gift the world?
- What roles could you create for yourself that would facilitate you in making that gift?
- How could you make it more likely that this role will find you?

A particular kind of powerful question is the benchmark or touchstone question. This is one that an individual, team, or organisation can use as a backstop in making difficult decisions. It is deeply connected with personal and shared values. I first encountered the concept at Clark's the shoemakers, where any decision to spend money was tested against the question "But does it sell shoes?" Doing up the boardroom failed the test. Investing in employee development and welfare passed it.

Over the years, I have helped create numerous benchmark questions for others – and occasionally for myself. The changes in these questions reflect the changes in me and in my priorities. Every few years, I take time to review whether my benchmark question is still relevant and meaningful. An early example was: "Is this what my clients need?" At a later stage: "Will this make me respect myself more or less?" And currently, I am prone to ask both: "Will this be fun?" and "How does this relate to the legacy I want to leave?" It's not necessarily that one question replaces another: it's simply that the significance changes with circumstances, age, and perspective.

## Questioning perspectives

Observation of effective mentors and coaches at work indicates that they have the talent of keeping dialogue moving, primarily through switching perspectives. They rarely allow the learner to remain in the same mental state for long. They constantly shift the nature and style of the questions they ask. Analysis of how they change perspective suggests that they move around the quadrants of the matrix See Figure 2.1 below.

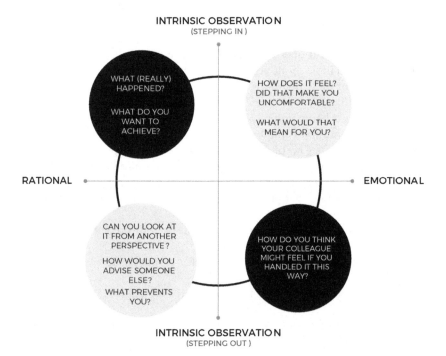

*Figure 2.1* Stepping out and stepping in.

*Table 2.2* Debate, discussion, and dialogue

|  | *Debate* | *Discussion* | *Dialogue* |
|---|---|---|---|
| Purpose | Promote a single perspective or opinion | Achieve a compromise | Co-creation |
| Relation to others | Ego-based | Recognise alternative perspectives | Ensuring all voices heard |
| Nature of conversation | Listening for fault or illogicality | Problem-solving | Deep listening, learning |

*Stepping into* the box is about acknowledging the individual's own perspectives, joining them to try to understand what they are thinking and feeling and why. Some people may come at an issue from a purely rational viewpoint, not wanting to explore their emotions for fear of what they might discover about themselves. Others may simply be too caught up in the emotion of a situation to think about it rationally.

*Stepping out* of the box is about helping them to distance themselves from the issue, either to examine it intellectually from other people's or broader perspectives; or to help them empathise with and understand the feelings of other protagonists in the situation under discussion.

To truly understand and deal with an issue, it is frequently necessary to explore it from each of these perspectives. A small insight into one perspective can generate progress in another and a skilled coach/mentor uses frequent shifts of questioning perspective to generate these incremental advances. In general, experienced coaches/ mentors will not spend more than four or five questions in the same quadrant. Moving from one quadrant to the next may require a bridging question (for example, *How helpful is this emotion? Or What emotion would you like to be feeling right now?*). Moving diagonally, rather than to an adjacent quadrant, tends to be too big a jump in most cases.

### There's never enough dialogue

Debate, discussion, dialogue – these are terms that are frequently confused. One of the first challenges for me was to try to sort out what the differences were. The table above captures the results.

Heading up an employee communications company, I naturally found myself actively engaged with the International Association of Business Communicators, where I learned that even professionals were so bound up by their cultural assumptions that they didn't communicate well. For example, the simple phrase "bring this to the table" meant one thing to a North American audience and completely the opposite to a European or South African audience

– leading to great resentment on both sides. There was no mechanism for recognising these conversational dislocations!

The potential for linguistic confusion was drilled home for me in other contexts. For example, a US-based multinational called me in to investigate why there was so much conflict around the results of the employee opinion survey. It quickly became apparent that no-one had checked whether the way people in different countries interpreted the meaning of the questions was consistent. So, to the question: "Do you feel challenged by your work?", North Americans would assume that it meant "Are you engaged with and energised by it?" Whereas Europeans, and particularly the English, would assume it meant "Are you struggling to cope?"[1]

One of the most profound of the communication studies I engaged with looked at how employee communications functions added value. The communication professionals typically measured success by factors such as awards for the employee journal. But these factors had a marginal impact on the effectiveness of the employee communication function. What did make a difference was how well they facilitated conversations between the leaders and the rest of the organisation – for example, in the flow of information, especially about the purpose and the quality of listening.

## The influence of context on how people communicate

As a very junior manager, I was sent on a leadership course that included a psychometric on communication style. It was loosely based on bits of the Myers-Briggs Type Indicator. I was naïve enough at the time to accept that both had a credible scientific underpinning. The first indication that they didn't was the realisation that the fault lines between different styles of communication we observed didn't match the personality profiles. Then several client companies asked me to explore a frequent occurrence in their performance appraisal systems. When managers rated direct reports as poor on communication, direct reports responded that, in reality, it was the manager, who was the poor communicator.

We engaged with a research team at the Birkbeck College, London, to investigate what was happening and subsequently develop a situational model of communication. Among the things we learned was that clarity of communication is often low because:

- People place different filters, based on culture, personality, or experience, on what they hear
- People often speak before they have sorted out in their mind *what they want to say* and *what impact they want it to have*. (Then they are surprised by the other person's reaction!)
- People are reluctant to cause themselves or others pain or embarrassment by pointing out directly things that they think are wrong
- People do not recognise their own or other people's stereotypes

- People often lack the verbal dexterity to express ideas concisely and accurately, or in language appropriate to the recipients
- Good communication requires an appropriate balance of intellectual observation/ analysis and emotional involvement. When the balance is disturbed, in either direction, communication is disrupted
- When there are too many ideas to be communicated at the same time, either the speaker or the receiver (or both) is likely to suffer from "channel overload."

These seven causes of low clarity in communication apply equally to individuals and to organisations. In both cases, considerable improvements can be made by a planned approach that helps the individual or organisation to address each factor as a development issue. Developing the competence of dialogue requires changes in both behaviour and process.

### *A tale with a moral (or two) to illustrate the concepts*

If there was one thing Arthur Harding prided himself on, it was being a good communicator. His verbal instructions and memos were always clear and unambiguous and even his e-mails were usually carefully crafted. Arthur was also a pretty good networker. He always knew who it was important to know and made sure that he kept in regular contact with them.

So, it was a double whammy for him to be told from two separate sources within the same week that he was actually a very poor communicator. As he confided to a friend at the gym after work, "It was the first time I'd done one of these 360-degree feedback exercises and I'm not sure I want to do it again. After all the effort I put into communicating, my staff and some of my colleagues say they don't think I'm any good at it. Worse, when I took it to my boss, he said he didn't think I communicated well either. I've been communicating all my life and suddenly I'm no good at it! When I asked what I could do about it, he said maybe they could find a course to send me on. Saying I don't communicate is like saying I don't think, or I lack judgement – I can't prove otherwise and I can't get my mind round what I have to change."

John paused before answering. "What sort of courses are on offer?"

"Well, the main one seems to be about presentation skills. But that's something I *know* I'm good at. I can't see that offering me anything that's going to make a radical difference in the short term," replied Arthur.

"You are probably right," John acknowledged as they climbed down from the exercise bikes and headed for the rowing machines. "Is there any pattern to when you communicate well or badly? After all, communication is a *situational* skill. You can be brilliant at communicating in one situation, but terrible in another."

"Give me an example."

John thought for a moment. "Let's say you are giving me an appraisal. You'll be listening to me – at least I hope you would – but it would be in a very different way from the way you're listening now or the way you'd listen to the audience if you were giving a speech. What makes a good communicator is being aware of the different situations and adapting how you respond in each of them."

"Doesn't that make it even more difficult to improve?"

"Not really, if you can identify those situations, where you most need to make changes. Stick with listening, for example. I'll bet you listened closely to what your boss was saying, because it was of real interest to you. But would you want to improve your listening skills for when we meet Luke, in the bar later? Remember how you described him to me last week as the club bore? Communication experts have identified nine different clusters of communication situations which managers commonly encounter. If you want to show some rapid improvement, identify and focus on those situations, which are most frequent and important in your job."

Back at work, Arthur sat down with a sheet of paper and tried to identify the communication situations he had to deal with. Then he talked his list through with his team and added a few more. Talking with them and with his boss, plus a couple of peers he trusted, he ranked these in order of importance. Then, using some notes John had e-mailed him about communication skills, he asked for feedback about how he used each of those skills in those priority situations. The results, he told John the next time they met at the gym, were quite sobering. "I learnt that I've got one problem that arises across all the situations – I don't give people sufficient time to think through what I've said. And I'm not good at getting other people to say what they think at team briefings. But I'm pleased to say that people think I'm good at giving instructions – it was such a blow to my ego when I thought that wasn't so."

The problem now, he explained, was how to tackle these improvement issues. "They are all so specific to me," he explained, "that I can't find a course that will help. I've looked at getting a coach, but that's expensive and what I really need is a chance to practise."

"Are there other managers who could be in the same boat?" asked John.

"I'm sure there are, although they may not all know it. You think maybe there's room for a mutual help group?"

It took a lot of courage to send out the e-mail asking if any other managers had a similar issue with communication, but Arthur was surprised by the number and enthusiasm of the responses. Several wanted to know more about how he had classified his different communication situations and almost all said they wanted an unthreatening environment, where they could practise specific skills in situations, that were important to them.

"So, I took all the responses to HR and asked them if they could help," he reported back to John. Once they got over the shock, they were very helpful. They provided a facilitator, who gave us some more theory about good communication, but mostly created opportunities for us to rehearse communication situations with each other. I came away with a lot more confidence about being able to demonstrate some real improvements. What worries me most, though, is how I'm going to sustain it. I've been on so many courses, and come back with good intentions that disappear when the pressure is on back at the coalface."

John's reply was not what he had expected. "How do you think communication works? Forget the theory, what's the bottom line?"

"Well, one person talks and the other listens. Then they might reverse roles," Arthur replied.

"So, if it takes two to tango, both parties need to put effort into communicating effectively. Would it make you feel better if you got them to consider how they can contribute to improving communication with you – in other words to how they might share the responsibility?"

"Yes, it would. And maybe I can get them to give me feedback on the spot, if they don't feel we're connecting. That way I can continue to tie my efforts down to something specific each time."

Over time, Arthur worked his way down his priority list, to the point where he was working on communication situations, which were more relevant to the job he hoped to be promoted to. He also found that he had become quite comfortable about giving other people direct and real-time feedback about their communication. "I find myself using the phrase *help me to understand* a lot," he told John. "That way, instead of telling someone they aren't communicating well, I'm sharing the blame, and they respond – well, better than I used to."

Arthur's story is based on an amalgam of several people, but it illustrates some basic truths about training people in communication skills. In particular:

- Most people resent being told they can't communicate. All too often, the problem lies as much with the other person. Recognising mutual responsibility is essential in creating appropriate learning attitudes
- Working on a few, targeted situational skills of immediate relevance to the individual is likely to produce better and faster results than attending generic training (in, for example, presentation or listening skills)
- Sharing concerns and learning with colleagues, who have similar issues, provides a sheltered environment to practice and the encouragement to do so
- Reinforcement in the workplace works best when it is focused on situational priorities

These should not be revelations to an experienced trainer, yet most organisations still structure their communication training along generic, one-size-fits-all lines. Twenty-first-century organisations are becoming increasingly reliant on the quality of their communication – indeed a study **item** carried out with the International Association of Business Communicators demonstrates a very strong link between communication quality and business performance – to the extent that it is now a significant competitive differentiator. Traditional training approaches are unlikely to achieve the breadth and depth of change in communication competence that is required. Time for a radical rethink on how to help the many Arthurs in our organisations.

## Communication style

We also identified eight archetypes of communication style, built around four dimensions (See Figure 2.2). These are not the only factors that define how people habitually communicate, but they do seem to capture the most significant. If we created a diagnostic tool around them, I have long forgotten it – and we certainly didn't put the model to rigorous testing to establish norms. The archetypes were:

- *Expander v Focuser.* Expanders tend to be intuitive thinkers, fascinated by ideas and things new. They often have great difficulty keeping to the subject, because they constantly see new possibilities. They can be very good at extrapolating from relatively thin data, sometimes making leaps of logic that only they can follow – but may often be broadly correct. They can often appear to other people as rambling and incoherent. Their favourite phrases include "Yes ... and ..." and "Here's another way of looking at the issue ... ."

  Focusers like to concentrate on one thing at a time and deal with it thoroughly. The vaguer a concept is, the more they feel the need to narrow the discussion, until there is something they can pin down. They are not necessarily without creativity, but they do not tolerate uncertainty and ambiguity well. They need to have a clear agenda for the discussion or dialogue. Their favourite phrases include "Let's be clear what we mean," "Let's get back to the point," and "What are we trying to achieve here?"

- *Tortoise v Hare.* Tortoises like to think before they speak. This may be partly from a concern not to embarrass themselves, but it is primarily a matter of needing to assess and weigh as they go along. They need to be sure they have understood each step of an argument before they proceed to the next. Tortoises often leave much unsaid. Depending on the circumstance, they can be seen at the extremes as "deep thinkers" or as dullards. They may switch out of a discussion for a while to ponder a statement or concept, then switch back when things have moved on. Their favourite phrases include: "Can we just stop and think about where we're going with this?" and "Can we just back up a bit?"

  Hares talk fast and a lot. They may often be perceived by tortoises as shallow, as overly concerned with presentation at the expense of content. They often see the implications of an argument one ahead of other people and may make their mind up about what to do before they have listened fully to the arguments. They may be seen most positively as decisive and productive, but others may see them as impetuous. Their favourite phrases include: "We have too many meetings here" and "This is getting too detailed."

- *Logician v Empath*. Logicians are determined to ensure that discussions are intellectually sound. They like to see the framework of a concept and test it against their perception of reality and coherence. They can be seen at their best as rigorous; at worst, as cold, pedantic, and argumentative. They accept no statement at face value and they may appear to others to pursue insignificant details to distraction, because something does not fit their pattern of logic. They are more concerned with being right than with building consensus. Their favourite phrases may include: "Where's the proof?" or "I don't think this hangs together."
- *Influencer v Conciliator*. Influencers like to get their own way. They are clear about their objectives for communicating and sometimes aggressive in achieving them. They employ consensus building only as long as it leads towards the answer they intended. They expend a lot of energy trying to bring others around to their viewpoint. They may be seen positively as visionary and results-oriented; negatively as obsessive, confrontational, and egotistical. Their favourite phrases include: "I can't see your problem" or "We (meaning I) need to make a decision."
- Conciliators are concerned to keep the group together and united. They are less worried about the outcomes of a discussion than the process by which decisions are reached. They are prepared to subordinate their own

*Figure 2.2* Communication styles.

views to those of the group, or to the other person in a one-to-one discussion, if that will ensure a broadly acceptable outcome. They will always prefer negotiation to confrontation. From a negative perspective, they may appear weak and unassertive; from the positive, they help to ensure that decisions taken have a broad commitment necessary from all parties if those decisions are to be implemented effectively. Their favourite phrases include: "We're all in the same boat" and "Let's not over-react ... ."

## Learning conversations

In my early experiments with mentoring, I observed dozens of mentors, both beginners and experienced, holding mentoring conversations. I was looking for discernible patterns in the flow of conversation and at the same time observing the quality of the conversations through the lenses of:

- Animation (were they both engaged?)
- Generation of new thinking
- Clarity about the learning and what the mentee was going to do with it.

The pattern that emerged was as follows:

- Firstly, the mentor re-established the human connection. They rarely started with "What do you want to talk about?". Rather, they established an interest in the person before getting to the issue the mentee wanted to explore. This is in stark contrast to the GROW model, where the focus is on the issue first and foremost – with being "person-centred" added as an afterthought
- Secondly, they encouraged the mentee to talk around the issue, exploring it from multiple perspectives – like adjusting a telephoto lens until the picture is sharp and clear
- At intervals, they would encourage a summary, with both drawing out themes they observe. This might lead them back into further exploration – commonly, there would be multiple cycles, like climbing a tree to check where they were
- Next, before getting into any form of solutioneering, the mentor would say or do something that would reinforce the mentee's self-belief. The Pygmalion Effect, in which someone takes on daunting tasks because someone, who they trust, believes in them, is in play here. This sense of belief in the mentee's potential wasn't always expressed in words – it was often an unconscious mental connection that was nonetheless patent to both the mentee and an observer
- When they did begin to look at how the mentee could respond to the issues they had identified, the longer they had spent in exploring the context of the issue in stage two, the simpler and faster the mentee was able to articulate his or her alternatives and what they would do next. Often, this

was what they would think about more deeply later – it wasn't essential to find a solution within the mentoring dialogue

- Finally, the most effective mentors ensured that the mentee summarised at the end. The less effective mentors often summarised for the mentee, taking control and inadvertently imposing their own ideas of what was important

The ending of learning conversations – and indeed conversations in general – also proved a rich area for observation and experimentation. Zoom and other virtual platforms have given us an opportunity to observe just how difficult people find it to conclude a conversation. It often becomes an awkward, fumbling dance with subtle and not-so-subtle clues being offered until both sides feel enough of the social niceties have been fulfilled to let go. One of the simplest and most effective tools I developed is the four Is, which stand for:

- Issues: what topics did we explore?
- Ideas: what new thinking emerged?
- Insights: what do we now see differently?
- Intentions: what are we going to do with our learning?

These four simple questions are now used not just by coaches and mentors but in thousands of companies across the globe to capture the content of meetings.

## Four questions to enhance the quality of meetings

I've observed hundreds of team meetings and I'm still amazed at how constrained the conversations are. There are a number of factors at work here. People don't like to give contrarian opinions, because they don't want to create discomfort, or be seen as disloyal. The more powerful and more extroverted people in the meeting tend to do most of the talking, so the potential contributions of the less powerful and the introverts often don't get heard – especially when whoever is chairing the meeting keeps watching the clock.

To overcome these problems, I introduced to teams I worked with – and to leaders to take back to their teams – three questions to ask before opening up any important topic, where different perspectives will enhance the quality of decision-making. Before any discussion takes place, everyone is asked to reflect upon:

1. What do I want to say about this issue? (Or what do I think needs to be said?)
2. What do I want to hear from others?
3. What do I want us to achieve from this conversation?

Everyone reveals their responses to the three questions before any discussion starts. The result is that the discussion is more focused, more respectful of other people's needs – and usually much shorter! When it is clear that a consensus is emerging, the person chairing the meeting can check with everyone:

- Did you say what you wanted to say?
- Did you hear what you wanted to hear?
- Did you achieve what you wanted to achieve?

But there is one last step that adds value to the discussion and that is *What hasn't been said that needed to be said?* This allows unvoiced concerns that arose during the conversation to be brought into the open.

## The seven conversations of leadership

A study in London in the first decade of this century measured what happened in offices, when managers spent just ten minutes each morning in brief individual conversations with team members – brief catchups and human reconnections without significant content. Team morale, work throughout, psychological safety and other positive factors increased as a result.

I had learned the importance of social dialogue when the company I led ran into a sector-wide downturn. We acquired a former competitor and moved to a smaller office – which meant that a third of the staff worked mostly or entirely from home. For these isolated employees, keeping in touch with the social news was a major need. Those coffee machine conversations that provide the social glue weren't available to them. So we developed a range of ways of keeping them in touch, including making sure that meetings started with the personal exchanges and gossip they were missing.

Social dialogue is just one of seven kinds of dialogue that leaders can beneficially stimulate within their teams. Each of the seven has increasing levels of depth and impact. Not included in this model are transactional conversations, such as asking for directions or giving instructions, as these are not dialogue.

Technical dialogue is an opportunity for the leader to explore with team members work processes, policies and systems. This might be to explain them to a newcomer and check their understanding, or to work out together how to improve processes.

Tactical dialogue helps people work out practical ways of dealing with issues in their work or personal life. This might encompass, for example, how to get round a difficult stakeholder in another team or how to prioritise workload.

Strategic dialogue takes a broader perspective, helping people put problems, opportunities and ambitions into context. It generates different perspectives and alternative scenarios. It may also involve testing strategies against values and comparing likely short-term, medium-term and long-term outcomes. It may create radical, game-changing alternatives.

Dialogue for self-insight shifts the focus away from doing and towards being. It may involve giving feedback, working with diagnostic tools, or co-learning as in a mentoring relationship. It enables people to understand their own drives, ambitions, fears and thinking patterns.

Dialogue for behavioural change is mostly about planning and monitoring how someone brings about changes in thinking and behaviour. It allows them to meld insight, strategy and tactics into a coherent programme of personal adaptation

Finally. integrative dialogue connects planning for personal development with their sense of identity and purpose. It enables them, for example, to develop greater balance in their lives and to resolve inner conflict. It's about helping someone become a whole person.

In multiple workshops, we have helped leaders at all levels in organisations reflect on which of these conversations they feel most comfortable with and which they engage in most. Everyone has preferences for some over others and many people are avoidant of one or more kind of dialogue. Knowing this gives them the opportunity to develop their skills in that area. Not surprisingly, the deficits for corporate leaders typically lie in the deeper levels, though many leaders may also not be too hot on the social dialogue!

## The four conversations of systemic talent management

The starting point for my research in the early 2000s was the question: "If HR practice in succession planning and talent management works, how come the wrong people so often get to the top?" The answer, after hundreds of inter-views with both senior executives and HR professionals, was straightforward. Not only did much of HR practice not work; in many cases, it was part of the problem rather than part of the solution. One of the reasons that this was the case was that so much of HR practice was (and still is) grounded in linear thinking, when the relationship between an organisation and its employees comprises a complex, adaptive system – in constant evolution and flux. The concept of systemic talent management emerged as a pragmatic approach to working with the complexity of that relationship.

Whenever I see a systemic failure, I ask "What is the conversation that should be happening, but isn't happening?" In this research project, it led me directly to four kinds of conversation. The more of these four conversations that happened, the more aligned the organisations and their employees seemed to be and the more rapidly and effectively they were able to realign around changed situations. The four conversations were:

- *Employee with self.* The employee's conversations with themselves, to raise self-awareness and awareness of the context, in which their career is taking place

- *Employee with manager.* The employee needs to have honest conversations with key stakeholders – and their manager, in particular – about how to maintain the pace of learning and gathering of experience that will help them grow into new roles
- *Organisation with its talent generally.* The organisation can align its aspirations and those of talented employee by engaging them in regular, frequent dialogue aimed at helping them create more informed personal career strategies and the organisation identify new opportunities to use the energy of its talent wave in achieving competitive advantage
- *The informal communication infrastructure.* This is the ultimate in distributed leadership – people at many levels in an organisation coming together through dialogue using virtual media, to provide leadership on emerging business issues. This appears increasingly to be where most innovation in organisations happens, rather than through the formal structures – though there are not enough studies to confirm this adequately

## How communication creates value in organisations

My work in corporate social responsibility, corporate governance and communication zeroed in on stakeholder communication in the mid-1990s. The model below (Figure 2.3)[2] was the result of interviews with internal communication professionals and CEOs. It aims to capture the essence of how an effective communication strategy supports business outcomes. The outstanding features of this system are its complexity and the volume of stakeholders involved. At that time (and still to a large extent now) communication functions in organisations focused on different stakeholder groups linearly and individually. Addressing the whole system and facilitating communications between stakeholders is more challenging, but holds out greater possibilities for an organisation to navigate in a VUCA environment. In Chapter 5, I present a model of the psychological contract that facilitates some of the required conversations.

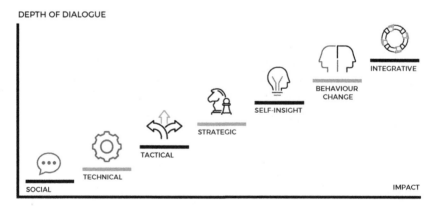

*Figure 2.3* Seven modes of dialogue.

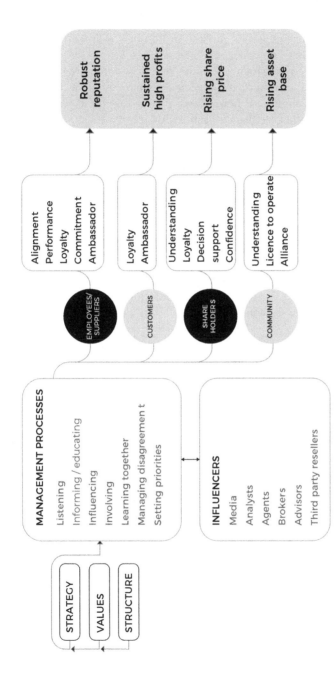

*Figure 2.4* The communication chain.

## How words create ideas

I am a dedicated logophile – I love words and especially neologisms. The power of words is illustrated by the example of an isolated tribe in a remote area of the world, whose vocabulary for numbers is limited to one, two, and many. So, they have no concept of mathematics. For ideas to become communicable, they need names and, for complex ideas, often a whole new vocabulary. Bizarrely, if we don't have a specific word for a colour, we don't "see" it.

The English language is rich in large part because of its wholesale adoption of words from other languages, each with a set of associations. The worlds of coaching, Human Resources, leadership, and mentoring similarly benefit from the insights and challenges of vocabulary from diverse languages and cultures.

Amongst my neologisms[3] I am fondest of are:

- Pracademic – the combination of practitioner and academic that produces research with practical value
- Screenager – teenager constantly on electronic gizmos
- Bambidextrous – lack of physical coordination, analogous to a newly born deer
- Snortsman – athlete on drugs
- 4-life-coach – once they get their hooks into you …
- Welfie – selfie showing how well-off you are

It's also fun to put new meanings to old words. For example, in reviewing the implications of coaching as a profession versus coaching as a vocation, it was clear to me that a middle ground was needed. The word I co-opted was pro-vocation.

Some of my favourite acronym coinings include:

- OSM: *Oh Sh … Moment* – that sudden tsunami of understanding that comes from a powerful question
- DNA: *Desperate Need for Alcohol*
- FKT: *Fast Knowledge Transfer (skinny coaching and mentoring focused on a simple transfer of knowledge or information)*
- QUAD: *Quick and Dirty*

There are also so many words that are unique to other languages; or at least unknown in English. Linguistic diversity is a diamond mine of new concepts, which can be applied to learning and self-reflection. An article in *New Scientist* introduced me to the fascinating word *rawa-dawa*, which comes from the Mundari language of the Indian subcontinent and means "the moment of suddenly realising you can do something reprehensible and no-one is there to witness it." Maori is just one of several languages that have a word that means simultaneously to learn and to teach. (In Victorian England, the ruffian who says "I'll learn you!" is looked down upon, yet has a point!) *Pena agena* is a

Mexican phrase that means the sense of shame for someone else's behaviour or lack of action.

The point of this short section is that we are all limited by the vocabulary available to us. I believe strongly that expanding our vocabulary is key to expanding our minds.

## Summary

Communication and particularly dialogue holds the key to all the other areas explored in this book. From leadership (leadership is the conversation that moves mountains) to coaching and mentoring, everything relies on the quality of communication. The leaders I coach and the coaches I supervise all quickly learn that, at some point, I am always going to ask: "What's the conversation that needs to happen here?"

## Notes

1  I still chuckle whenever the stewardess on an American flight says that we will be landing "momentarily." Will the plane stop or just pause briefly? Will I have to jump out while they throw my luggage onto the tarmac behind me?

2  Eileen Scholes and David Clutterbuck, (1998) Communication with Stakeholders: An Integrated Approach, *Long Range Planning 31(2) 227–238*.

3  Neologisms come from all sorts of places. One of my favourites was coined by my learning-disabled son, Jonathan. When his elder brothers went out for the evening, he said "They're going out drunking."

# 3 Corporate leadership and governance

The relationship between leadership and governance is complicated. Organisations need leaders at every level. Leaders take responsibility for making things happen within a defined area. Governors (directors) have responsibility for the whole enterprise. Executive directors tend to have both responsibilities at the same time.

My interest in leader development stemmed from engagement in a number of programmes to mentor future leaders and leaders in transition from one role to the next. Working increasingly with top teams and taking on various non-executive directorships also led me to involvement with corporate governance in multiple countries.

In this chapter, I explore how the **role of leader** is evolving, some insights into **the key qualities of a leader in a VUCA world**, and how to **assess a leader's potential to grow**. I also share experience of what an **effective board** looks like, the importance of **contrarian perspectives**, the **skills of a non-executive director**, and the concept of **boardroom roles**.

I've held a variety of leadership and board roles, both in my own companies, in private and public sector organisations, and in not-for-profits. I've observed hundreds of board meetings, often in a context, where I was expected to give feedback. I've seen highly competent chairpersons take a board through a complex and demanding agenda with skill, ensuring that topics are dealt with openly and from multiple viewpoints; and the opposite, such as the martinet who stopped all discussion on each topic as the allotted time ran out.

On the way, I worked with the finance company 3i to research what an effective board meeting looks like and found a role in educating directors. The latter included working with top teams in the Singapore state sector, helping directors of Czech and Slovak newly created companies adjust from a Communist centrally planned mindset to a commercial one, and designing with the then UK National School of Government its *Stepping Up to the Board* programmes and a framework for board assessment. Looking back, I am surprised that I wrote (or co-wrote to be more accurate) only one book in this area – *The Independent Board Director*, with Stephen Waine.[1]

My learning journey in leadership started when I was called into the editor's office at *New Scientist*, where I was a young journalist, and told I was the

DOI: 10.4324/9781003323990-4

*Table 3.1* My learning journey: leadership

| *My learning journey: leadership* | | |
|---|---|---|
| Leadership is a personal quality | Leadership is collaborative | Leadership is collective and symbiotic |
| Leaders command and control | Leaders consult and listen | Leaders curate the team environment on behalf of the team and its stakeholders |
| Leadership is about what you do | Leadership is about what you enable others to do | Leadership is about influencing the system |

*Table 3.2* My learning journey: governance

| *My learning journey: governance* | | |
|---|---|---|
| The Board creates strategy | The Board tests and approves strategy | The Board provides the moral guidance from which everyone can evaluate the strategy |
| The Board is accountable to shareholders | The Board is accountable to stakeholders and society | The Board is accountable to future generations |

new trade union representative. It wasn't a role I had any aspiration to, but someone had to do it! I was sent on a leadership training course, with half the attendees being union officials and the other half being first-line managers. The perspective of management was traditional with an overlay of listening skills. A few years later, working for another journal, I was given my first-line manager role, leading a team of translators from different cultures. One of my first tastes of how tough it was occurred when Spanish speakers from Spain and South America asked me to arbitrate over correct wording. (Even worse, when the same thing happened over Arabic translations!) I realised quickly that I would never have the skills to make or arbitrate such decisions. What I could do was help them take responsibility for working it out themselves. I was later lucky enough to encounter the remarkable Einar Thorsrud, the Norwegian pioneer of semi-autonomous work groups. He and his institute practised what they preached – the CEO role rotated every couple of years. Thorsrud introduced me to cases of companies which had made semi-autonomous work groups function well – including a factory making automobile mirrors in Bolivar, Tennessee.

Some groups of workers in this factory were given the opportunity to self-manage. They had a stretching daily target, but if they completed it early, they could take the rest of the day off – which for most of them meant valuable time to work on their small farms. They soon got into a routine that allowed them to quit after five hours instead of eight. Other employees, initially suspicious that they were cutting corners, regularly came to check the quality of their output, but it was the highest in the whole factory.

I encountered many other cases, where traditional, hierarchical leadership had been replaced in different forms. When Finnish forestry workers were supported in becoming independent contractors, owning their machines, downtime – which had been a plague – disappeared. They now did maintenance in their own time. I learned that not only was effective leadership consultative and collaborative, but it was also symbiotic – dependent on the system, of which it is a part, and contributing to that system. When leaders think the important parts of their role are about making decisions and giving direction, they miss the point. They can have a far more positive impact by creating an environment where others can step up and take the lead; and by being role models for doing so. In this way, they influence the whole system; and the system responds by freeing them up to add value in much more productive ways.

In the year before I sold my communication company to the staff in a buy-out, I began to wonder whether I had gone too far in the role of curator. Had I become more of an absentee landlord? I would come into the office and feel I was in the way. Now I recognise that the value I had created lay in part in the fact that they didn't need me.

I can also look back at my own style of leadership and recognise that it lies at one extreme of a spectrum. At one end lies the leader, who values structure, order, and containment. At the other is the visionary, constantly seeing new possibilities and setting new hares running. (Yes, I'm the second!) Another analogy I have found useful in this context over the years is that between the chief and the shaman, elegantly described in *The Corporate Tribe* by Danielle Braun and Jitske Kramer.[2] The chief's role is about "staying focused, getting results, streamlining work processes, being attentive, planning and control." The shaman is "the leader of change … teaching, facilitating dialogue, making sense of current circumstances and explaining the future …" The chief's style of leadership is linear, they assert, while the shaman's is more circular. Instinctively, I have sought out partners who have provided the counterbalance. It's that duality, the yin and yang that seems to make for effective leadership. I'm not saying that you can't have both qualities in the same person, but it's asking a lot of them! Various studies of entrepreneurs have come to similar conclusions – the idea that all the characteristics of leadership need to be found in one individual, while beguiling and appealing to the high narcissist, is only tenable by exception. It's the complementary characteristics of the leadership *team* that make for consistent leadership quality. I am working with a leadership team right now, where the founder-entrepreneur is a cross between Action Man and a mystic. In his role as founder and majority shareholder, he holds the power. Yet, he wants to diminish his role, so he can move on to the next visionary project. For that to happen, the team as a whole have to discuss with him how they will complement his strengths and what he needs to do to let them grow into a confident collective leadership. It takes courage on both sides but I have seen many teams rise to the challenge – as indeed is happening in this case.

The book *Doing it Different*[3] captured many stories of different, more inclusive styles of leadership. The starting point was a recognition, in many sectors, that there were companies that took pride in not being like their competitors. They sought difference through having and protecting a unique philosophy, through dismantling the organisation, by creating environments where work could be fun – yet at the same time having the systems in place that made delivering the customer promise an unquestioned priority. The leaders of these companies were often larger than life, "whacky" characters, who exemplified the values they wanted to create. Among the lessons from interviewing these were that the values they held were not learnt at business school – they came from life experience – and that being a role model was one of the most important parts of the leader's role.

It's been a similar journey in the context of governance. The role of a director starts with collective responsibility for the well-being of the organisation. In a commercial company that responsibility is exercised on behalf of the shareholders. It doesn't necessarily mean the survival of the organisation – it may be in the shareholders' best interests to wind the company up. In other sectors, the stakeholders are more diffuse. One of the lessons of recent decades is that the best interests of the company or organisation are not served by placing too much emphasis on one stakeholder at the expense of others. Like everything else, governance has become a lot messier than it used to be.

Good governance has evolved to encompass multiple competing perspectives, among them:

- Profit versus value-creation (short-term versus long-term; financial security versus wider societal impact)
- Performance versus capability (what we deliver now versus what we will be able to deliver in the future)
- Focus on the organisation in isolation versus focus on the organisation as part of an ever-evolving system

One implication of this is that strategic planning is too important to leave to the leadership team and the Board alone. While a clear sense of direction is needed to align everyone around the same objectives, the radar at the top of the organisation is limited in what it can see.

Another implication is that the gradual evolution of strategic attention and responsibility, which has shifted away from shareholder to stakeholder, is about both breadth and depth. *The Good Ancestor*[4] put into simple terms what I had been wrestling with for several years – how to incorporate the dimension of time. The question "What do you want your grandchildren's children to say about you?" encapsulates the challenge beautifully!

My very first book, in 1981, was about corporate citizenship. Its focus was on how companies could benefit from demonstrating strong moral leadership, through enlightened people practices, courageous responses to ethical challenges, and so on. I am increasingly convinced that moral leadership, directed both within the organisation and externally is now as important as fiscal probity. Yet director training rarely addresses this issue in depth and coaches frequently fear intruding into this sensitive area. My question to you, as you read this, is "What can you do to change that situation?"

To help, here are my **seven questions for social action:**

- What is it that needs to be said today, that will be too late tomorrow?
- What is it that needs to be done differently today, that will be too late tomorrow?
- What kind of role model does the world need you to be today?
- What will your grandchildren thank you for and blame you for when they inherit the world you helped to create?
- If you want to be remembered for doing the right thing when it needed to be done, what might you do differently today?
- What will it take to bring the long-term consequences of today's decisions into stark clarity and what is your part in making that happen?
- How can you connect with and influence others, so the whisper of a lone voice becomes the roar of a crowd?

## The role of a leader

Google Scholar lists nearly four million mainly academic articles and books on leadership skills and qualities – and that's pretty much all in English. Add non-English papers and the popular literature and we are probably looking at ten million or more perspectives on leadership. The one thing they all have in common is that they are all different!

We don't know what leadership is. We do know that:

- It is culturally dependent, with a few universal threads such as integrity
- Perceptions are constantly evolving. Textbooks on leadership from the 1970s emphasise command and control and the cult of the heroic leader, while today they are more likely to focus on empowerment and exhibiting human qualities
- Being the titular leader is not the same thing as leadership. Many of the functions traditionally seen as reserved for the leader can be distributed amongst the team
- Extroverts don't necessarily make good leaders. Indeed, INSEAD studies suggest that direct reports rate introverted bosses as marginally more effective
- Processes for selecting and promoting leaders are typically deeply flawed. Not only do existing leaders tend to assume that potential leaders are people like themselves, but the manipulative skills of sociopaths allow them to subvert the most well-meaning of succession planning processes

My own definition of leadership is very simple: *leadership is the conversation that moves mountains*.

One of my earliest studies of leadership was as part of a wider study that explored how some companies managed to thrive long-term, while others didn't. The inspiration was Tom Peters' *In Search of Excellence*. Walter Goldsmith and I improved on the research method and focused on UK companies in *The Winning Streak* (1985). A little over a decade later, in 1997, we reprised the study. Most of the excellent companies had either been taken over and absorbed or lost their way. A key realisation for us was that leadership had become a lot more complex over the period. The challenge for leaders was increasingly systemic – how to balance multiple conflicting forces. The balances we identified then were:

- Control versus autonomy – how they give people the maximum freedom to get on with the job and act as if they were owners of the business, yet exert just enough control to ensure that things work smoothly
- Long-term strategy versus short-term urgency – thinking long-term while maintaining urgency and action in the present
- Evolutionary versus revolutionary change – how can we ensure an effective balance between gradual, incremental change and rapid extensive change?
- Pride versus humility – how can we sustain justified pride in our achievements without slipping into dangerous complacency?
- Focus versus breadth of vision – how can we focus on the core business and new opportunities at the same time? (What we might call a bifocal perspective.)
- Values versus rules – how do we get people to do the right thing with the minimum of rules and controls?
- Customer care versus customer count – how to balance customer volumes against the need to make every customer feel uniquely served?
- Challenging people versus nurturing people – how to get extraordinary performance out of ordinary people
- Leaders versus managers – leadership as a role; management as a function
- Gentle versus abrupt succession – how to make executive and leader succession relatively seamless, balancing continuity against the need for a new direction

One of the more recent studies explored the dynamics of the highest-performing teams in one of the world's largest technology companies. The formal leader clearly played a major role in creating the environment for high performance. They were able to do so by being "positively vulnerable" – secure and confident both in themselves and their team members. We called them "secure leaders." Among the characteristics we identified were:

- Leaders, who are secure in themselves, don't feel the need to control. It is relatively easy for them to trust others, because if mistakes happen, they have big enough shoulders to share responsibility

- They recognise that trying to manage a large team is an impossible and fruitless task. Rather, they aim to support team members in managing themselves
- These leaders don't expect to be kept informed about everything, or to reroute information between members of the team. Instead, they expect team members to ensure communication happens between them and to tell the manager when there is something he or she needs to know
- These leaders see part of their role as protecting the team from distractions from outside; equally important is ensuring that everyone understands and is aligned with the overarching team goals
- Their self-security makes them open to (and welcoming of) feedback from team members. They have a "growth mindset" – focused equally on their own development and that of the team
- They *care* – both about the team goals, but also about each of the team members as individuals. They make time for human interaction
- They are role models for corporate values. They are aware that they, too, are a work in progress and they are fully comfortable with that perception

An earlier study I conducted into talent management identified that much of the leadership activity that happens in organisations happens outside the formal structures. To try to understand what was happening here, I reduced the exercise of leadership to three essential functions:

- Identifying an issue (problem, opportunity, or simply interesting) that required attention
- Identifying alternative ways of addressing that issue and selecting the most appropriate
- Making it happen – ensuring the necessary resources are in place, clarifying roles, gaining the active engagement of others, and measuring/monitoring progress

Classical assumptions are that the person with the title of leader does all of these things. Yet the reality I observed within organisations is that much of this activity took place outside of the formal structures – frequently within self-organising groups on the intranet. And almost always under the radar of the talent management and succession planning systems. How could this happen? Simply because the traditional myth of leadership is that we expect all three functions to be exercised by one person. What we were observing then was a factor that has become increasingly obvious – effective leadership lies less in the individual than in the collective. Even great leaders struggle to excel in all three functions. They compensate by building around them a team of others, who bring complementary strengths.

The problem with giving special status to the titular leader is that he or she feels obliged to live up to the heroic image projected onto them. Leaders at all levels across the globe are falling victim to debilitating imposter syndrome – a direct consequence of trying to live up to impossible expectations.

A solution is to redefine leadership as a collective activity, in which the titular leader has responsibility for a small core of roles, to which others may be added according to context. I spent several months trying to find evidence-based articles about what leaders actually do – as opposed to what competencies or traits they should exhibit. What little literature we did find, I shared with workshop groups and asked what they thought only the appointed leader could do. We found only two functions where the groups could not identify examples of distributed leadership: liaising with higher levels for resourcing and authorisation; and protecting the team from interference from outside.

Context does matter, of course. So, depending on the skills and confidence of the team, the small core of titular leader roles can include, for example:

- Creating a climate of psychological safety, where people are able to step up and take accountability
- Role modelling the behaviours, such as co-coaching and self-development that promote good teaming (i.e., leading by example)
- Creating time for reflecting together
- Mentoring
- Monitoring the energy in the team and intervening supportively whenever it is low

Much also depends on the nature of the leader's interface with the team. Is he or she:

- Within the team, doing similar tasks and with similar responsibilities, but "first among equals"?
- Outside the team (perhaps managing several teams) providing direction and monitoring performance but not engaging in any of the team's tasks?
- A hybrid of these two positions?

The style of leadership is likely to be different in each case. For the leader outside the team, it might be normal to have privileged information that is not shared with the team. If the leader is inside the team, then withholding that information could easily damage psychological safety, if it came to light. The leader, who is part inside and part outside, may find himself or herself in an impossible position!

## Key qualities of a leader in a VUCA world

A vast amount has been written about the competencies of coaches and mentors, and even more about the qualities of great leaders. Much of this is contradictory and dependent on circumstance or context. Research into the desirable traits of both coaches and leaders, for example, shows significant differences in expectations and perspectives arising from cultural factors. There seems to be a whole industry devoted to creating new descriptors of these traits: authenticity, connectedness, learning agility … and so on.

Some time ago, I set myself the task of cutting through the fog. My question for research and reflection was *What lies at the core of an optimally functional human being, who is tasked with (or takes upon themselves the task of) influencing others to achieve a greater good?* There are, of course, potentially limiting assumptions in this question. Not all leaders have a greater good in mind – many on the sociopathic spectrum seek only personal advantage. Moreover, the greater good is in itself a slippery concept. Optimal functioning is also a concept, which may have different interpretations. I have taken for granted, for example, the inclusion within this term of a reasonable level of intelligence, as well as a lack of any serious mental disease, but ignored any aspects of physical disability.

These constraints accepted, in my reading and conversations, especially with coaches, who I supervise in their professional practice, I have sought a consistent pattern that integrates multiple perspectives (philosophy, religion, the science of adult development, well-being, and the literature of coaching, mentoring, and leadership). What emerged are four core virtuous traits or qualities, which seem to underpin optimally functioning coaches, mentors and leaders. These are:

- **Compassion.** Compassion is a much more positive and useful trait than empathy. Empathy is about feeling *with* someone, and can easily lead to emotional overload, distancing and in extreme, desensitisation. Compassion is feeling *for* another person and brings with it the desire to alleviate their pain. Key components of compassion are self-awareness, kindness, self-compassion, acceptance, and equanimity. In a current study of high-performing teams, one of the key observations is that the leaders of these teams tend to have a much greater sense of personal security than their counterparts in less successful teams. They have confidence both in themselves and in others, are forgiving of mistakes (their own or other people's) and, because they have trust in themselves, are able to extend trust to others, empowering them to take decisions and self-manage. Self-compassion reduces the likelihood of depression, dysfunctional self-criticism, and physical illnesses. It is also believed to improve immune system functioning
- **Curiosity.** Curiosity incorporates creativity, for an incurious mind does not easily put concepts together to generate new ideas. Curiosity causes us to explore our inner worlds (why and how do I think, feel, behave, and function?), how we interface with the world outside of us, and how that world itself functions. Key components of curiosity include mindfulness, higher order reasoning, and learning orientation
- **Courage.** Courage is the capacity to do the right thing, while being aware of the personal and wider risks. Key components of courage include clarity of one's own values, a deep sense of ethicality, being positively self-critical,

being able to let go and move on, and resilience to setbacks. Courage also encompasses the will to work with dreams (generated or espoused through Curiosity) until they become reality. It allows us to take tough decisions, to have conversations, and to avoid dealing with issues we would rather avoid, and to behave in ways closer to the person we aspire to be

* **Connectedness.** In South Africa they have a word *Ubuntu,* which translates as "I am because we are." It can be hard in individualistic cultures, such as the United States, to recognise that interconnection. I cannot be a leader, if no-one will follow me. Or a follower, if no-one leads. The reality is that most of us are not very well connected with ourselves, let alone with other people or, wider still, with the ebbs and flows of the tides of human society, the environment, or beyond. Our human brain is designed to filter out most of what we could pay attention to, if we chose. The alternative is what happens at the most debilitating end of the autistic spectrum, where sensory overload becomes intolerable. We'll explore more on this in Chapter 5, which is all about human connectedness

Whether we are acting as a coach, mentor, or leader, our primary role is to help people make better sense of their internal and external worlds, so that they have more constructive choices for decisions they make about themselves and on behalf of others. In effect, we use our compassion, curiosity, courage, and connectedness to stimulate and support theirs. When we see failures of leadership, while the attributed cause may be related to a lack of knowledge or skill, the root cause in every case I have examined can be attributed to a lack of one or more of these four qualities. Poor decisions, for example, typically come from not wanting to acknowledge alternative perspectives or information (lack of curiosity and low connectedness) and/or the inability to challenge myopic thinking (lack of courage), and/or ignoring or underestimating the impact on stakeholders (lack of compassion and connectedness).

Much the same appears to hold true in coaching and mentoring. In observing hundreds of coaches, we observe a broad correlation between evidence of self-awareness and self-compassion and the depth and quality of the coaching/mentoring conversation. The most effective coaches and mentors are deeply interested in the other person and how they see their circumstances – the client is not a problem to be solved, but a world to explore together. They have the courage both to release control of the conversation and to ask those difficult and penetrating questions that access the "beneficially painful" aspects of the client's world. And they achieve presence by the strength of their connection with both the human being in front of them and the systems around the client.

Becoming compassionate, curious, courageous, and connected doesn't happen overnight. It takes time, reflection, and practice. I have started to ask myself regularly *What did I do (today or this week) that made me more compassionate, more curious, more courageous, more connected?* I conclude that I am still a "work in progress"!

Let's look at these qualities in a bit more detail.

### Curiosity

*Harvard Business Review's* September–October edition in 2018 devoted several articles to curiosity. Egon Zehnder measures seven leadership competencies (results orientation, strategic orientation, collaboration and influence, team leadership, developing organisational capabilities, change leadership, and market understanding). Curiosity is the best predictor of leadership strength in all of these.

When highly curious executives don't achieve the level of competence to advance to the C-suite, it is usually because they have less exposure to stretch assignments and job rotations.

Particularly relevant experiences are: working for several companies, serving more diverse customers, working abroad or on a multicultural team, experiencing more business scenarios, and managing larger teams.[5]

Another article in the same edition, by Francesca Gino, reported on the benefits of curiosity:[6]

- Fewer decision-making errors – generating alternatives reduces confirmation bias
- Innovation – "the most curious employees [in a call centre] sought the most information from co-workers and the information … boosted their creativity in addressing customers' concerns"
- "We view tough situations more creatively … curiosity is associated with less defensive reactions to stress and less aggressive reactions to provocation"
- Natural curiosity is associated with higher job performance
- Reduced group conflict. "Curiosity encourages members of a group to put themselves in one another's shoes and take an interest in one another's ideas, rather than focus only on their own perspective."

A third article proposed five dimensions of curiosity:[7]

1. Deprivation sensitivity – recognising a gap in knowledge, the filling of which offers relief
2. Joyous exploration – being consumed with wonder about the fascinating features of the world
3. Social curiosity – talking, listening, and observing others to learn what they are thinking and doing
4. Stress tolerance – a willingness to accept and even harness the anxiety associated with novelty
5. Thrill seeking – being willing to take physical, social, and financial risks to acquire varied, complex, and intense experiences

The first four are all claimed to be strongly associated with improved work outcomes.

Curiosity is also closely associated with learning agility, which W. Warner Burke of Columbia University breaks down into nine dimensions: Flexibility (openness to new ideas and solutions), Speed (being able to act quickly), Experimenting (trying new behaviours), Performance Risk-taking (taking on new challenges), Interpersonal Risk-taking (seizing differences in opinion as opportunities to learn), Collaborating (partnering with others, who can offer additional perspectives and knowledge), Information Gathering (actively looking out for relevant information and developing networks that provide it), Feedback Seeking and Reflecting (taking time to think things through).

Intriguingly other studies suggest that curiosity activates much the same regions of the brain as physical hunger. When we talk about people having "a hunger for knowledge," it's closer to the truth than you might think![8]

### *Courage*

Acting with courage is one of the attributes most closely associated with effective, transformative leadership. Yet coaches and mentors frequently find that clients are torn between doing what they believe is right and fear of the consequences of so doing. Courage is sometimes wrongly associated with being fearless, but more accurately it is about working with and overcoming fears.

The capacity for bravery brings with it multiple advantages, including increased self-confidence, authenticity, openness to other perspectives and new experiences, and being more able to seize career and other opportunities as they arise. There is also evidence to correlate courage with higher levels of happiness. People who can't overcome their fears tend to be less ambitious.

There's an impact on other people too. The level of bravery that a leader exhibits creates the climate under which their teams work. While bravery isn't always associated with team effectiveness, timidity is generally an indicator of team mediocrity. And fearful leaders tend to micromanage.

Coaching and mentoring conversations can help people recognise and confront their fears. They can also help people learn to *value* fear. The emotion of fear evolved as an instinctive protective mechanism, to ensure we recognised and attended to threats. Survival often depended on allowing fear to take control momentarily, to avoid threats. Fear becomes dysfunctional when we are unable to take back control.

The good news is that we can do a lot to increase our level of courage. Among practical steps are:

1. Step back from the fear with curiosity. What specifically am I afraid of? Voicing the fear, first to oneself then if appropriate to others allows us to relax its grip on our emotional and physical responses to the perceived threat.
2. Identify small steps and experiments you can make that allow you to "put a toe in the water."

3. Make the mental link between situations in which you exhibit bravery and those where you feel fear. The benefits can work both ways – sportspeople sometimes identify unexpected ways in which they can tweak their performance by attending to suppressed fear about things that might go wrong.
4. Notice when you are being brave and give yourself credit for it. The more often you do it, the easier it becomes.
5. Find role models for "modest bravery" and try to learn from them. Modest bravery is about having the courage to act authentically under pressure. It's *not* about making a lot of noise.
6. Manage stress. The higher stress levels are, the less able we are to control instinctive fear reactions and the bigger obstacles appear.
7. Ask yourself the question: "Who am I being brave for?" When we stand up for a principle, we are seeking a wider impact than just for ourselves – and this strengthens the link between doing the right thing and speaking up.
8. Bring into play the multiple resources you have. Articulate why you have concerns (for yourself or others) and the emotions involved – a passionate narrative has far more impact than "I don't want to complain, but …". Seek security in numbers – if you have a concern, then others are likely to share it and together you will have a much louder voice. Rehearse with others how you will take a stand.

Courage is a trait that can be learned. Which is fortunate, because the complexity of issues facing clients at all levels in organisations increasingly requires leaders who will cut through the confusion and demonstrate courageous, concerned leadership.

### Compassion

Coaching textbooks are full of advice for leaders and coaches to develop their skills of empathy. It might seem to make common sense, but this advice doesn't seem to be based on any credible evidence. In fact, the contrary may be true – too much empathy may be a dangerous and unhealthy addiction linked closely to burnout.

The problem is much wider, however. Researchers have coined the term "emotional contagion" to describe how distress exhibited by one person – even a stranger or a fictional character in a movie – causes negative emotional and physical reactions in another. Empathetic overload can cause us to avoid helping situations, because we cannot cope with the effects upon ourselves.

What is needed in most situations is not empathy, but compassion. Whereas empathy is about feeling *with* another person, compassion is about feeling *for* them. Neurologically, empathy and compassion use different brain resources.

Being compassionate allows us to take a step back in terms of emotional entanglement, focusing on both the person and their situation. Empathy traps us in the mode of "how would I feel and what would I do, if this happened to me?" and pushes us towards solutions that alleviate our own anxiety or distress. Compassion focuses our attention on relieving their suffering.

Compassion leads us towards considerations, such as:

- What does this person most need right now?
- What has to change for them to progress out of this situation?
- What resources do they have within themselves to climb back to normality?
- What positive change is possible in the client's context?

So how can you develop compassion? Various approaches to compassion training have emerged in recent years, based on a mixture of perspectives and practice from neuroscience, Buddhist meditation, and mindfulness. Central to all these approaches is that compassion is less an emotion than a mindset. The lesson from all of these is that compassion can be learned and enhanced. Experiments with clinicians and students in secondary and tertiary education also point to significant health benefits from becoming more compassionate, ranging from improved cardiovascular function, to enhanced immune systems and reduced inflammation.

We can categorise the process of developing compassion into three elements:

- Widening the scope of who we are compassionate towards
- Learning to be more self-compassionate. (Self-compassion gives us emotional strength and resilience, so we recover more quickly from embarrassment and a bruised ego. That in turn makes it easier for us to admit and address our failings.)
- Creating the environment where we can be compassionate towards others and ourselves

### Widening the scope of who we are compassionate towards

In general, the wider the scope of our compassion, the easier it is to adopt a compassionate approach as a coach. Neurological studies suggest that we find it easier to be compassionate to "in-groups" – family, friends, people we perceive to be like us. The more distant or "alien" to us, the less attention we pay to suffering and the more judgemental we tend to be. So sympathy for refugees can be muted by rationalisations such as, "Why can't they sort the problem themselves?"

We can widen the scope of our compassion by seeking to understand the perspectives of out-groups who are suffering. The best way to do this is to engage in dialogue with them, showing "empathetic curiosity" about them as individuals and about the situation, in which they find themselves. Listening to their stories has a powerful and durable impact on our emotional memory.

We can also raise our awareness of our own compassion limits. When we find ourselves irritated by a client's attitudes or behaviours (or those of anyone we encounter), we can ask ourselves: *Would I be feeling like this, if I were more compassionate towards them? How might greater compassion on my part help them think and behave differently?*

More generally, we can develop wider compassion by reflecting on:

- What kindness could I offer to someone, towards whom I feel disapproval?
- How compassionate is my ideal self?
- What's the most generous thing I could think or do right now?

### Learning to be more self-compassionate

We all tend to beat ourselves up about our weaknesses and mistakes – being "our own worst critic." Even people who seem to have high self-esteem have agonising conversations with their inner critic. Being self-compassionate is not about silencing our inner critic; it evolved as a tool of survival and continues to play a valuable role in our development as individuals. However, like any other organ or system in human beings, the inner critic becomes dysfunctional, if it becomes overactive.

You can enhance self-compassion not by ignoring your inner critic (it will still be hard at work in your subconscious!) but changing how you listen to it. Assign it a name and a personality – treat it as if it were a real person. Approach the conversation with curiosity – "I want to understand what you are telling me and why." Make it as real a dialogue as you can. Now *thank* your inner critic for their attempt to be helpful and tell them why you aren't going to accept their advice or point of view this time. Shift now to a dialogue with your self-compassionate self – the very opposite of your inner critic. Finally, if you still feel anxious, use your coaching skills to facilitate a conversation between your inner critic and your self-compassionate self.

Being self-compassionate isn't about denying our mistakes, bad thoughts, or weaknesses. Rather, it is about coming to terms with them and accepting that we are all "works in progress" – organisms developing through trial and error. If we are not making mistakes, we are not growing. Focusing on how we let ourselves or other people down or didn't live up to our values doesn't help us to grow and improve (which is what the inner critic is supposed to support). Much more effective is to do what we would do with a client – focus on what learning can be extracted from the experience.

Useful questions to ask ourselves from time to time, when we reflect on our practice or when we experience a period of self-doubt, include:

- What can I forgive myself for?
- What simple kindness can I do for myself today (or in this situation)?
- What would someone, who deeply loves me, say to me right now?

*Creating an environment where we can be*
*compassionate towards ourselves and others*

By environment, I don't mean here a physical location. You can be compassionate towards other people anywhere. The environment is mainly to do with what is happening, both within and immediately around you. Compassion flourishes best in a state of calm, even in the midst of chaos.

*Connectedness*

I explore the concept of connectedness more deeply in Chapter 5. I define four arenas of connectedness:

- Connection with oneself – self-awareness, interception, and more
- Connection with others – other-awareness, emotional intelligence, networking etc
- Connection with the system(s) in which others are nested – systemic awareness
- Connection with the wider eco-system – eco-system awareness

The question "What makes a whole person?" has preoccupied me for many years. I haven't found an answer, but it seems evident that wholeness is inextricable from connectedness. Much of psychological theory revolves around the related concept of completeness. Is wholeness or completeness achievable? If so, what does it look like? Is it possible to be complete without being connected at all four levels? If there is an answer, it probably lies not in the realms of science, but within philosophy or the intersection between science and philosophy.

## Assessing a leader's potential to grow

One of the big failings of talent management is that it still places more emphasis upon the capabilities a leader has now than on his or her ability and capacity to develop the capabilities they will need for an unpredictable future. I was asked by the Saudi Ministry of Health to design a set of criteria for assessing leaders' capacity for rapid learning. The aim was to use these as part of the strategy to allocate developmental resources. There is no foolproof method for predicting leadership potential – other than putting people in a leadership role, supporting them, and observing how they perform. Rather than rely on diagnostics, I opted for identifying key areas that could be explored in an interview. The five that emerged constitute a framework for a deep conversation. These were:

- *How they manage their learning.* In particular:
  - Do they have a track record of both developing themselves and developing others?

- Do they demonstrate an ability to reflect upon their experiences to acquire both learning and wisdom?
- Are they able to plan their future learning in the context of developing the leadership skills required for more senior roles?

Indicators:

Low: focus on technical knowledge, with little attention to self-development as a leader. Little evidence of *passion* for developing others (even if the role includes training). Takes a simple, linear perspective of self-development.

High: focus on developing leadership skills in self and others. Takes a complex, adaptive systems perspective of self-development.

- *How they manage their strengths and weaknesses.* Effective leaders have clarity about their strengths and weaknesses – and when overuse of a strength can become a weakness. They also focus less on "fixing" weaknesses than on being "good enough" in these areas and building around them people with complementary skills, who can compensate for those weaknesses

Indicators:

Low: unable to articulate strengths and weaknesses clearly. Does not appear to "own" them. Has no clear strategy for managing them.

High: has reflected deeply on own strengths and weaknesses and has a well understood strategy to manage these.

- *How they focus their energy.* Effective leaders recognise that they can't do everything and that their energy is a finite resource. So, they use their energy on tasks that they find motivating and which align with their mission or purpose. The research around this area is captured well by Alex Linley (*The Strengths Book; Average to A+*) People with high leadership potential tend to learn this lesson early in their careers – they become noticed for their achievements and they achieve because they focus their energy on what is important

Indicators:

Low: little sense of what motivates them or how they apply their energy to key tasks.

High: strong sense of what motivates them and how they apply their energy to key tasks.

- *The clarity of their mission or purpose.* They know what they want for themselves and for a larger cause. Sociopathic leaders are obsessed with creating positive outcomes for themselves; effective leaders place more emphasis on achieving a cause (and may still place some lesser emphasis on outcomes of benefit to themselves). The evidence for the importance of passionate commitment to a cause goes back to *In Search of Excellence* and beyond. Warren Bennis' work on management versus leadership also emphasises the importance of this factor

Indicators:

Low: little sense of connection between what they do and serving a broader/higher societal purpose; if a connection exists, it is in generalisations, rather than specific ways in which they wish to bring about change. This might be described as "part of the job, not part of my personal identity."

High: strong sense of connection between what they do and serving a broader/higher societal purpose. Strong integration between their personal identity and specific changes they want to bring about.

- *How they make change happen and reflect upon the process of facilitating change.* Effective leaders have a clear concept of how to bring about change within the context of their environment. As they experience success or failure, they reflect upon and redesign their approach to change management. The literature on inner-directed and outer-directed personality has relevance here – our belief in our ability to make change happen and our sense of personal responsibility for positive change. Without this belief, people can only be administrators, not leaders, no matter what the job title says

Indicators:

Low: a sense that making change happen is the responsibility of other people. Sees failure to achieve a change as a reason to give up. Invests little in developing "networks of influence" to support change.

High: takes personal responsibility for change, even when it is not in their specific job role. Takes setbacks as new challenges and innovates to find ways around them. Passionate about developing networks of influence.

When drawing on these five factors, I am vigilant in *not* applying them as some kind of test, but as a way of understanding more of the whole person. The HR consultancy industry is driven in large part by the desire to compartmentalise and make judgements on people and on encouraging people to do the same on themselves. This I feel does an injustice to them!

## The effective board

I got my first taste of being a director when I became chairman of a start-up venture with a colleague, Mike Long, in the early 1980s. We took advantage of a government loan guarantee scheme to seek seed capital, hiring one of the middle-sized international accountancy firms to help us prepare the pitch and make introductions to banks. All six of the banks we approached offered us the cash! An early lesson was that non-executive directors (NEDs) were either great assets, keeping us aware of issues we might otherwise not have paid attention to; or a complete waste of space.

Over time, I began to work with boards in a wide range of areas and to acquire NED roles of my own in sectors ranging from business to government and not-for-profits. I developed a fascination with the quality of board conversations, observing that they were often "dire-log" rather than dialogue. One research project involved interviewing dozens of CEOs and directors of entrepreneurial businesses about their experiences of board meetings. The good practice guidelines developed from that study are still widely used today.

My growing practice in corporate governance led to roles supporting the Czech government in making the transition from state-owned businesses to a modern, capitalist economy. A lifetime of working in centrally controlled environments, where all decisions were pushed upwards, ill-prepared senior managers for directorships. Abandoning all bureaucracy at once was too big a step – these managers needed time to grow into the roles of leaders and strategic thinkers. At the same time, I also found myself running workshops in Singapore for the CEOs of state-owned businesses, which were already very commercially oriented.

Studying boardroom dialogue led me to develop a framework of boardroom roles. In part, this came about as a result of criticism by directors that Belbin's team roles – used indiscriminately by some consultants – were only partially relevant. While an executive group can and should be a team, a board with NEDs has a different role and function of oversight that requires them to maintain an outside-in perspective. That's why most boards have limitations on the duration an NED can serve – to prevent them from becoming so deeply embedded in the system that they lose their independent viewpoint.

The UK National Health Service was a fertile ground for experimentation as it moved towards a business model of boards. Amongst the projects I learned most from were developing board observation templates and measures of board effectiveness, and mentoring programmes to support boardroom diversity (which is still a big problem). I also designed and delivered the *Stepping Up to the Board* programmes for the then National School of Government.

My focus on the transition from senior executive to director continues. Mentoring between aspiring directors and experienced directors turns out to be remarkably effective. In the areas of finance and human resources, the success rate of aspiring directors in achieving promotion is close to 100%. A study I carried out in 2021 explored the question *What do you know now as an HRD that you wish you had known before?*

The HRDs were remarkably candid about their own naivety before they joined the Board. Many of them stressed the importance of understanding what they needed to learn and what they needed to let go of. For example: "[Being a director] is a completely different role with different responsibilities … you need to understand the business in more depth and be more visible to the senior leadership team. Attend board meetings to gain greater insights. Network with HRDs and find a good mentor to start preparing for the change. The role is more about influencing others and role modelling good leadership."

Boards typically operate in a climate of secrecy. Newly appointed HRDs therefore lack "context about historical organisation decisions … which unfortunately you don't get exposed to until you're in the room."

Directors in the study recommended that aspiring HRDs should prepare for their extra responsibilities by "being exposed more to the requirements of company directors, the obligations and accountabilities" well before they take up the role. Learning how to view issues through the perspective of a board and good governance – by spending learning time with experienced directors from a variety of disciplines – allows the aspiring HR director to adjust his or her mindset. At the same time, they stressed the importance of understanding all the other functions around the Board table and especially finance – being able to understand the business as a whole.

Political astuteness (as opposed to behaving politically) was seen as a key competence.

The perceived status of HR as a function that creates value indirectly is felt more strongly at an HRD level than at a department head level. Amongst pertinent comments: "You are evaluated on business not professional contribution … You're in the marketing business. Having a vision is not enough. You need to be able to articulate it and sell it at every opportunity."

Respondents saw educating other directors as a key part of the HRD's role, along with building strong networks within and outside the organisation.

Just as the new HRD has to adopt a different mind-frame, they also need to extend or enhance their skill set. Among a quite daunting array of suggested competencies were:

- Actively "let go" of the old job and hand out responsibilities to your team. Internal progression makes this more difficult and people are used to you delivering on a range of fronts
- Learning to adapt communication style for C-suite; e.g., being more commercially focused, using problem statements before introducing initiatives for better engagement, getting things done relies heavily on credibility and influence
- To listen more. To be less controlling. To enjoy the job more. Be a bit more relaxed
- The challenge is about managing the self more and managing others less in an HRD role
- Stakeholder management
- How to make a good strategy land
- Not being restricted by existing thoughts and processes is paramount – both in earning credibility and being able to drive new ways of working
- Keeping a focus on the people agenda, particularly during C-suite meetings
- You are there for a reason – to be an advisor and to make decisions. Be ready to make decisions with maybe only 80% or less of the information. Get used to making decisions objectively and calmly. You will be questioned on your decisions, so be ready to talk through why the decisions were made

Many comments under this theme related to achieving a long-term, systemic perspective and moving from tactics to strategy. One respondent describes it thus: "The transition from a tactical mindset (in the moment, people-focused and usually reactive, despite work on more proactive aspects such as talent and succession planning) to a strategic one (macro, always starting with the business strategy and goals, translating to HR and talent strategy, developing initiatives, and testing them against the business strategy and goals)."

## The high-performing board

The value-creating framework here below takes a systemic perspective of board functioning. Effective, high-performing boards demonstrate excellence in three key areas:

- Structure (how they are composed and influenced; clarity of role)
- Process (how they manage key tasks, such as auditing, appointments, and strategic oversight; the trade-off between management and direction)
- Behaviour and competence (how they exercise "collaborative independence"; the quality of boardroom debate; the exercise of leadership)

To provide a complete picture of board effectiveness, an evaluation process needs to address issues such as:

- Clarity of purpose for the Board and how and it fulfils that purpose in practice
- The quality of board meeting dialogue
- The balance between cohesion and constructive dissent (as opposed to cosiness v conflict) between board members
- How genuinely strategic the Board is
- How well connected to the organisation the Board is
- The quality of relationships with stakeholders, both internal and external (including the reputation of the Board in the eyes of employees)
- The quality of environmental (in the widest sense) awareness and analysis
- How the Board makes decisions (and whether it makes enough decisions)
- Clarity of distinction between managerial and directorial roles amongst executives
- Induction and "onboarding" of new directors
- Nature and quality of the Board Development Plan (or whether it has one!)
- The scope and quality of the appraisal process (both outcomes and how the Board and its members achieve them)
- The depth of knowledge of other disciplines by executive directors
- How the Board ensures that different viewpoints are heard and that various stakeholder interests are understood and taken appropriately into account

### Evaluating board structure

Issues here include:

- The size of the Board
- The constitution and its relevance to the operating environment and purpose

- Clarity of role of both executive and non-executive members
- Linkages with other institutions (e.g., other levels of the Board)
- The number, scope, and relevance of sub-committees
- The composition of the Board in terms of complementary skills, perspectives, personality, and experience

The critical question is: *Does the structure facilitate the Board in delivering the performance, with which the organisation is tasked?*

### Evaluating boardroom processes

Issues here include:

- The scope and relevance of policies relating to board tasks
- How well the implementation of these policies is monitored
- The management of risk
- The effectiveness of decision-making
- Avoidance of groupthink and dominance by individuals or sub-groups

The critical question is: *Does the Board manage itself in a way that supports the delivery of the performance with which the organisation is tasked?*

### Evaluating director behaviour and competence

Issues here include:

- The ability of the Board to sustain appropriate levels of strategic and collaborative dialogue
- The Board as a role model for the values of the organisation
- The degree, to which the directors individually and jointly demonstrate experience, expertise, and judgement in fulfilling their key roles

The critical question is: *Is the Board making effective use of the talent available to it?*

## Boardroom roles

Boards are not teams – at least not when they consist of both executive and non-executive members. Teams require a high level of interdependence; boards require "collaborative independence." When executives come together, they can be a team. When joined by non-executive directors, the group dynamics change to emphasise oversight. The realisation that board roles were not the same as team roles emerged from observation of board meetings.

Each of the roles identified in Figure 3.1 can be expressed positively or negatively. Each may be undertaken by more than one member, but the team

| Role | Positive aspects | How many people on the team exhibit this characteristic? | | | | | | | Negative aspects |
|---|---|---|---|---|---|---|---|---|---|
| | | Very strongly | Quite strongly | Occasionally | Neither | Occasionally | Quite strongly | Very strongly | |
| Organiser | Makes sure people have information they need; keeps an eye on Boardroom procedure; ensures issues unresolved at previous meetings are not forgotten | | | | | | | | Can overemphasise process at the expense of purpose (efficiency v effectiveness) |
| Focuser | Ensures meetings maintain their strategic focus; assists in route setting | | | | | | | | Tends to give inadequate attention to how strategy will be made to happen; seen by others as impractical |
| Challenger | Questions the basis of assumptions and assertions; queries at the conceptual level; interested in *why*? | | | | | | | | Stirs up debate for its own sake; enjoys conflict and argument; unable to be a team player |
| Probe | Questions the mechanics and processes; interested in *how*? Asks "Is it logical? Will it work? Does it hang together?" Good at identifying gaps in information supplied | | | | | | | | So concerned with tactics and operations that he/she is unable to think strategically |
| Discloser | Brings underlying conflict to the surface, so it can be discussed and resolved | | | | | | | | Doesn't understand when to leave alone |
| Honest broker | Prevents and helps resolve conflict; works a lot behind the scenes; seeks conciliation, compromise | | | | | | | | Over-conciliatory; so concerned with keeping the peace that he/she buries problems |
| Architect | Creative thinker with the capacity to expand and articulate the Board's ambitions for the company | | | | | | | | Seen by others as having head in the clouds, not in the real world |
| Builder | Highly creative; develops and integrates other people's ideas as well as own | | | | | | | | Lacks creativity, ideas of own; may need time to consider ideas before developing them, so can be seen as resistant to them |
| Lateral thinker | Idea-generator able to open up alternative ways of tackling/viewing issues | | | | | | | | Produces too many way-out ideas indiscriminately; more interested in novelty of symmetry of ideas than immediate relevance |
| Conscience | Concerned with ethical and moral dimensions of the Board's decisions; good at relating discussions back to the corporate values | | | | | | | | Can be dogmatic and lacking in business sense |
| Summariser | Good at condensing wide-ranging discussions into concise statement | | | | | | | | Tends to over-simplify |
| Mentor | Experienced director who helps newer members fit in and maximise their contribution | | | | | | | | Can be over-protective, intrusive |
| Ambassador | Communicates board's view to the outside world (investors, employees etc); enhances reputation of the Board to others | | | | | | | | May present own views rather than the Board's |
| Bulldog | Tenacity to keep pursuing important issues time after time until they are resolved | | | | | | | | Tends to pursue trivia at the expense of the really important; doesn't know when to let go |

*Figure 3.1* Boardroom roles.

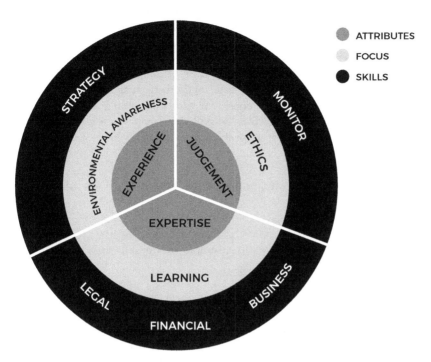

*Figure 3.2* Director competencies.

will be stronger when a) every role is taken by at least one member and b) each role is valued collectively. One of the ways the model can be used is to invite everyone to reflect upon a board meeting. Could the conversation have been better, if some roles had been given greater prominence?

### Director competencies and characteristics

There's no one formula for an effective director. Like leadership, it's very contextual. Nonetheless, over time in the 1990s, I developed a framework for the core attributes, skills and focus of effective directors, based on extensive interviews with both executive and non-executive directors. (Figure 3.2)

*Experience* may be specific (knowledge of the business/sector; or of a situation, such as acquiring businesses). Or it may be broad – for example, of working in different cultures, different sectors, or being on other boards.

*Expertise* is about the specific skills the director brings to the role and how they use them.

*Judgement* is about the exercise of wisdom – extrapolating from experience and expertise to make and influence decisions.

Each of these core areas supports other essential characteristics of the effective director. Experience gives the director a sense of what is happening in the external world – an awareness of business, market, technological, and social trends can be seen as *environmental awareness*.

*Strategic thinking* is informed by both experience and environmental awareness. It is, in essence, the organisation's pre-emptive response to emergent
change.

Good judgement involves a moral dimension. Without judgement, it is difficult for the director to maintain a strong sense of *ethicality*. The director must
recognise ethical issues, have appropriate methods to analyse them and their
implications, and derive solutions consistent with their own and the organisation's values. He or she also needs to be skilled at *monitoring* – knowing what
to look for, why, and how deep to probe into issues. The director needs to be
able to monitor:

1. Financial performance (e.g., profit and loss, shareholder value added, cash
   flow)
2. Progress of major projects
3. Other key external indicators (e.g., sales, customer loyalty)
4. Other key internal indicators (e.g., employee opinion surveys, retention
   of talent)

The director's expertise on appointment is a critical factor in his or her appointment. Thereafter, however, it is important for him or her to continue to *learn*
– about the business, about the skills and capabilities of the other directors, and
so on.

More specifically the director needs to continue to develop his or her expertise in the fields of *legal, financial, and general business*. The latter now increasingly includes expertise in human resources, technology, and sustainability.

## Summary

As I look back over my evolving understanding of leadership and governance,
I am embarrassed by my initial naivety. The concept of the charismatic leader
is seductive – what would a movie be without a hero? But leadership is not
about the individual leader; it is about the system that creates the leadership
environment. Great leaders as individuals enable the system to exhibit positive
leadership. The same applies to corporate governance – the role of the Board
is to create the conditions under which leadership can flourish wherever it is
needed.

I have also, of course, reflected on my own leadership style and approach,
which has been described as "empowering and enabling, while constantly
teetering on the edge of abdication." (Harsh but fair!) Certainly, at this
stage of my personal development and career, I am more of a shaman than
a chief.[9]

I am intrigued about how some of the most important innovations in modern society – such as the internet – have emerged without obvious leaders.
What they have had instead is *instigators*. Instigators often demonstrate innovation and energy, but show little desire to lead, at least in the sense of wanting

to control how things develop. They work on the assumption that if an idea (or meme) is sufficiently powerful, people will adopt it. The combination of shaman and instigator is a comfortable one for me.

## Notes

1 Clutterbuck, D and Waine, S (1994) *The Independent Board Member*, McGraw-Hill, Maidenhead.
2 Braun, D and Kramer, J (2019) *The Corporate Tribe*, Routledge, Oxford.
3 Clutterbuck, D and Kernaghan, S, (1999) *Doing it different,* Orion, London.
4 Roman Krznaric, (2020) *The Good Ancestor*, WH Allen, London.
5 Fernandez-Araoz, C, Roscoe, A and Aramaki, A Harvard Business Review, p61 September-October 2018.
6 Francesca Gino, *Harvard Business Review*, pp. 48-57. September-October 2018.
7 Kashdan, TB, Disabato, DJ, Goodman, FR and Naughton, *Harvard Business Review*, pp. 58-60. September-October 2018.
8 Lau, L, Ozono, H, Kuratomi, K, Komiya, A and Murayama, K Hunger for Knowledge: How the Irresistible Lure of Curiosity is Generated in the Brain *Nature Human Behaviour* doi: 10.1038/s41562-020-0848-3.
9 Danielle Braun & Jitske Kramer, (2019) *The Corporate Tribe* Routledge, London.

# 4    Mentoring

I've been lucky to have mentors at most key stages of my life from my mid-teens. The first, mentioned briefly in Chapter 2, was my English teacher, Wilf Tallis. He kindled in me a deep curiosity beyond the curriculum. In lessons, he would deviate into what seemed (but never were) random excursions into higher maths, architecture, astronomy … I learned to be attentive to the connectedness between disciplines and bodies of knowledge.

In the world of work, I was "adopted" as a young journalist by a grizzled and apparently grumpy old man in his sixties, who took the first article I produced on joining *New Scientist* and returned it to me covered in red ink. And I had been so proud of it! Momentarily, I was annoyed. Then I realised how much more elegantly the words flowed. Six months later, my articles came back untouched. Worried that I had somehow offended him, I invited him to the pub. He reassured me: "You don't need my help anymore." A decade later, I modelled much of my own mentoring on this experience, when I hired young journalists to work alongside me in researching and writing books and reports. After a time, I would encourage them to create their own projects, with a view to moving on to roles elsewhere that would take them into the next phase of their career and professional growth.

In between, three mentors at McGraw-Hill made an impression on me over my ten years there. The first recognised that I had ambitions towards management. He asked me to observe managers in the company – what did I notice? I realised that none of them sported long hair down to their shoulders. He wasn't telling me what to do – simply raising my awareness, so I could make an informed decision. A haircut later, I was on my way! The second was my boss' boss, who took me on visits to advertisers and other influencers. We spent some of this time discussing my role and aspirations; but more talking about the kind of issues he was grappling with. When I later got promoted, I went to thank him. He told me he had not intervened – precisely because he was my mentor – but that I had been promoted because I was manifestly thinking like a manager at the next level. I had absorbed new and more complex ways of thinking largely unconsciously.

My third mentor was utterly useless – except in one valuable intervention. He represented everything that was complacent and US-centric in the corporate

DOI: 10.4324/9781003323990-5

*Table 4.1* My learning journey

| My learning journey | | |
|---|---|---|
| US definitions of mentoring are universal | Return to the European roots of mentoring | Mentoring as a diverse and multicultural phenomenon |
| Mentoring is hierarchical | Mentoring as co-learning | Wisdom of the system |
| Mentoring is instrumental | Mentoring is developmental | Mentoring is liminal |

culture. We communicated only briefly when he was passing through and only had a few minutes to spare. Then he had me fly to New York for a lunchtime meeting in his club, where he explained for me how the corporate politics worked. I came away with an understanding that the opportunities for progress as a non-American living outside the States were severely limited. I flew home with a determination to move on and become an entrepreneur.

During every major transition in my career since, I have sought out a mentor to give me new perspectives, challenge my assumptions, and give reassurance when I needed it. Those transitions included selling a business for the first time, disengaging from a business relationship with a sociopath, and learning to be a coach supervisor. My co-author David Megginson and I would co-mentor, walking across the Yorkshire hills, sometimes creating and honing new tools and techniques.

My interest in mentoring as a topic for research and education came from interviewing Kathy Kram, a US academic, who undertook her PhD research into 22 informal mentoring relationships. I began to research and consult in formal mentoring. Entirely by coincidence, Kathy and I both published our books at the same time, in 1985. Kathy's book became the basis for most subsequent research into mentoring in the US; my *Everyone needs a mentor* did the same for Europe. Without intending to, we had created a schism in mentoring practice and research. Kathy's interviews revolved around asking people about a broad range of helping relationships, within a North American cultural context. As a result, she conflated the roles of mentor and sponsor. The European tradition, by contrast, retains the association of mentoring with the achievement of wisdom (the original mentor being the goddess Athena, in Homer's Odyssey) and recognises that sponsorship and mentoring are two different and largely incompatible roles – a perception reinforced by the findings of my own PhD research 15 years later. In the story, Athena the goddess of martial arts does behave in a sponsoring manner – but the subtlety of the story is that it reflects the concept of a split personality 3,000 years before it appears in modern psychology. It is now widely accepted that sponsorship and mentoring are two related but very different helping styles. Mainstream corporate practice tends to support this division, although some academic studies continue to appear that don't "get it." This is in large part because of the cultural dominance of social science research by a handful of US academic journals unable to escape from their own gravity wells!

European and US mentoring also evolved different language to describe the relationship. US literature typically refers to a protégé (someone who is protected), which emphasises the power of the mentor and ingratiation behaviours by the more junior partner. European literature refers to a mentee (someone who is supported in their thinking) and emphasises empowerment.

Since those early days, mentoring has expanded into dozens of different applications. From an initial focus on privileged young men, mentoring has expanded to cover almost any situation where a person is going through a transition. This transition can be of a role (for example, promotion to first line manager), identity (for example, becoming an adult) or circumstance (for example, returning to work after maternity leave). One of my favourite applications is ethical mentoring, in which anyone who feels they face an ethical dilemma or are the victim of unethical practice, can work through the issues and make better decisions as to how to address them. The mentor comes with a toolkit to support their thinking.

Similarly, reciprocal mentoring is a powerful tool for bringing about systemic change in organisations. Reverse mentoring, where a junior employee mentors a senior executive, has its origins in companies such as General Electric, where executives would keep a fatherly eye on the careers of young technical professionals who would educate the executive in the use of technology. The concept rapidly evolved to one, in which the exchange became one between the executive and either a Black and Minority Ethnic employee or another group, such as women hitting the glass ceiling. The junior person would help the more senior understand the world from their perspective – which at least in theory resulted in the executive being more aware of their privilege and the needs of minority employees. The junior person in return got to understand how the organisational systems worked, so they could better navigate within them. The problem, of course, was that this tended to perpetuate the existing system with all its racial or gender biases. Reciprocal mentoring therefore encourages mentors and mentees individually and collectively to work together to change the system.

Another area, which has enormous potential to change society for the better, is mentoring in schools. Typically, mentors are teachers or other adult volunteers. However, our experiments around the world show that schoolchildren can themselves be highly effective coaches and mentors to their peers. The education materials we have built around the *very Kid Needs a Mentor* project include a chapter on how to mentor your parents.

### Defining a learning conversation

This simple model (Figure 4.1) emerged from an analysis of the similarities between coaching and mentoring. It captures the essence of the "chemistry" of

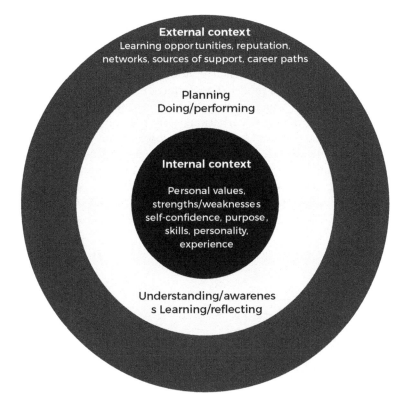

*Figure 4.1* The developmental conversation.

a person-centred learning dialogue. The conversation involves working to and fro between the internal context (knowing yourself) and the external context (being aware of what is happening in the world around you). Both coaches and mentors help the other person become more aware and achieve greater clarity in these two contexts. Then they help them integrate their new understandings from both contexts to facilitate different and better paths forward and clearer, more values-based decision-making.

The model also helps to clarify the principal difference between coaching and mentoring. Coaches tend to focus marginally more on the internal world and mentors marginally more on the external environment. This is not the result of any significant difference in approach or philosophy: it happens because mentors usually come with greater relevant experience of the mentee's environment. This allows them to achieve different intuitive insights, to empathise more with the mentee's situation, and to use their knowledge to craft powerful questions that would not occur to someone without context-specific insight.

## Mentoring in the spectrum of helping styles

The model below (Figure 4.2) dates from the earliest days of my research in mentoring, when coaching was still primarily a form of instruction and modern coaching was only just emerging as a serious alternative to traditional learning methods. It still has general validity. Most sports coaching, for example, remains in the instructional model. The distinction between sponsorship and mentoring continues to widen, with increasing recognition that the two roles – one power-based, the other co-learning – are not compatible. At the same time, the distinction between developmental coaching and developmental mentoring has become less clear. The European Mentoring and Coaching Council, the only professional body to encompass both disciplines, sees both disciplines as drawing on the same basic set of competencies. Mentors, however, need to have additional competencies – in particular, the skills of contextual understanding, role modelling, and experience sharing.

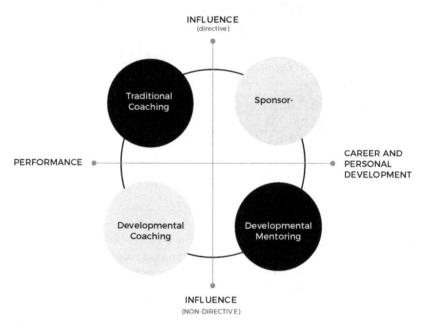

*Figure 4.2* Coaching versus mentoring.

## Problems with mentoring research

It's unfortunate that the quality of research in mentoring generally has been poor, in spite of the vast volumes of studies. In the early 2000s, I developed six tests. These are:

- *Definition*

Is it clear what kind of relationship is being measured? Some research mixes participants in structured programmes with those in informal relationships and some even with relationships, where one party does not realise they are part of a mentoring duo. Some papers mix within the reporting line and outside it (leaving aside the argument as to whether it is possible to be a mentor in a boss-subordinate relationship).

There are, of course, dozens of definitions of mentoring, yet many studies fail to be precise about which definition they are following. Unless it is clear which model is being followed in a particular piece of research, it is often impossible to draw conclusions with confidence, or to make comparisons with other studies. Meta-studies and literature reviews may compound the problem, because they tend to begin from the (false) assumption that everyone is measuring the same phenomenon.

The issue is made even more complex by the recognition by some researchers in the area that multiple, simultaneous mentoring relationships are also a common factor. Clearly, the dynamics of one relationship within a web of others may be different from those of a single, intensive mentoring dyad.

To maintain the validity of research in mentoring, it is necessary in my view to provide a precise definition of exactly what kind of relationship is being measured and to ensure that all the samples lie within that definition. Some research has attempted to get around this problem by asking people about broad helping relationships, but then the data is too general to apply meaningfully to specific types of a mentoring relationship. Mentoring is a class of phenomena and each phenomenon needs to be investigated in its own right.

- *Context*

A wide variety of contextual actors can affect the relationship and the scheme. At a minimum, these will impact upon the intent (their own or that of third parties, such as the organisation) mentor and mentee bring to the relationship. Other contextual variables include the level of training participants receive, the way in which they are matched (with or without an element of choice), and whether the relationship is supported as it develops (for example, by additional sources of learning and/or advice). Additionally, differences in race, age, or gender may exert an influence.

Trying to account for all the contextual variables that might apply, especially when a research sample is drawn from many organisations or schemes would be very difficult to do without vast sample sizes. This suggests the need for relatively narrow selection criteria – for example, senior managers, in company-sponsored mentoring relationships of at least six months' duration with a paid external, professional mentor; or young males 12–15 from deprived backgrounds at risk, paired with male role models between 10 and 20 years older. The more variables subsequently introduced (e.g., gender variation), the larger the sample size will need to be to draw conclusions with confidence.

- *Process*

Process provides another set of variables. It is clear, for example, that e-mentoring differs in some fundamental aspects from traditional face-to-face mentoring. Simple process factors, such as frequency of meetings, can have a major impact on outcomes. At the very least, studies need to allow for or try to eliminate such variables. Studies attempting to link personality to the success of mentoring relationships, for example, would be better grounded if they also investigated the degree to which personality factors resulted in specific behaviours, perceived as helpful or unhelpful to the maintenance of the relationship and to the achievement of its goals. (This classification into maintenance- and achievement-oriented behaviours appears to be very relevant across the whole area of mentoring relationship dynamics.)

- *Outcomes*

Much of the research literature uses Kram's functions of a mentor (or the subsequent recasting of the functions by Noe[1]) as measures of outcomes. Yet the functions are a mixture of behaviours, enablers, and outcomes and so for the most part unsuitable for this use. Moreover, outcomes are almost never related back to goals/intent. The reality is that different types of mentoring relationships have different expectations of outcomes; and so do different dyads within the same programme. Failure to recognise these means that the purpose of the relationship is ignored – which suggests the research fails the sixth test, that of relevance.

- *Limited perspective*

It is also remarkable how few studies attempt to measure outcomes for both parties. Yet mentoring is an interaction between two partners, with the outcomes highly dependent on the motivation of both.

- *Relevance*

The so-what test is a standard element in guidance on research design, but it seems often to be honoured mostly in the breach. I recommend anyone designing future studies to convene at an early stage of research design a panel of practitioners – those, who the research is intended to inform and benefit – to help shape and ground the project.

My own research and concept development have covered extensive areas of mentoring, taking a contextual perspective wherever I can. In the rest of this chapter, I explore some of the themes that have had the greatest impact, including:

- **Phases of the Mentoring Relationship** – how the relationship develops over time
- **Structure of the Mentoring Conversation** – how an effective mentoring conversation flows

- **Significant Unresolved Issues** – a way of understanding what people bring to coaching (and to supervision)
- **Personal Reflective Space** – the model of how people think through their SUIs
- **The Mentoring Quadrangle** – the interaction of the key relationships in a formal mentoring programme within an organisation
- The **Executive Mentoring Framework** – a holistic perspective of the developmental conversation at this level
- **Measuring the Impact of Mentoring** – for both participants and organisations
- The **Mentor as Role Model**

On this learning journey, I have had to change my thinking multiple times, as indicated in the table at the beginning of this chapter. The six tests have played a significant role in helping me question my assumptions. In particular, I learned that a volume of literature doesn't necessarily correlate with evidence-based practice, when cultural context is taken into account. If we had a similar volume of papers related to mentoring in Islamic cultures, compared to North American studies of mainly North American cultures, we would have a very different evidence base. Over time, my appreciation of the diversity of mentoring narratives has been an important source of enrichment for my personal practice and of connection to traditions in many other cultures and especially first nations, such as the Maori of New Zealand.

The first formal mentoring programmes were hierarchical in nature – for example, experienced executives and novice leaders. The US model emphasised a social exchange: a helping hand up the ladder in return for loyalty. But from the earliest days of my studies of mentoring programmes and relationships, it became clear that mentoring is most effective as a form of learning exchange. In current programmes of reciprocal mentoring, we now pay much more attention to the potential for the learning relationship to become a partnership to achieve change outside of the dyad itself. With knowledge of systems from above and below, it becomes much easier to bring about positive organisational change, especially in the context of diversity and inclusion. This parallels an evolving perception of the role of mentoring – from achieving goals, to much deeper levels of learning and becoming, to being a continuous series of liminal states. By the latter, I mean that we are always in transition, although we may not be fully aware of the nature of the transition. Through mentoring, we not only gain greater clarity about the journey travelled, but an appreciation of the waypoints where we stop to reflect on where we are and where the path might take us.

## Phases of the mentoring relationship

Kathy Kram's study of informal mentoring relationships[2] identified four stages. My work with formal programmes found five overlapping phases: (Figure 4.3)

*Rapport building*: Getting to know each other and build trust

*Direction setting*: Evolving a purpose for the relationship (which may be very different from the mentee's initial intent)

*Progress-making*: Rapid learning and co-learning – the core phase of the relationship

*Winding up*: Recognising that the relationship has achieved much of what was intended and that the mentee needs to cast off and bring the formal relationship to an end

*Moving on*: Mentor and mentee achieve a "friendship of equals"

Although this seems like a linear progression, in practice the phases overlap. Over time, the mentee may revisit their developmental and career objectives, which may in turn affect the purpose of the relationship. In the winding up stage, it is important to avoid gradually drifting apart, as this is associated with negative recollections of the relationship.

## Structure of the mentoring conversation

Long before the ubiquitous GROW (goal, reality, options, will) model of coaching emerged, I started to observe mentors in action to try to understand what a good mentoring conversation looked like. It didn't take long for a clear pattern to emerge. Effective mentors:

- Start by making sure that both they and the mentee are in the right frame of mind for a creative, open conversation. Often this is simply a matter of some initial small talk to create a relaxed atmosphere, but some pairs use more formal approaches, such as a couple of minutes' meditation
- Help the mentee articulate and explain the issues for discussion. This usually means holding back on talking about their own experience and also recognising that the presented issue may not be the real issue. By spending time delving into the context, understanding the situation from multiple perspectives, questioning assumptions, and looking for hidden patterns, the mentor and mentee develop a deeper mutual understanding of the issue that ensures that any solutions generated will be soundly based and congruent with the mentee's values and feelings
- Initiate a summary when it seems that a sufficient understanding of the issue has been reached
- Reinforce the mentee's self-confidence and self-belief, before moving into solution mode
- Help the mentee to explore a range of possible solutions or ways forward and to test each against their personal values and long-term ambitions
- Encourage the mentee to summarise the mentoring conversation overall. This is important, because it emphasises that responsibility lies with the mentee, rather than with the mentor

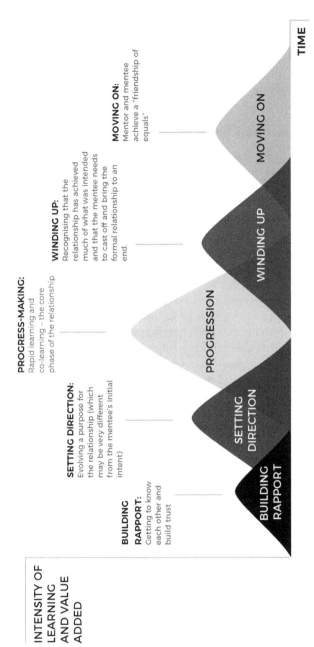

INTENSITY OF
LEARNING
AND VALUE
ADDED

TIME

**BUILDING
RAPPORT:**
Getting to know
each other and
build trust

**SETTING DIRECTION:**
Evolving a purpose for
the relationship (which
may be very different
from the mentee's initial
intent)

**PROGRESS-MAKING:**
Rapid learning and
co-learning – the core
phase of the relationship

**WINDING UP:**
Recognising that the
relationship has achieved
much of what was intended
and that the mentee needs
to cast off and bring the
formal relationship to an
end.

**MOVING ON:**
Mentor and mentee
achieve a "friendship of
equals"

BUILDING
RAPPORT

SETTING
DIRECTION

PROGRESSION

WINDING UP

MOVING ON

*Figure 4.3* Phases of the mentoring relationship.

One big difference between GROW and this conversation framework is that GROW did not originate out of any solid research. While it's sometimes useful for mentors to be aware of GROW, it represents one, minor form of conversation among many. While a mentee may have a broad sense of purpose for where they want to go in life, the immediate goal is typically quite vague – and is likely to evolve substantially as they begin to understand themselves and their context. In mentoring, *What do you want to achieve?* is often of far less significance than *Who do you want to become?*

## Significant Unresolved Issues (SUIs)

One of the earliest informal studies I conducted explored how people decided what to bring to their mentoring and coaching sessions. Of course, there was a great variety, but they all fell into the category of "things I need to get my head around." People rarely mentioned goals. Rather, they referred to anxieties. Even ambitions and opportunities contained a level of anxiety – for example, am I going to miss out or not get the benefits I should from an opportunity?

From this emerged the concept of an SUI – a Significant Unresolved Issue. Over decades, I experimented with hundreds of mentors and mentees, getting them to list the things they needed to think or work through and the level of anxiety they felt about not yet having done so. After a while, I scaled these, with 10 for being in a total panic and 1 being something you'd like to have time to attend to but where the consequences of not doing so are minor. Attempts to create a working index – for example, a general average score that people could use to recognise when they needed to step back and find time to think – proved impractical. However, most people can benefit from regularly listing their SUIs, with levels of anxiety for each item, and observing the patterns that emerge. These patterns are different for everyone, but being aware of them allows us to pause and create reflective space – either on our own or with a trusted other, such as a mentor.

## Personal reflective space

One of the big problems with coaching frameworks is that they focus on what the coach does to (or ideally, with) the client. But both coaching and mentoring are two-way conversations, in which both parties have contributions to make and responsibilities to fulfil. It became obvious to me that the developmental conversation would be most powerful, if it replicated the natural conversation people had with themselves when (See Figure 4.4) they reflected on an issue of importance to themselves. What emerged from individual and group interviews was a very consistent pattern of what happens when we "have a good conversation with ourselves."

The first lesson was that such conversations require a level of tranquillity – the time and space to devote quality thinking time to an issue. People find this time in all sorts of ways – driving home, walking the dog, in the gym or swimming pool, in the shower, ironing, and so on. The second was that when we allow it to and have the right external conditions, our brains automatically select one of the most pressing anxieties, or SUIs, for us to silently chew over. We begin to ask ourselves questions about this SUI, to *frame* it. Why is it important now? What am I concerned about? What's different? Who else is involved? What am I afraid of?

Framing gradually gives way to a deeper level of reflection. Who else shares responsibility for this? What assumptions am I making? What am I not noticing? What am I avoiding? We call this stage *implications*.

Toing and froing between framing and implications eventually (like rubbing two sticks together) produces a flash of *insight*. Suddenly, we see the issue differently and more clearly. That allows us to *reframe*, seeing the issue in a different light. That in turn generates new possibilities or *options*; and, having resolved the issue in part or whole, we are motivated to *action*, deciding what we are now going to do differently.

If you do your deep thinking walking or running, you may notice that the closer you get to insight, the slower you move. You may even stop entirely at the point of insight; then gradually pick up pace again as you process your new understanding. This is because the closer to insight you get, the harder your brain is working and taking from your blood the oxygen that would otherwise be going to your legs. As your brain drops down a gear or two, the blood oxygen can return to your muscles. Clearing anxieties in this way makes you more effective, less stressed, and more focused.

In working through personal reflective space, whether alone or with a mentor, the quality of dialogue is critical. The type of questions used, their relevance, and their capacity to stimulate reflection and understanding, are all important. So, too, is the nature and depth of reflection – in particular, how well intellectual analysis and recognition of emotional values are integrated.

The example questions below follow the basic curve of the PRS diagram:

### Questions to focus on one issue

- What's keeping you awake this week?
- What's your biggest fear/concern?
- What have you been avoiding thinking about lately?
- What's on your conscience?

### Questions to frame the issue

- What has prevented you from sorting it out before now?
- How frequently does this issue arise?
- What is the pressure to resolve/avoid dealing with this issue?
- What are the assumptions that you/others are making?

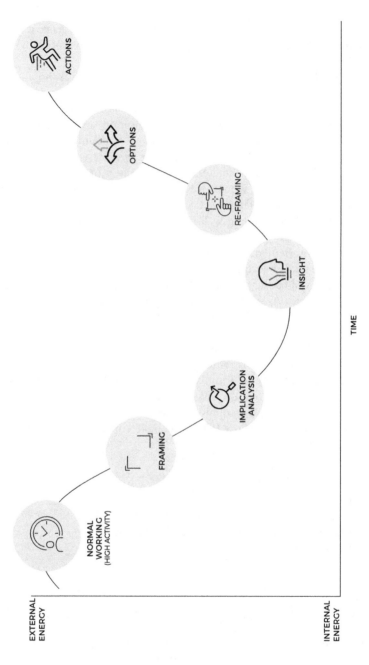

*Figure 4.4* The journey through personal reflective space.

*Questions to analyse implications*

- Why does it matter? (to you, to others)
- What's the current impact? (on you, on others)
- What's at stake? (future impact)
- How does this fit with your values?

*Questions to facilitate insight*

- What are your responsibilities in this?
- What have you been abdicating?
- What's the question no-one wants to ask/be asked?
- What patterns are repeating themselves?

*Questions to aid reframing*

- How do you now see the issue differently? (If I asked you to restate the issue, would you use different words?)
- What's important to you now?
- What if you did the opposite of what you do now?
- Could you redefine each of these problems as an opportunity?

*Questions to stimulate the creation of options*

- Assume you have no limitations on how to tackle this, what would you do?
- What would [role model] do?
- What's the worst thing you could do?
- What's the best thing you could do?
- Is a partial solution acceptable? (How good is good enough?)

*Questions to stimulate action*

- What are you going to do about that?
- When do you want to have achieved this?
- When and how will you get started?
- Do you have the courage and commitment to do what you now know needs to be done?

## The mentoring quadrangle

This simple diagram Figure 4.5 has been adopted widely around the world. It forms the basis for conversations that need to happen to make a mentoring relationship within a formal programme work well. It's also a good example of how my and other people's thinking has evolved. In the earliest iterations,

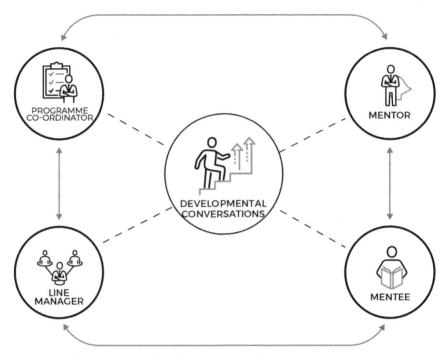

*Figure 4.5* The mentoring quadrangle.

it was assumed that all four parties would input into determining developmental tasks for the mentee – an assumption that originated from US practice. In European practice, however, this would compromise the mentor's role and the emphasis is much more on the conversations that need to happen to make the relationship productive and value-adding for all parties. The current thinking is that the four protagonists form a system, which is itself part of other, larger systems, and that everyone involved has a role to play in both supporting the mentoring relationship and managing the system.

## Executive Mentoring Framework

In the book *Mentoring Executives and Directors*, David Megginson and I interviewed both executive mentors and their clients to map what the role at this level involved. We found that there were four frequent foci, and that a mentoring relationship could involve any combination or all of these four over time or in some cases simultaneously (Figure 4.6).

*Transition* took many forms. For example:

• Promotion into a new more senior role
• Onboarding as a new executive in a new company

- Passing the baton to a successor (as in a founder-entrepreneur stepping back)
- Taking over from a predecessor with a very different leadership style

The role of a mentor is like a guide through difficult terrain. Their experience of similar transitions allows them to provide the mentee with timely conversations that help the executive think through the next steps on their path and link where they are with where they envision they are going. The destination and the journey rarely match our preconceptions, so the mentor helps us reflect and learn at each stage.

*Personal growth* also has many facets. The more complex the executive role becomes, the wider the range of developmental needs executives face. One of my favourite exercises with senior leaders is to ask them to tell me about their early careers and how much energy they put into learning at that time. If they made mistakes, what was the cost of these to the organisation? Then I ask them about the cost of mistakes in their current role and how much energy and time they put into learning now. Mostly, they get the point that the intensity of learning needs to be similar or greater the higher up they go!

By and large, executive mentoring does not focus on a specific skill or performance-related competency – that seems to be reserved for coaching. Executive mentoring is much more about becoming aware and evolving as a person. There is a strong link with the continuous process of becoming more mature and more connected as an individual. However, there are occasions when the executive seeks a role model or wise head to help them adjust to a change in requirement for their job role. An example of this is the specialist manager, who has never previously been required to think strategically. Or,

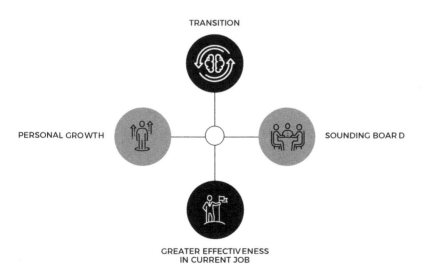

*Figure 4.6* Executive mentoring styles.

in my own career, when I first had to lead an acquisition and merger. In such cases, the mentor supports the executive in achieving *greater effectiveness* in their current, evolving job role.

As a *sounding board*, the mentor uses his or her experience to help the executive mentee think out loud. Being an effective sounding board requires:

*   Identifying the issues that are relevant to a decision
*   Establishing the questions that need to be asked to achieve clarity about the issues and options available
*   Providing context that the mentee doesn't have, if appropriate
*   Helping the mentee test their logic and be clear about the values they want to apply

## A model of executive mentoring processes

Our interviews with mentors and their executive mentees also gave us insights into the complexity of the conversations. The model below (Figure 4.7) summarises how mentor and mentee work together to build a deeper understanding

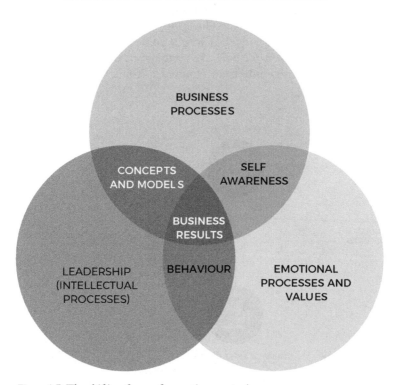

**A MODEL OF EXECUTIVE MENTORING PROCESSES**

BUSINESS PROCESSES

CONCEPTS AND MODELS

SELF AWARENESS

BUSINESS RESULTS

LEADERSHIP (INTELLECTUAL PROCESSES)

BEHAVIOUR

EMOTIONAL PROCESSES AND VALUES

*Figure 4.7* The shifting focus of executive mentoring.

of the executive's internal and external contexts. Whether they own the business or are an employee, the executive knows that achieving business results is how they will be measured, first and foremost. How they achieve those results is also important, but typically a subsidiary factor. The question *How can you contribute more?* lies at the heart of achieving results.

Three areas contribute especially to the leader's ability to deliver business results. Being intellectually competent for the executive role is essential. That doesn't mean the executive has to have a super-high IQ. He or she does need to have the ability to comprehend the complexities of the decisions they have to make. When we are aware of the limitations of our own intellect, we can surround ourselves with people who bring complementary intellectual skills. Executive mentoring helps the executive understand their own thinking patterns and grow in capacity by recognising increasing layers of complexity. In the current working environment, being able to manage and embrace uncertainty is an intellectual competence many executives are struggling with. Key questions here are:

- What and how do you think?
- What thinking capacity and capability does your job role require?

Emotional intelligence is of course equally important. About a third of all cases brought to me by coaches in supervision relate to clients who have EQ deficiencies. Being able to connect with both our own and other people's emotional needs and values is essential in motivating change. When individual values clash with those of the organisation the executive needs both courage and self-awareness to negotiate a route through the complexities of corporate politics.

Linking the IQ and EQ perspectives is how the executive behaves. Can they learn to be more vulnerable? To listen more? To demonstrate that they care for others? The ability to influence others in service of business goals depends on what those people experience in their interactions with the executive.

Business context is the third of the key circles. It addresses the question: *How do you understand what happens in the business?* This is partially about having effective networks but also about having clarity about how all of the functions fit together.

Linking business context and leadership is the ability to observe and communicate the patterns that underlie how the business functions. One of the great benefits of executive mentoring is that the mentor enlarges the executive's toolkit of models and frameworks to explain and see the patterns in the business. These might relate to strategy, decision-making, human psychology, or any of dozens of facets of business science and practice.

There is at least face validity for the assertion that executive mentoring conversations that address all of the perspectives in the model achieve more for the executive and their organisation.

## Outcomes of mentoring

Given the amount of money invested in a mentoring programme, it's to be expected that there will be a requirement to demonstrate results. Over time, I developed two models to address this – one relating to outcomes for the participants and one for the organisation.

For both mentors and mentees, four key measures emerged from the research:

- Career outcomes relate to changes in job role and promotability. These may include promotions, sideways moves that broaden experience, track record, and reputation. For mentors, a frequent outcome is the enhancement of their own reputation as developers of talent
- Learning outcomes relate to the gaining of new knowledge, skills, and expertise; greater self-awareness; and advances in personal maturity. They may include improved political and leadership skills
- Enabling outcomes relate to changes that will facilitate learning and career outcomes. For example, having a clearer personal development plan, building stronger networks, or investing in authentic reputation management
- Emotional outcomes relate to factors such as self-confidence, emotional self-management, or self-respect

For the organisation, measurement was much more complex, depending on the purpose of the programme. Here, we found that mentoring measurements fell into four categories, illustrated in the table below.

- *Relationship Processes* – what happens in the relationship. For example: how often does the pair meet? Have they developed sufficient trust? Is there a clear sense of direction to the relationship? Does the mentor or the mentee have concerns about their own or the other person's contribution to the relationship?
- *Programme Processes* – for example, how many people attended training? How effective was the training? In some cases, programme processes will also include data derived from adding together measurements from individual relationships, to gain a broad picture of what is going well and less well.
- *Relationship Outcomes* – have mentor and mentee met the goals they set? (Some adjustment may be needed for legitimate changes in goals as circumstances evolve.)
- *Programme Outcomes* – have we, for example, increased retention of key staff, or raised the competence of the mentees in critical areas?

## The mentor as role model

Both my research and that of others highlighted that mentors tended to be role models and that this was an important part of the value they added. Role modelling is very powerful, because it is an instinctive form of learning. The mirror neurons that lie at the heart of the process are core to our ability to socialise, to understand other people, and to work in groups.

I was fortunate enough to have some very strong role models, including the great pioneer of management studies, Peter Drucker. What I found surprising was firstly that mentors rarely understood the degree to which role modelling happened and secondly the tendency to default to passive role modelling. In our mentor training we spend time helping mentors and mentees understand the risks of negative or inappropriate role modelling. For many, asking *What would you be a good role for? And a poor role model for?* is the first time they have reflected on this aspect of how they influence others.

Here's a cautionary tale I often use. The mentee was a young female, part of a mixed group of 15 male and female graduate hires. Highly intelligent, she was also very shy and lacking in self-confidence. She was matched with a mentor, who was an assertive, well-regarded senior executive under the assumption she would make a good role model. The mentee certainly changed, trying to be like her mentor. But the mentor's quiet, authoritative assertiveness became in the mentee unsubtle aggressiveness, especially when she felt she was being patronised by male colleagues. An embarrassing altercation with a senior male executive in the staff restaurant put her career with the company on the line – a situation addressed successful by changing the mentor and providing counselling.

What had happened here was that the mentor had focused on transferring behaviours but without the necessary judgement of how and when to use them. She was in effect saying, "Be like me" rather than "Be yourself but adapt some of my strategies to your own needs and personality." The mentee was too young and too inexperienced to understand the power dynamics of the relationship and what was appropriate in her situation.

The model of role modelling emerged from a literature search and simply listening to people's experiences. It has never to my knowledge been empirically tested but has at a minimum high face validity when there is a significant power differential between two people in a learning relationship. The junior partner in such a relationship goes through several stages of adaptation:

- *Acceptive awareness*: identifying, sometimes from a distance, someone who appears to have qualities you would like to have
- *Admiration*: getting to know this person better and comparing yourself to them; wanting to be like them
- *Adaptation*: consciously or unconsciously adopting their perspectives, values, and behaviours
- *Advancement*: exerting your critical faculties to integrate their mental models with your own, rather than accepting them wholesale
- *Astute awareness*: seeing the role model as a whole person, with frailties as well as strengths; becoming clear about what to accept from the role model and what to reject

Among the lessons we have learned about role modelling are:

- When we have a high level of unconscious competence, it's harder for us to explain what we do and harder for others to imitate us. Mastery at this level involves much more than specific skills or behaviours. Mastery comes from integrating multiple areas of knowledge and competence; and from breaking the rules rather than complying with them. In general, it won't work for a beginner to try to role model themselves on a maestro
- Conversely, the things we know we aren't great role models for can be the source of greatest learning for the mentee. That's because knowing we don't have innate strengths there, we have developed coping strategies – so we are good enough. When the learner is still at the stage of developing their coping strategies, role modelling can be highly effective
- Proactive role modelling is a leadership skill that hardly ever appears in leadership programmes or textbooks but is vitally important. I like to ask leaders: "How do you exemplify the company values in how you interact with others?" "How do others see you as an exemplar and champion of the values?"
- Role modelling becomes much more effective when mentor and mentee discuss it openly. Mentees reach astute awareness much more quickly when the mentor puts his or her strengths and weaknesses into context

## Summary

The territorial skirmishes between coaching and mentoring in the 1990s and early noughties seem increasingly irrelevant in hindsight. Coaches lose much of their efficacy, if they do not embrace and learn from mentoring – and vice versa. This realisation can be immensely liberating. For coaches, having permission to use their whole self in support of a client's learning allows them to relax into the conversation and be truly present without the constant nagging that their coaching might not be "pure" enough. For mentors, being able to access the vast array of tools and techniques available to coaches increases their confidence and allows for a much higher degree of experimentation.

## Notes

1 Noe, RA (1988) An investigation of the determinants of successfully assigned mentoring relationships, *Personnel Psychology*, 41 457–479.
2 Kram, K (1985) *Mentoring at work: Developmental relationships in organizational life*, Scott, Foresman, Glenville Il.

# 5 Human connection

## Reflection

When I look back on my learning journey, it begins with a lack of connectedness. Having a name like Clutterbuck (so easily turned into insults) and being the brightest in my junior school class made a recipe for being picked on and bullied. At the age of nine or ten, I decided I'd had enough of this. Confronted by the school bully on the way home one day, I made a stand. He was a good head taller than me, but somehow it didn't matter. We both went home with bloody noses and I had a torn jacket. I was never bullied again. I and Michael (I remember his surname, but it would not be right to name him) became friends of a sort. I recall that I learned he had a home life I would not have wished to experience and somehow understanding this made me more forgiving.

I hated team sports. In football I would be put in goal, where I would read a book (with obvious consequences in terms of attending to the play). I loved individual sports, such as running, where the only competition was with myself. And I retain a love of solitude, especially when walking. When I want to centre myself, I return in my mind to a hill pass in the centre of Ireland. In front and behind me are deep, largely unpopulated valleys and just a few metres above me the underside of clouds drift sedately from one valley to the next. In that tranquillity, I am able to quietly dismantle the Lego bricks of my thinking and my emotions and reassemble them.

Then, in the world of work, I had to learn to get things done through other people. My solution (instinctive, rather than thought through) was to try to involve them in my thinking processes. When that didn't work as well as I had hoped, I learned to create conditions, where the thinking and creativity happened in the space between us. Over time, I learned to incorporate other systemic perspectives. So, enabling others to perform at their best involved helping them understand the systems, in which we are actors together. Coach supervision and more recently team coach supervision have provided me with the tools to do that.

Similarly, my first experiences managing people from multiple cultures left me deeply confused. It had never occurred to me beforehand that people who spoke Spanish would have radically different perceptions depending on whether they were from the New World or Old World. I spent my first few

DOI: 10.4324/9781003323990-6

*Table 5.1* My learning journey

| My Learning Journey | | |
| --- | --- | --- |
| Strength comes from self-sufficiency | Strength comes from collective intelligence and collective action | Strength comes from understanding the connectedness between people, cultures, and systems |
| Difference is a problem to be managed | Difference is a blessing to be embraced and grateful for | Whether difference is a problem or an opportunity depends on the degree of connectedness |

weeks in role trying to mediate on technical issues of language where I had zero expertise. By the time I had become deeply involved in mentoring and coaching, however, I had developed a clearer understanding of how diversity – used with a genuine appreciation of the value of alternative perspectives and experience and high levels of curious and empathetic listening – led to better decisions. In my two co-authored books on diversity mentoring, it became clear just how rare a genuine appreciation of the value of difference is. Without realising it, much of my practice has evolved to helping people see situations and themselves through the eyes of others.

One stark realisation was that we can't address issues of discrimination and bias in the system without first addressing our own ways of thinking. That holds true also in our mediating roles as coaches and mentors. Equally, we can't address these issues effectively on our own, nor even as a pressure group that has "voice." Only when multiple co-learning conversations happen across the system can we change the system. The greater the level of connectedness we can create, the easier it is to transmute the "problem" of diversity into opportunities.

The Southern African word *Ubuntu,* meaning "I am because we are" which I referred to in Chapter 3, is a sentiment that encapsulates so much of my reflections and sense-making. I trace my deep reaction to any form of injustice back to a seemingly inconsequential event at the age of six or seven. I intervened to stop two older boys from bullying a smaller one. A teacher stepped in, didn't bother to inquire what was going on, and punished me along with the two bullies. Somehow, I processed this not into resentment at any injustice done to me – I became surprisingly resilient in that respect – but into deep empathy with other victims of injustice.

A recent research study I encountered (Kardas et al)[1] asked people to approach strangers and have either a shallow, transactional conversation with them or a deeper conversation from curiosity about the other person. The research participants by and large expected to be happier with the shallow conversations and had more fears about the deeper ones. The opposite actually occurred. Once they had overcome the initial hesitation, they found the deeper conversations made them feel much happier than the shallow ones – and the more they got to know the other person, the more they liked them.

I have a theory that social scientists are drawn to study topics that relate to missing connections in their lives. It's just that – a theory that I have never had time to validate. I had very little connection with my father. He had been a prisoner of war in Japan and was one of only a handful of survivors. He returned to England a broken man, both physically and mentally. One of the broken pieces was his ability to connect. He died when I was 21 and before I had the skills to create the connection myself. The echo in me is the strong emotional reaction that I have towards any form of cruelty between humans. The killing fields and torture prison in Cambodia affected me deeply. I had to step out from the tour and sit quietly reflecting. As I write, the details of Russian soldiers raping, torturing, and murdering civilians in Ukraine feel like the victims were my own family and friends. The emotional connection is very strong. At the same time, I am intellectually intrigued by what happens in the minds of the perpetrators. How do they lose all human connection to their victims and to their ideal self?

I define two dimensions of connectedness: connection with yourself and connection with others. Both can have multiple layers – so, for example, connection with others may relate to close friends and family, work colleagues, societies, social causes, ecology, and so on. Inner connectedness is about how we connect with our selves, which is typically nowhere near as deep as we think. Take the phrase "I know it like the back of my hand." Without looking at it, try to describe the back of your hand – the shape and patterns of the veins, where the hairs are and any skin marks. Most of us fail this simple test!

Science has now identified more than 30 senses – far more than the six I was taught at school.[2] Many of these relate to internal functions, such as breathing, heart rate, or several kinds of touch. I was introduced to meditation and what is now called "mindfulness" in my early twenties. I have found my own ways of adapting the concepts, including reflecting while walking and multiple short "moments of stillness," where I can focus attention internally. This led me in the early 1980s to interview dozens of people about how they found time to think about issues that were causing them anxiety and led to the models of **significant unresolved issues** (SUIs) and **personal reflective space** (PRS) in Chapter 4. Unlike the GROW model, which derives from assumptions about how collaborative reflection *ought to* look like, PRS describes what actually happens in moments of internal reflection, with or without an external agency.

Another useful framework, which stimulates higher levels of internal awareness is the simple construct below:

- Thinking about how you think (meta-cognition)
- Thinking about how you feel
- Feeling about how you think
- Feeling about how you feel (meta-emotion)

In this chapter, I present some models and perspectives for enhancing self-connectedness. These include **emotional mapping, several models to put**

**self-awareness into context, a framework for understanding the whole person**, and the **worry index.**

External awareness is the other part of connectedness. Humans are not born with a "theory of mind" (the ability to recognise that others may not experience what we do). We develop it on the journey to adulthood. Our capacity to recognise other people's emotional states may be reduced by autism or enhanced by the neurodiversity of being a Highly Sensitive Person (HSP). However, for neuro-typical people, the limiting factor in our external awareness appears to be the degree of curiosity we have. Mindfulness exercises can be helpful here, too. Simply stopping and noticing. It's a bit like walking a route along which we would normally drive – we "see" so much more. It's because our brain works hard to filter out what it assumes not to be immediately relevant – unless we are on the autistic spectrum, where sensory overload becomes a problem. Neurodiversity is much more common than we think. It's only recently, after many years working with people on the spectrum, that I realised that I am mildly dyspraxic. I can't clap in time, for example!

My work with teams over the past 30 years and more continues to reinforce the view that most problems are caused by lack of connection and can be resolved by having connected conversations. Connected conversations involve dialogue, in which we are open to learning about ourselves by learning about and from others. It's impossible, for example, to appreciate the nuances and impact of "white privilege" unless you listen to the stories of people who are the victims of it. Multiple studies indicate that collective decision-making and teamwork produce better results than when individuals act on their own or pass responsibility up the chain to an "all-knowing" leader. The term "collective intelligence" has been around for some time now, but I refer also to **collective wisdom**.

My love of travel – I have been to more than 120 countries so far – is as much about experiencing the people as the scenery and the exotic foods. How do they see the world differently and what can I learn from them? A learned skill is to have conversations with people, in their own environment, when neither of us understands each other's language. This is a conversation that comes from within, where words are relatively unimportant. (Lesson number one is that saying things more loudly doesn't help communication; speaking more slowly and more softly does.) One particularly poignant moment for me was when I was invited to join a Maori community on New Zealand's North Island. I didn't try to understand the words of the ceremony in the longhouse – just the emotions that were expressed within them. The sense that I now *belonged* was overwhelming. I had now become part of their narrative and they of mine. If only we could replicate this in the corporate world!

Link a strong sense of justice with a keen interest in the differences and similarities between people and my engagement with diversity and inclusion was inevitable. From the obvious macro-inequities that fuel gender and racial discrimination, I have grown in awareness of the micro-inequities – the accumulation of tiny factors that result in people feeling that they belong less and in closing opportunities to them. We are back again to what we notice. I may fume at the long immigration queues to enter the United States, but I scarcely notice the similar queues of "aliens" at London's Heathrow airport. Many of the projects I engaged with were for the public sector and especially for the health services and the police. Working with a large police force in the UK, we investigated why it was so much more difficult for anyone who was not white, male, and heterosexual to progress through the ranks. We learned that a key mechanism was the quality of developmental conversations people received. When a senior person gave feedback to someone they felt to be "like themselves," they tended to be open, forthright, and take more risks. The more they felt the other person to be different, the more stilted developmental conversations were and the less robust the feedback. These behaviours were driven in part by a desire not to offend and in part by the fear of being called out for some transgression of political correctness. This and other research led to the concept of **diversity dialogue** – building the skills to have meaningful, authentic conversations across the barriers of difference. They also led to one of the most useful tools in helping people become aware of how their own anxieties prevent such conversations – the **diversity awareness ladder**.

I have been blessed by having a son with a learning disability. Jonathan, the youngest of my four sons, has both autism and Down's syndrome. I have learned so much from him. I am more patient, more aware, more connected with a wide range of diversity. I'm proud of his achievements, such as competing in the Special Olympics invitation games (as a skater), that illustrate how possible it is to overcome tremendous disadvantages, with courage and appropriate support.

The ways people connect are many and varied. I have frequently been drawn towards shining a light into darker corners – for example, **how we react to vulnerable others**, or working with **imposter syndrome**, or **polarisation**. I also look at one aspect of how coaches connect with clients – **Clutterbuck's 13 questions** form a useful checklist for rapidly getting to know another person.

**Laughter** has played an increasingly important part in my professional and personal life. It connects people in ways that build understanding and inclusion. Humour is an essential element in the learning environment – from the classroom to the coaching or mentoring relationship. When we researched the qualities that mentees looked for in a mentor, having a sense of humour was regarded as essential.

I have divided this chapter into two sections. The first looks at connecting with self; the second with connecting with others.

## Connecting with the self

### Putting strengths and weaknesses into context

I am a strong believer in the power of positive psychology, especially when compared with the deficit models that permeate so much of HR and consultancy practice. Performance in my analysis comes from the combination of three elements: aptitude, energy, and contextual awareness. All three are potentially improvable, but the potential for mastery is greatly reduced if any one of the three is missing and doubly so if two are absent. These elements reinforce each other, either positively or negatively. We avoid things that don't energise us, so our aptitude is never developed. If we aren't aware of what we are doing or what is happening around us, any energy we do expend is likely to be misdirected, which leads us to give up easily. And so on.

The matrix of strengths and weaknesses below (Table 5.2) provides a useful way of contextualising them. When we find that a strength serves us well, we tend to apply it in more and more contexts. Then we find that, in some contexts, it doesn't give the results we expect or want. (My sense of humour is both an asset and a liability!) Personal qualities that are highly functional can be dysfunctional when taken to extreme. So, for example, having lots of energy gets things done and can motivate others; but excess, unfocused energy is a symptom of ADHD (attention deficit hyperactivity disorder).

Another useful way of looking at our strengths and weaknesses is the matrix (Figure 5.1) of how much a task is needed (that is, should be done by us) and how energised we are by it. In an ideal world, we would spend all of our working time doing tasks that energise us and contribute significantly to the goals we are working to. In practice, when I ask people to analyse how they spend their time and energy, the proportion ranges from between 10% and 75%. (If you think you reach 100%, consider tasks like filling in expenses forms or tax returns!) There is usually a substantial amount of time spent on things that aren't needed but are satisfying. For example, the manager who keeps doing tasks that really would be better done by his or her team, because solving technical problems or making sales still gives them a buzz. That's not to say that we should always have zero effort in that quadrant – sometimes these activities amount to "play" time that allows us to restore our energy for other tasks.

Tasks that we aren't good at and don't need to be done by us should ideally be dropped or delegated. That's not always possible but recognising the extent of them gives us some opportunity to minimise them. The final quadrant, tasks

*Table 5.2* Strengths and weaknesses

|  | *Strengths* | *Weaknesses* |
|---|---|---|
| **Developed** | Where you are already a high performer | Fatal flaws, e.g., self-destructive tendencies, arrogance |
| **Emerging** | Where you have some successes, but need greater knowledge or consistency | Strengths you tend to overuse, or use in the wrong places |
| **Embryonic** | Things you feel drawn to do, but have not had a chance to develop capability | Things you feel adverse too, but have not had great exposure to |

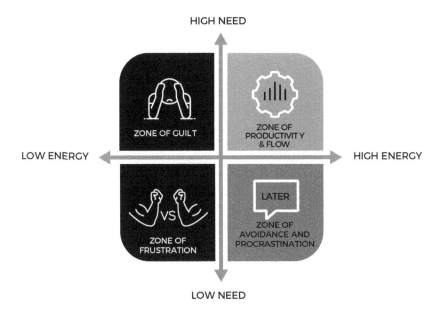

*Figure 5.1* Need versus energy.

that are important for us to do, but which we are not energised by, is the most problematic. It's here that creative approaches are most valuable. For example, many tasks can be broken down into smaller elements, some of which may be more motivating than others. Who else could support us by taking on those elements that are least motivating? Tactics, such as bundling together tasks we are reluctant to do, for a binge of anxiety clearing, can also help.

*Self-awareness reality checker*

The self-awareness reality checker (Figure 5.1) is another framework for structuring reflection around relative strengths, weaknesses, and aptitudes.

### Finding your values

Ask someone to define their core values and you may often get a blank stare in return. It's an abstract question that needs reflection and time to work through. The values matrix (Figure 5.3) is a simple way to structure a conversation about values, making them easier to articulate. Talking through each of the quadrants typically provides lots of verbal clues, from which value statements can be extracted.

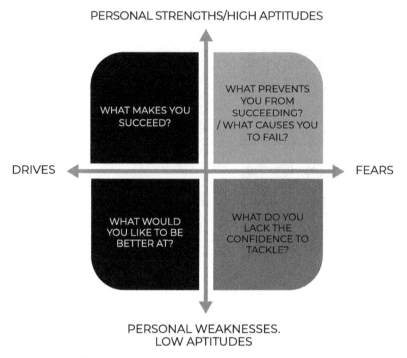

Figure 5.2 Building self-awareness: reality checker.

### Emotional mapping

Emotional mapping emerged from my realisation that, when people present an emotional issue, they are typically aware only of the strongest emotions. Other, less noticeable emotions are drowned out, yet may unconsciously haunt us long after – unless we recognise and manage them. Identifying other component emotions can:

- Help us see the issue, which has given rise to the emotional response, from different perspectives
- Identify contradictory emotions – and hence encourage a greater depth of analysis and insight
- Permit the examination of each emotion individually, so that we can determine how we want to deal with it

The simplest way to use the emotional map is to underline all the emotions we are feeling about an event or issue. Sometimes this may involve only two or three cascades; at other times, a really difficult emotional situation may involve

IDENTITY • RESPONSIBILITY

SELF

WHO ARE YOU
WHO YOU ASPIRE TO BE
WHAT MAKES YOU FEEL
GOOD/BAD ABOUT
YOURSELF

YOUR RESPONSIBILITY
TOWARDS OTHER
PEOPLE

OTHERS

HOW DO YOU WANT
OTHERS TO
PERCEIVE YOU

YOUR EXPECTATIONS OF
OTHER PEOPLE'S
RESPONSIBILITY
TOWARDS YOU

*Figure 5.3* The values matrix.

ten or more different cascades. As a coach, I might ask a client if they are experiencing other emotions, which aren't on the map.

Before I proceed to any form of structured analysis, I ask the client to reflect upon their responses. What learning can they extract immediately? A typical reaction is that they had not realised how complex their feelings were and/or that they had some of the marked feelings at all.

Then I ask them which feelings they'd like to explore first. We examine those feelings one by one, with questions such as:

1. What does the word "despised" (or whichever word the client has chosen) mean to you?
2. What makes you feel like that?
3. What inner need drives that feeling?
4. Is this a "good"/appropriate feeling?
5. How long, if at all, do you want to hang on to this feeling?
6. If you'd like to change the feeling, what would you like to change it to? (Typically, but not always, this will be another word or phrase from the same cascade.)

7.  What would be the likely consequences of such a change?
8.  What could you do to make that change happen?

Positive emotions often form part of a general negative mix of feelings. Helping the client focus on these positives may energise them sufficiently to accept and deal with stronger negative feelings.

Tackling component emotions one by one is similar to tackling the components of a rational puzzle. If the big picture is too complex to tackle at once, breaking it down into manageable elements is a practical way of "eating the elephant." However, it is important to retain the bigger emotional picture in mind. The solutions identified for each component emotion must be capable of integration into a coherent way forward, which the client can understand and commit to.

### Self-awareness and self-belief

The matrix of self-awareness and self-belief arose out of an analysis of coaching and mentoring conversations that centred around imposter syndrome. Imposter syndrome has attracted a lot of study in recent years, especially in the context of race and gender. It appears that the more people feel they belong in an environment, the less susceptible they are to imposter syndrome.[3] And of course, vice versa, which is why attention to imposter syndrome is so important in the context of diversity and inclusion.

As so often happens in the coincidence of ideas, the idea that there might be an upside to imposter syndrome arose for me from two sources simultaneously. The first was a discussion during coach supervision of the role of self-doubt in how coaches approach assignments. Having what we might call *balanced self-doubt* keeps coaches on their toes and constantly curious.

The second source was a short section in the latest book from Adam Grant at the Wharton School; in his book *Think Again*,[4] Grant points to studies that suggest a strong positive link between performance and self-doubt. He outlines three key benefits of self-doubt:

1.  It makes us work harder and avoid complacency
2.  It makes us work smarter, by prompting us to rethink our strategy
3.  It makes us better learners, by seeking support and ideas from other people

On the other hand, there is plenty of evidence that dysfunctional reactions to self-doubt lead us to:

4.  Micro-manage in vain hopes of asserting control over outcomes
5.  Work less smart, because we are afraid to admit our fears and weaknesses
6.  Learn less, because we are afraid to ask for help

All of which pointed me back to the model I developed in the 1990s, which helped to put high and low self-awareness and high and low self-esteem into

*Table 5.3* An emotional map

| | | | | | |
|---|---|---|---|---|---|
| Calm<br>Placid<br>Content<br>Relaxed<br>Laid-back<br>Angry<br>Furious | Bored<br>Uninterested<br>Disinterested<br>Curious<br>Intrigued<br>Stimulated<br>Inspired/radiant | Friendless<br>Deserted<br>Alone<br>Welcome<br>Included<br>Supported<br>Engaged | Distressed<br>Miserable<br>Sad<br>Numb<br>Pleased<br>Happy<br>Joyous | Cynical<br>Suspicious/wary<br>Unconcerned<br>Open<br>Confiding<br>Trusting | Hating<br>Disliking<br>Ignoring<br>Neutral<br>Liking<br>Caring<br>Loving |
| Drained<br>Tired/wary<br>Idle<br>Interested<br>Energised | All at sea<br>Unsure of myself<br>In control<br>Masterful | Despised<br>Ignored<br>Respected<br>Valued<br>Proud | Aimless<br>Confused<br>Purposeful<br>Decisive | Overwhelmed<br>Frustrated<br>Keeping the lid on<br>In control<br>In the flow | Frivolous<br>Whimsical<br>Thoughtful<br>Serious |
| Cowed<br>Compliant<br>Assertive<br>Rebellious | Contemptuous<br>Disrespectful<br>Respectful<br>Admiring | Terrified<br>Afraid<br>Threatened<br>Secure<br>Confident | Inferior<br>Equal<br>Superior | Transparent<br>Open<br>Reserved<br>Mysterious | Self-contemptuous<br>Self-pitying<br>Realistic<br>Good about myself<br>Arrogant |
| Vengeful<br>Judgemental<br>Accepting<br>Forgiving | Trapped<br>Constrained<br>Manipulated<br>Empowered<br>Liberated | Ignorant<br>Uninformed<br>Informed<br>Knowledgeable | Disappointed<br>Unimpressed<br>Impressed<br>Delighted | Betrayed<br>Let down<br>Supported<br>Strongly supported | Sick<br>Not at my best<br>Not bad<br>Healthy |
| Ugly<br>Plain<br>Pleasant<br>Attractive | Discouraged<br>Unmotivated<br>Encouraged<br>Determined | Resentful<br>Unappreciative<br>Appreciative<br>Grateful | Self-sacrificing<br>Generous<br>Self-interested<br>Selfish | Stupid<br>Uninspired<br>Clever<br>Inspired | Hopeful<br>Unconcerned<br>Worried<br>Despairing |

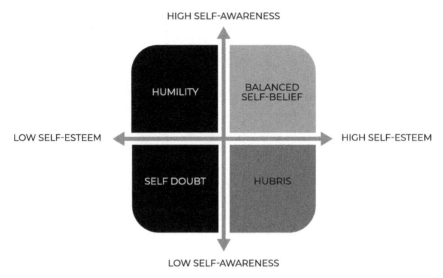

*Figure 5.4* Self-awareness and self-esteem.

perspective. A combination of low self-awareness and high self-esteem is asso-ciated with the "dark" traits of personality. High self-awareness and low self-esteem produce humility. While humility can be a very positive quality, in excess it prevents people from having the level of assertiveness necessary in leadership roles. We often talk about people being "self-conscious," mean-ing that, while aware of their abilities, they hesitate to use them. Self-doubt is the product of both low self-awareness and low self-esteem. Again, a certain amount of self-doubt can be helpful, but too much can be a real career blocker. The ideal combination comes with both high self-esteem and high self-aware-ness. Here, too, an appropriate balance is important. It's possible to have too much pride and even too much self-awareness.

The four C's of great leaders and great coaches – Compassion, Courage, Curiosity, and Connectedness – have a role here. Having compassion for our-selves gives us freedom to be wrong. It takes courage to ask for help and curi-osity to seek better ways of doing things. And it takes connectedness to build around us a support network of people, who will give us both honest feedback and guidance.

So, what does it take to achieve balanced self-doubt? Some useful questions to ask include:

1. What am I in danger of becoming complacent about?
2. What assumptions about myself and my practice/role have I not chal-lenged for a while?
3. How can I increase my self-compassion and be kinder to myself?

4. What conversations could I usefully have with my idealised self?
5. How effective am I at using self-doubt to stimulate continuous learning?
6. What would help me feel a great sense of "I belong here"?
7. How can I cultivate and nurture my network of collegial support?
8. How will I know when I have a reasonable balance between complacent arrogance and self-doubting humility?
9. What experiments are waiting for me to try out, for my benefit?
10. Where is the laughter in the system that can help me put myself into perspective?

### Self-empowerment

Empowerment was the management buzzword of the 1990s. I joined the bandwagon with *The Power of Empowerment,* a book of case studies.[5] An immediate understanding was that you can't empower anybody except yourself – you can only create the conditions, in which they are able to self-empower. Then I became less interested in the general concept of empowerment and much more interested in the context of self-empowerment, particular with respect to diversity in the workplace diversity. In a typical, well-designed corporate mentoring initiative, mentors and mentees come together after six months or so to review both the relationships and the programme. The model below came out of listening to their sense-making around empowerment and disempowerment in the mentoring relationship.

The level of ambition which people from non-privileged backgrounds felt they could achieve within the corporate environment was shaped partly by the biases and systems of others, and partly by their own. The model below gives a structure for conversations to identify the different kinds of restraint on ambition and develop strategies and tactics for overcoming them.

### Know thyself

In my iconoclastic study that led to the concept of systemic talent management, I identified four areas, where employees need to be particularly self-aware and accountable, if they are to manage their careers well:

- Identity (Who am I? Who and what defines me?)
- Purpose (What do I want to achieve? Who do I want to become? What do I want to contribute? What are my values and my motivations?)
- Context (How do I and my environment interact? What possibilities and limitations arise from environment?)
- Strengths and weaknesses (Where does my energy lie? What kinds of tasks and roles am I best suited for? What are my developed and latent capabilities?)

Together, they offer a simple but very practical framework for periodic career self-assessment, either on one's own or with a coach or mentor.

## PERSONAL EMPOWERMENT

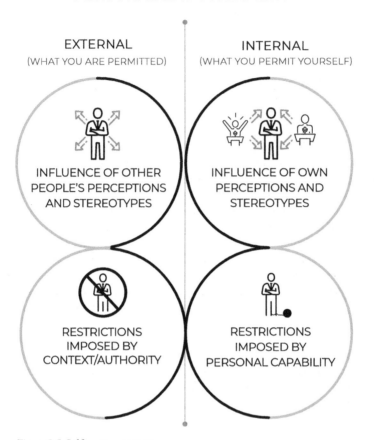

*Figure 5.5* Self-empowerment.

### Six life-streams

There are now a lot of models and tools relating to work-life balance, such as the wheel of life. When I decided to write a book on the topic,[6] my wife made it very clear what kind of role model she thought I presented! One of the problems with the whole topic of work-life balance is that it is all in the eye of the beholder. What can seem to one person as dreadfully unbalanced can seem to another to be the perfect equilibrium. The key is the *sense* of work-life balance – do we feel in control and do we feel fulfilled by the way we portion out our time and energy?

Some years before, I had built on the work of Ed Schein and others to develop a framework of six life-streams – aspects of our lives that need attention for well-being. The six are:

1. Job: how we earn a living, pay the bills etc
2. Career: how we aim to progress and use our skills and aptitudes
3. Social connection: relationships with family and friends
4. Health: how we keep fit and well
5. Intellectual self-fulfilment: what we do to keep our mind active outside of work
6. Community: how we connect with society and give wider meaning to our lives – for example, through volunteering or faith associations

Burnout often happens when people invest all their attention and energy in their job and career, but don't build strong emotional capital in other parts of their lives. So, when things go wrong at work, they have fewer resources to fall back upon. To achieve a well-balanced life requires us to feel we are making progress in most, if not all, of these life-streams. People often have personal development plans for their job and career, but may not regularly plan and review progress in the other life-streams. The questionnaire in Appendix 4 is designed to help them do so.

### Understanding the whole person

One of the big challenges for coaches and mentors in the context of diversity and inclusion is that we tend to make assumptions about where other people are like us and unlike us. So, the breadth of areas in which we seek to understand the other person tends to be limited by our expectations. This model (Figure 5.6) emerged from an analysis of themes identified through a variety of techniques to establish and compare the values held by partners in learning relationships. The top of the pyramid may look familiar – it is the triangle of meanings of value within the model of the psychological contract, adapted to focus on the values themselves rather than the social exchanges based upon them.

Worth in this context is about how we find satisfaction through achievement. Success we can define as "achieving what we value" – which could be, for example, financial reward, happiness, or learning. The common factor is that they all hold *intrinsic value* for us. Respect, on the other hand, is about *extrinsic value* – the recognition we acquire from others. Respect and self-esteem are two sides of the same coin. Being respected by others enhances our sense of self-worth and efficacy. Our self-esteem and self-belief influence how ambitious we are in the goals we set and the expectations we have of ourselves. Both are also affected by the attitudes we have – for example, towards the role of work in our lives, or the appropriateness of self-promotion. These, in turn are, of course, at least partially cultural in origin and both created and reinforced by cultural assumptions and beliefs. All of these factors overlap and come together to define where the person is in their capability and capacity to engage in self-development. Whether someone undertakes this analysis on their own or with the help of a coach or mentor, it provides clarity that permits more considered, more individualised personal development planning.

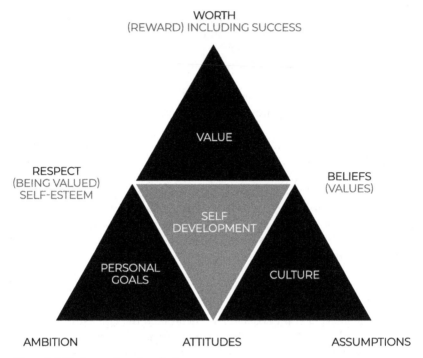

*Figure 5.6* Understanding the whole person.

### From collective intelligence to collective wisdom

What makes a fully functioning human being? A fully functioning team? A fully functioning organisation? Philosophers, psychologists, educationalists, and experts from many other disciplines have been theorising these questions for thousands of years. It is still an evolving quest, but one pragmatic way of expressing where we have got to in terms of the fully functional individual is the concept of Me-Q, which combines several different kinds of skill and awareness.

$$\text{Me-Q} = \text{IQ} + \text{EQ} + \text{SQ} + \text{Wisdom}$$

IQ (cognitive ability), EQ (emotional intelligence), and SQ (spiritual intelligence) each provide valuable insights that contribute to helping individuals be purposeful and effective in how they live, work, and play. But they only become collective intelligence with the addition of wisdom, which can be defined as the understanding that comes from reflection on experience. Wisdom is the ingredient that enables the transition from IQ, EQ, and SQ as limited, narrow lenses on the world to the holistic, unbounded horizon of collective intelligence. So much so that it might better be described as *collective wisdom*.

IQ becomes cognitive maturity when we learn to think about how we think and to integrate direct and indirect experience in ways that reveal patterns and systems.

EQ becomes emotional maturity when we learn to observe and reflect upon our feelings, sensing the patterns and interconnections between our emotions and those of other people, and between how we feel and what we do.

SQ becomes spiritual maturity when we become aware of the connectedness between ourselves and the forces that have created humanity – physiological, environmental, and cultural.

These basic building blocks provide the foundation to observe fully functioning teams, organisations, and societies. **TQ** (team intelligence) is the equivalent of Me-Q applied to the team environment. Close in concept to Amy Edmondson's "teaming," it involves the ability of people within a team to collaborate instinctively, pooling knowledge and insights, sharing emotions and caring for each other, learning together, and engaging in effective decision-making. Team members may individually be intelligent, emotionally aware, and connected to a purpose, but those assets need wisdom to achieve the full potential that comes from integrating them. In order to see the patterns and systems that determine whether it delivers more or less than the sum of its parts, the team needs to reflect on its individual and collective experiences – intellectual, emotional, and spiritual.

**We-Q** applies the same principles to organisations. It is much harder to achieve, because of the number of people involved, the greater complexity of the issues to be addressed and the limitations on the size of group, in which people can comfortably practice teamwork. Collective wisdom:

1. Captures and integrates the learning and innovative thinking that takes place across the organisation
2. Engages the intellectual power of everyone in the organisation to solve collective problems – regardless of who has formal responsibility for the issue
3. Harnesses the emotional power of members by focusing them on endeavours that capture the imagination and energise them; and by developing a strong sense of collective identity

The reflection that underpins wisdom requires a different approach to the norm of organisational consultation, which is typically an up-down-up, hierarchical conversation, outside of the normal operational routines. Rather, it is a constant, iterative, living, unending conversation that ignores departmental, functional, or hierarchical boundaries. It is encouraged and nurtured but not managed by the organisation's leaders.

**HQ** or Intelligent Humanity describes what happens when a society behaves with high levels of collective intelligence. Jared Diamond's wonderful book, *Upheaval*,[7] describes several examples of how nations have achieved this feat to reinvent themselves. The Covid-19 epidemic is an example of this kind of collective intelligence in operation on a global scale. Scientists across the world collaborated, sharing data amongst rivals in ways previously unimaginable, to defeat a common threat. (Then politicians became involved and acted to put the interests of their own nations first.) It is hard to see how the many other global threats to humanity can be resolved without collective intelligence – unless we invest in building collective wisdom based on positive examples of global collaboration.

The journey to maturity of Me-Q is hard enough. Through team coaching, we are gradually acquiring the ability to develop greater TQ. But the question remains: how do we develop the We-Q and HQ the world needs in time to avert the catastrophes that immature, unwise, collective intelligence has contributed to?

### The worry index

One of the benefits of looking back at the development of my thinking and practice is that I rediscover things I had completely forgotten. The worry index is one of these. Originally developed as a tool to help internal communications departments recognise and address concerns of employees during periods of acquisition or merger, it has multiple applications in change management generally and in individual coaching. The underlying principles are that:

1. People often fail to articulate their worries – either to themselves or to others
2. We are often oblivious to other people's worries – so worry-induced behaviour may seem irrational to us

The example below is the original worry index for a company going through a takeover. Surveying employees and holding focus groups identified the concerns they had and allowed the company to address them.

*The worry index for an acquisition*

*Security*

1. Am I going to be made redundant, either now or in the future?
2. How many other people will be made redundant?
3. If I remain, how secure is the job and will my conditions face reduction?
4. If I am made redundant, will I be able to get another job?
5. What are the likely impacts on career opportunities?

*My job*

1. Will I get a new boss, and if so, will I like him or her?
2. Who will assess me?

3. Will I have to change jobs or work harder?
4. Will I have to work with different people?
5. Will I have to relocate?
6. How will my performance be measured?
7. With all this going on, will I be able to take my holiday as planned?

*My prospects*

1. Will this affect my status?
2. Will it reduce/enhance my chances of promotion?
3. Will I have to learn new skills?
4. Is this my opportunity to show what I can really do?
5. What do I get out of it?
6. If I learn new skills, will those skills help me get another job if I need to?

*My values*

1. Is this the company I thought I was working for? What's happened to the caring attitude of the old company?
2. Do my contribution and loyalty count for nothing?
3. Will the company respect my home life?
4. Will I be happy if they move me out of my team?

Working with individuals, a coach, mentor, or leader can help the person create their own worry index, as a means of keeping track of and managing nagging doubts and self-doubts. Worry, of course, has negative impacts on our task concentration, sleep, general health, and relationships. And the more we try not to think about our worries, the more embedded they become. Naming them helps break this cycle. Standard coaching dogma suggests (without a lot of proof) that coaching assignments should start off by defining clients' goals. If, instead, we define and work with their worries, then goals will emerge. Dealing with the worries first creates conditions, where they will have the mental energy to envisage and pursue goals that are more ambitious and more closely connected with their values and sense of identity. Some of the questions that elicit the worries that people don't otherwise express include:

1. What keeps you awake at night?
2. What's scarily out of your control?
3. What concern do you have that do you not want other people to worry about?

A personal worry index starts with the areas of life and work a person is most worried about. These might include financial security, personal reputation, health (own and family), coping with work responsibilities, and so on. For each area, they identify a small number of questions that can put the worry into context. For example:

1. What's changing here (for better or worse)?
2. What do I need to pay attention to?
3. What can I do to alleviate this concern?
4. What plans can I put in place, so that I know what to do, if the worst happens?
5. What support can I call upon?

This pre-emptive approach to worry falls within what we now define as building resilience. It shifts the focus of worry from a detractor from performance and well-being to a good friend that makes us a more aware person recognising and dealing with potential problems before they arise.

After all, much of the time, the things that hurt us most are the unexpected, unpredictable ones that we haven't worried about!

### Connecting with others

A dominant theme throughout my work in coaching and mentoring has been working with difference. It's a human trait to gravitate to people, who we perceive to be like ourselves. When we are in such a group, we ascribe more positive qualities to it than to "outsiders." In doing so, we diminish ourselves by narrowing perspectives and restricting the growth that comes from interactions with different perspectives and narratives.

I grew up in a society, immediately after World War Two, that was far from diverse. At school in North London, I do not recall a single non-white face. The only source of cultural difference was from a large Jewish minority. Homosexuality was illegal and not talked about. It was an all-male establishment and if any thought were given to feminism, well that was sorted with giving women the vote, wasn't it? It was a safe, protected place – and, from a diversity perspective, utterly sterile. Then I was introduced to an Indian family, who had just arrived in England, and was asked to help the son, roughly my age, to get to know the capital city and adjust to his new home. I discovered that the world of people was much more complex than I had imagined. I regret now not using this opportunity more fully to experience my world through his eyes, but I didn't have the tools to do so.

Even at university, staff and students were mostly like me – except that the year I joined was the first my college had accepted male undergraduates, so there was a substantial gender imbalance. (We'll draw a curtain over the inevitable misadventures of that period!) Again, I failed to take advantage of the opportunity to see the world from a feminine perspective. The only difference I was consciously aware of was that of class. I was the first in my family to go to university for at least five generations, perhaps ever. (By the time the Clutterbuck dynasty had worked its way through the generations, the wealth had not trickled down to my branch of the tree!) It was only when, as a young journalist, I became interested in the dynamics of the workplace that it gradually dawned on me how important diversity of thinking was. I became a fervent champion of diversity in all its forms, first from a gender perspective, then racial/cultural, and ultimately from a cognitive and neurodiversity perspective.

The dominant theme for me was the value of engaging with and learning from other perspectives; how this could enhance our growth as individuals but also contribute to better decision-making, collaboration, and job satisfaction. My deep-seated value of fairness played a part, but my focus became how to help people connect with different others through honest and curious dialogue.

### Diversity dialogue

The authors of the book *Difficult Conversations*[8] point out that when we feel constrained from saying exactly what we think, it is the gap between what we are really thinking and what we say that makes a difficult conversation difficult. In essence, we are trying to have two conversations at once. Each difficult conversation, they say, is really three conversations:

1. The *what happened* or *reality* conversation (disagreement about the facts, responsibilities, expectations etc). Only by trying to understand the issue through both parties' eyes can dialogue happen.
2. The *feelings* or *emotional* conversation – what I'm feeling v what you're feeling. Trying to stay rational doesn't help, because "Difficult conversations do not just *involve* feelings, they are at their core *about* feelings." The key to learning dialogue is to understand, talk about, and manage feelings.
3. The *identity* conversation – what it means to us; i.e., what's at risk, what this says about us and our sense of self-esteem and/or identity. If we feel that our self-image is under attack, or conversely, if we accept the image of ourselves projected by someone else, the less the opportunity for dialogue.

The table below captures the essence of how I built upon these three conversations to relate them in particular to conversations across the barrier of difference. It led directly to the development of the following model, the diversity awareness ladder. The difference between general conflict, as explored in the *Difficult Conversations* book, and diversity related conflict, is that the former is most often personal, while the latter always has a systemic dimension. Among the systemic issues we identified were:

*Hierarchy gap* – It takes a lot of courage to say what you really think to someone more senior to you in an organisation. In some cultures, where respect for age is deeply ingrained, it may be even more difficult to speak out.

*Political correctness* – Studies of managers in a variety of environments show that they often fail to give honest feedback to BME colleagues, for fear of being seen to be non-PC. Lacking confidence in what they can and can't say, and how, these managers unintentionally discriminate, because they do not give BME colleagues the opportunities to correct ineffective or dysfunctional behaviours.

*Same words / different meanings* – Especially in English, words and phrases can have very different meanings. For example, the question; *Do you feel challenged by your work?* was answered positively by US employees of a multinational company and negatively by those in the UK and Continental Europe. The US employees interpreted "challenged" as being stretched and motivated; the Europeans as being unable to cope.

*Avoiding exploring own feelings, attitudes, and values* – Unless both parties can be open at this level, it will be difficult to develop real understanding.

*Problem denial* – Refusing to admit or being unable to acknowledge consciously that there is a problem can be highly dysfunctional. Taking personal responsibility can be very painful, when it means accepting that we are not meeting the ideals we espouse.

*Table 5.4* Normal versus diversity dialogue conversations

| Normal versus diversity dialogue conversations | | |
|---|---|---|
| Conversation type | Normal assumptions | Diversity dialogue assumptions |
| What is reality? | My view of the world is right | My view is one of many; I could benefit from understanding other people's perceptions |
| | I know what you intended | I know what I intended, but I can only guess at what you intended |
| | If there's poor communication/ performance etc, it's your fault | If there's poor communication/ performance etc, we have probably both contributed to it |
| Feelings conversation | We need to stay rational if we are to make progress | Only when we understand each other's feelings, will we be able to look at the issues really rationally |
| | I have to control and suppress my feelings | In order to manage my feelings, I need to be open about them |
| | It's my feelings that matter | It's both our feelings that matter |
| Identity conversation | I have to protect my self-image | I have an opportunity to understand and develop my self-image |
| | I feel incompetent/guilty/ unworthy | Nobody's perfect, but here's an opportunity to learn something that will help me get closer to it |

## The diversity awareness ladder

Getting to grips with our own stereotypes and implicit biases isn't easy. The intent of the ladder is to help us be honest with ourselves and to give us better options for connecting with people who we perceive as different to ourselves. It is a model of two conversations – the inner conversation, which represents instinctive, emotional responses to difference and is not normally spoken out loud; and the outer conversation, which offers a way of engaging with the other person to counter and overcome the concerns of the inner conversation. On the early steps of the ladder, people tend to avoid conversation with the "different" person or group – often for positive reasons, such as not wanting to offend by saying the wrong thing. When a client defines where they are on the ladder, they have a starting point for addressing the assumptions and concerns that prevent them having fully open conversations that genuinely value difference.

Our desire not to offend makes us cautious in what we do and don't say. Research into coaching and mentoring of people with disability or of different racial background found that coaches and mentors often either overemphasised the difference (for example, ascribing too much of what was happening to the client to racial prejudice by others) or avoiding it altogether (like the mentor, who never once in a 12-month relationship alluded to the fact that the other person was in a wheelchair). Both extremes have the effect of making the client feel undervalued and uncomfortable.

The principle behind the diversity awareness ladder is that, even we avoid talking to someone we see as different, there is still an internal conversation taking place, mostly unconsciously. To give a personal example, quite a few years ago, I was at an HR conference, with a large exhibition attached to it. In a prominent place within the exhibition was a stand for a publisher for the LGBT community. I made a mental note to talk to them about a mentoring project I had learned about in the United States, specifically aimed at gay professionals. I had walked through the hall several times before I realised I was about to do so again without stopping at this stand – indeed, I had unconsciously chosen routes that would not bring me immediately past it. That's when I asked myself what was the inner conversation I was having that was influencing my behaviour. I quickly understood that my internal voice was telling me that if I were seen on that stand, other people might make assumptions about my own sexuality. And that was enough to make me walk straight up there and have the conversation I had planned.

The more aware we are of our inner conversations about difference, the easier it is to change those conversations. And that gives us greater choices about the conversations we have with those people or groups. The diversity awareness ladder helps us understand both the conversations we have and those that we could have, if we have the courage. Defining where we are on the ladder gives us a starting point for addressing the assumptions and concerns that prevent us having fully open conversations that genuinely value difference.

*Table 5.5* The inner and outer conversations of the diversity awareness ladder

*The inner and outer conversations of the diversity awareness ladder*

| Stage | The inner conversation | The outer conversation |
|---|---|---|
| 1. Fear | What do I fear from this person? What do I fear learning about myself? What might I be avoiding admitting to myself? | What do we have in common? What concerns do you have about me and my intentions? |
| 2. Wariness | What if I say the wrong thing? Is their expectation of me negative and/or stereotyped? How open and honest can I be with them? | How can we be more open with each other? How can we recognise and manage behaviours that make each other feel uncomfortable/ unvalued? |
| 3. Tolerance | What judgements am I making about this person and on what basis? What boundaries am I seeking/ applying in dealing with this person? | How can we exist/work together without friction? How can we take blame out of our conversations? |
| 4. Acceptance | Can I accept this person for who they are? Can I accept and work with the validity of their perspective, even if it's different from mine? | What values do you hold? How do you apply them?How can we make our collaboration active and purposeful? |
| 5. Appreciation | What can I learn from this person? How could knowing them make a better/more accomplished person? | What can we learn from each other? How will we learn from each other? |

The five rungs of the ladder are:

**Fear** – characterised by low self-awareness and low awareness of others. At its extreme, the fear stage becomes bigotry – the deliberate avoidance of examining one's own beliefs and perspectives, for fear of undermining them. Having the inner conversation is essential in moving people on, allowing them to confront and understand their fears. The outer conversation is a stepping stone to doing so, but equally the inner conversation may stimulate more productive outer conversations.

**Wariness** – when the individual is sufficiently self-aware and aware of others to recognise that their fears are irrational, but lacks the confidence to be truly open with people, who they perceive as different. At this stage, for example, managers are often reluctant to give clear and open feedback to black or opposite gender direct reports, because they are overly concerned not to offend, or worried that they will be accused of bias. This isn't helpful for the team or the direct report.

**Tolerance** – people who express tolerance of other groups often can't let go of their own feelings of superiority. Tolerance involves no attempt to understand issues and events from the other person's perspective. It assumes that the tolerant person is right and the other person is misguided, sinful, or in some other way less worthy.

**Acceptance** – involves an understanding that the other person's perspectives are valid, well-intentioned, and reasonable, in their own context. Acceptance creates the possibility of working together in a truly collegiate manner, with differences put aside as simply part of the wallpaper.

**Appreciation** – takes the relationship and the conversation into the realms of mutual learning. The very fact of difference becomes a valuable opportunity to explore new perspectives and ideas, to test assumptions, and to create a new, more powerful sense of reality. Difference becomes a driver of change, self-awareness, and the creation of a wider, healthier, and inclusive community.

The critical steps in using the ladder in coaching, mentoring, or diversity awareness training are:

- Help the other person recognise their instinctive, often unconscious assumptions about groups of "others." (How they categorise a group may vary considerably.) Simple ways to do this include recalling times when they have had (or avoided) conversations with people from that group. How did they feel? What inner conversation was going on for them?
- Help them recognise the benefits of adopting a different inner conversation, which might lead them to a different conversation with people from that group
- Help them gradually replace the existing internal and external conversations with new, more inclusive conversations that show greater appreciation of difference
- Helping them embed these new conversations – and the new ways of thinking that underlie them – into their day-to-day responses to other people

## The psychological contract

Psychological contracts underpin most relationships at work. They are the unwritten rules and expectations people and entities have of each other – a form of social exchange. Various academic studies[9] in the 1990s showed how they address issues such as motivation, retention, and productivity. What people hear when the organisation sends out messages is modified by the filters they apply and these filters are to a significant extent influenced by the nature and the health of the psychological contract between each individual and the organisation, and between groups of employees and the organisation. What people are prepared to say is also influenced by the psychological contract. Where the contract is healthy, people are more likely to speak openly, to challenge poor practice and to take responsibility.

A key factor in the psychological contract is the perceived *fairness* of the social exchange. At the same time, the contract is about an exchange of *value*. Value in this context has three core meanings (Figure 5.7):

*Value as worth* refers to how each side creates added value for the other. For example, while the employee adds value to shareholders in the form of dividends and share price or other forms of capital appreciation, the company promises a decent salary, a pension and – often most important – an opportunity to gain skills and track record that will give the employee greater earning power, should they move on. A sense of equity is also important here – do employees feel that the reward system is fair?

*Value as respect* refers to how the employees feel about the organisation and how they feel the organisation regards them. How much pride does the employee feel working in this organisation? Is it an important part of their self-esteem? Do they feel that their contribution is recognised and seen as important by peers, superiors and customers? Is recognition perceived as merit based or on factors, such as who shouts loudest? All these add up to a sense of *being* valued.

*Values as beliefs* relates to the degree of alignment employees feel between the values they hold (about such things as honesty, how people are treated and social responsibility) and those espoused and exhibited by the company. Problems occur when people feel they are asked to leave their external values at the door when they come to work; or when they observe major differences between the values an organisation espouses and what it does in practice.

Some useful questions to investigate the worth exchange include:

- Do you feel appropriately rewarded for the work you do?
- Do people get treated equally on merit?
- Does the company invest appropriately in your development?
- Do you see a clear relationship between your investment in your own development and the opportunities open to you (in this organisation or elsewhere)?
- Is the work that you do sufficiently stretching to help you build competence and track record?

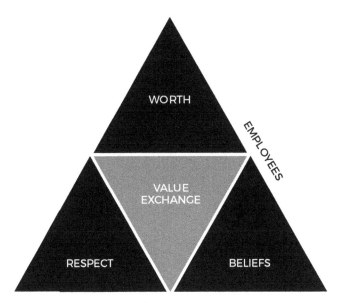

*Figure 5.7* The values triangle.

Some useful questions for the respect dimension of the psychological contract include:

- Do you feel that your contribution is sufficiently recognised?
- Are your ideas listened to and do you get credit for them?
- Do you think senior managers care about you and your peers?
- Are you proud of the work you do and the organisation you work for?
- Would you encourage your friends to work here?
- Is diversity genuinely valued or simply tolerated?

Some useful questions for the beliefs dimension of the psychological contract include:

- Do you feel you have to compromise at work on principles you'd apply in other parts of your life?
- Do you think that the leaders live up to the company values?
- Do you feel the company is honest and fair towards all its stakeholders?

The psychological contract isn't just about the employer–employee relationship. It applies to relationships between the company and all its stakeholders (Figure 5.8). Few companies spend time and resources defining and measuring these other psychological contracts, or if they do, typically assume they are discrete arenas of the business. Yet employees can be customers or shareholders, or related to them. I tried for several years to persuade companies to investigate how the psychological contracts overlapped, but never quite managed to do so. It's not difficult to identify instances, where contagion occurs between the psychological contract with one group of stakeholders and another. I recall a furniture retailer, which decided that telling customers the truth about how long it would take for their new sofa or table to arrive would lose sales. Sales staff were instructed to lie. Orders plummeted even further, because the beliefs dimension of the psychological contract with employees was broken.

A psychological contract survey for employees is reproduced in Appendix 3. The survey is copyrighted and free to use as a paper version, with attribution, but not as an electronic version.

### Relationships with vulnerable others

In any ongoing relationship, we fall into roles, which may not be obvious. Reviewing these from time to time helps keep us balanced and prevents those roles becoming "fixed."

One useful model is the triangle of *Protect – Exploit – Equate* (Figure 5.9).[10] Protect refers to the instinct to shield the learner from pain and/or to intervene on the learner's behalf. It has much in common with the parent–child dimension of transactional analysis. In this mode, we are part-parent and part-hero. We give advice, rather than help the learner work things out for themselves. It taps into all our deep instincts of protecting the vulnerable but can easily lead to being overprotective.

Exploit is the dark side. It is the instinct to manipulate others to our own ends and/or to take advantage of their weaknesses. We don't like to acknowledge this side of ourselves, but it comes to light in many, often subtle, ways – for example, when the mentor steers the mentee along a path that they wish they had taken. Mentors can sometimes create dependency in their mentees, not recognising that this is a by-product of their own needs for recognition and approbation.

Equate is where we achieve an appropriate equilibrium. It is not that we don't have the instincts to protect and exploit; they are still there, often both at the same time. The skill of equating lies in being fully aware of them and managing them. Once we get used to acknowledging these instincts, we can put them to better use. For example, if we observe an inclination to exploit, it may lead us to wonder whether other people have similar reactions to the mentee and what the implications might be for the mentee. What is there in their behaviour that makes others view them as exploitable? Similarly, awareness of our own urge to protect might stimulate a stronger focus on helping the mentee achieve greater self-confidence and self-belief.

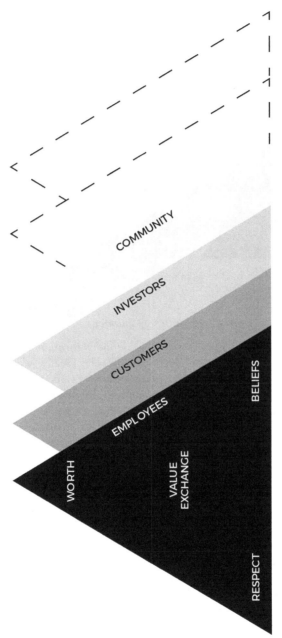

*Figure 5.8* The chain of value exchange.

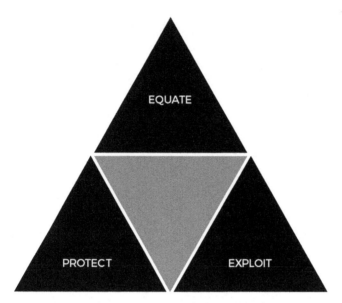

*Figure 5.9* Three ways to relate to vulnerable others.

### Getting to know a client: Clutterbuck's 13 questions

By far the fastest way to get to know someone is through an initial dialogue, in which empathetic curiosity plays a strong role. Ideally, we want to gain a multi-perspective, holistic insight that encompasses values, aspirations, culture, and both the current and historical contexts. The dialogue serves a dual purpose, creating awareness for both the coach–mentor and the client.

The following 13 questions and their subsidiary questions provide a framework, on which to build this kind of exploratory conversation.

1. How did you become you?
2. Who do you admire? (What does this say about you?)
3. What do you most care about? (How does this influence the choices you make?)
4. What are your core values? (How do you put them into practice?)
5. What do you fear most? (How do those fears affect your behaviour?)
6. What does success mean for you? (What is your purpose in life?)
7. What's the difference between your public and private selves?
8. Where do you find your energy and how do you focus it?
9. What do you still have to accomplish in your life? (What is your future story? Who do you want to become?)
10. How does what you want to achieve in the short term fit with your long-term aspirations?

11. What creates interference for you, preventing you from focusing on what's important to you? (How do you manage interference?)
12. What resources do you have/could you create to support your aspirations?
13. How do you think coaching/mentoring can help? (What are your expectations of me and of yourself?)

Of course, other questions and topics will emerge from the dynamics of the dialogue. However, these 13 questions are enough to establish the insights and rapport essential for beginning a journey of deep learning and transformational change.

### The importance of disconnect

Remember being in school, being asked a question by the teacher, and realising your mind was somewhere else and you have no idea what to say? Have you had the same experience at work meetings? Even if they didn't say, "You weren't paying attention," you feel guilty, embarrassed, and diminished. When I work with groups and teams, I try to establish a different norm. If something that has been said prompts someone to a relevant internal reflection, that should be valued. Those individual insights can contribute greatly to group or team creativity. Under the new norm, the person says: "I was having an inner moment. Could we go over that again, please?" Not only does this add to the psychological safety in the room, but much of the time other people also find it useful to have a recap.

I coined the term "moments of disconnect" (MOD) for a paper I was writing as part of my coursework for my postgraduate diploma studies in coach supervision.

Moments of disconnect I define as points in the coaching or supervision conversation when a temporary, unintended conversational disengagement occurs. Examples might be:

1. When there is a loss of rapport
2. When the supervisor feels the learning conversation has lost its energy
3. When the learning conversation isn't going anywhere

Here are three examples I drew upon. In discussing a successful coaching relationship, the coach voiced a concern that she would not be the right person to continue coaching this client once he became a chief executive. I left the door open to explore this concern, but she switched back to talking about the client's perspective about his job opportunity. The conversation lost much of its energy. Later I shared the feeling that she had walked to the edge of a cliff, shuddered, and walked away. By revisiting the moment of disconnect, we were able to confront and overcome some of her doubts about her self-efficacy coaching CEOs, when she had never been a CEO herself.

The second supervisee talked for much of the first session without saying anything. I felt increasingly uncoupled from the conversation. Eventually I understood that she was bringing to the session a whole raft of work-life balance and self-esteem issues that she did not know how to address and were preventing her from concentrating on the client case, which she was trying to present. Confronting the disconnection gave her permission to talk about these issues (she had felt guilty about wanting to raise them). Only when we had dealt with these issues was she ready to move on into the intended case discussions.

In another session, I found myself talking too much at one point. A disconnect had occurred between me and the coach – driven by feelings of projected panic from the client to the coach to me – and only when I recognised what had happened was I able to recapture the positive energy of our conversation.

### A model of disconnection management

Managing MOD requires the coach (or supervisor) to follow a logical sequence of reflections, consider a range of potential causes, and select an appropriate response. The basic framework I developed has seven stages.

1. *Who is aware of the disconnection?*
2. *Where is the disconnection located?*
3. *Do we have the conditions for sustained connection?*
4. *In what ways can we each describe the disconnection?*
5. *What is the impact of the disconnection?*
6. *What learning potential does the disconnection contain?*
7. *What action, if any, do we want to take as a result?*

In the first stage, awareness, something alerts us to the disconnect. It could be body posture, a strong, fleeting emotion, or simply a sense that rapport has broken down. A recent example brought to me in supervision was "I suddenly felt she was on autopilot." The other person may not be consciously aware of the disconnect, but there will be an impact on the flow of the conversation. Many coaches also miss signs that are obvious to a third-party observer. They are so bound up with following the process that they lose attention of the person. (This can be a particular issue with beginner coaches and NLP practitioners I observe.)

Having identified that there is a disconnect, we can look for where it is located. Is it within the client, who has come up against something painful he or she does not want to address? (And, if so, has the coach become alert to potential ethical and professional boundary issues?) Is it in the coach, triggering their biases and judgement? Is it in between them? Or is it in the system that surrounds the client and the coaching relationship? It's not necessary and sometimes not immediately possible to pin down the location, but the process of enquiry has started.

The conditions under which the conversation takes place are a good place to start. Was the potential disconnect built in from the start, because the client was not in an appropriate state of mind for the kind of conversation we are trying to have? Is there a hidden power issue here? Would a change of environment (e.g., getting out of the office and going for a walk) help? Where is their energy?

We get clarity when we describe what we observe. The coach can keep the description to himself or herself and park it as something to come back to. Or they can ask the client what they think the disconnect is. Or they can reveal their thoughts and feelings (their Gestalt) to stimulate client reaction. A key here is that a disconnect is both persons' responsibility.

Together, coach and client can now explore the impact of the disconnect on their conversation and emotions. It's important, of course, to maintain a judgement-free atmosphere – one of mutual curiosity that seeks learning in the moment. It's likely that this conversation will be tangential to the initial topic, but the coach treats the disconnect as an opportunity to learn rather than a problem to overcome.

The coach and client can now explore what to do with the insights gained. What are the implications for their future conversations? For conversations the client has with other people? For the topic with which this session began?

### Laughter

I've indulged my love of laughter in many ways, from competing with an Oxford don to writing limericks about hard-to-rhyme places, to writing humorous stories for children. I've found some very talented illustrators, who have captured the cheekiness of the narratives in the pictures that accompany them. For my first published children's story, in the late 1980s, I initially doubted my ability. I reached out to a role model I respected – the writer and comedian Spike Milligan. To my surprise and delight, he wrote me a long letter of encouragement and guidance. The stories[11] took shape one summer holiday, with me writing evenings and early mornings and trying them out with groups of children on the beach. There was no mistaking when they were engaged with when they were bored!

The advent of grandchildren brought me back into humorous writing in the past decade, with titles such as *Pegleg the Pirate* and *The Amazing Adventures of Hector, the Giant, Flying, Smelly Jellyfish.*[12]

The world of "people-who-make-others-laugh" is fascinating and holds many lessons for coaches and mentors. Great coaching is essentially *improv* on steroids. I invested in training as a stand-up comedian, with a view to improving how I used and delivered humour, then also learned the basics of *improv*, mime, and other dimensions of comedy. After a while, I became chair of the research committee at the London School of Comedy, overseeing research into using laughter to support social change (like keeping kids out of knife crime) and well-being (helping people with severe depression).

Using humour in a coaching or mentoring dialogue can be beneficial in many ways. Firstly, it helps to rebuild rapport at the beginning of a session. You might say, for example, "Tell me what has amused you most since we last met." This helps to the client to relax and to switch on their creative thinking faculties.

Secondly, humour can assist the process of helping the client taking a different perspective. For example, "What would your serious self say here and what would your frivolous self say?" Very often the frivolous self has things to say which have been suppressed by an inner voice saying: "I shouldn't be thinking like that." Bringing these emotions to the surface allows us to confront them.

Thirdly, humour helps in bringing to the surface repetitive dysfunctional behaviours or language. For example, if someone is prone to use phrases like "should," "ought to," or "must" (indicators of self-limiting beliefs). Once the client has been made aware, all it takes from the coach is a slight tilting of the head and a smile, to make the client aware that they are limiting their thinking. When clients can laugh at themselves, it is generally a sign that they are loosening their attachment to some image of themselves and that they are consciously or unconsciously trying to change a habitual behaviour or perception.

However, sometimes humour can be a defensive barrier – a technique to avoid dealing with uncomfortable issues or facing up to responsibilities. To an alert coach, the difference is usually obvious – the client deflects difficult questions by being flippant, for example. An appropriate approach here is to:

- Listen carefully to the words they use
- Reflect back to them what you are seeing and hearing
- Ask them to consider what impact their reaction might have on other people

I don't have many of the obvious traits of autism, but I do instinctively seek to find patterns, as described in Simon Baron-Cohen's *The Pattern Seekers*[13]. Watch closely any experienced stand-up comedian and you will see the patterns in their repertoire that provide rhythm. Audiences unconsciously tune in to the rhythm – and that's how the comedian maintains connection with his or her audience. (One of the easiest patterns to observe is how they use pauses.) The model below Figure 5.10 comes for me under the heading "Interesting – so what?". I include it in the spirit of raising self-awareness of your response to humorous stimuli.

### *A simple technique*

There is tragedy and comedy and tragi-comedy. The most common of these is tragi-comedy – people survive terrible events by finding the humour in them.

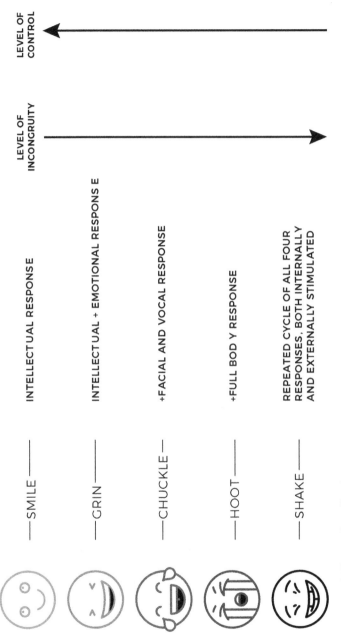

LEVEL OF
CONTROL

LEVEL OF
INCONGRUITY

INTELLECTUAL RESPONSE

INTELLECTUAL + EMOTIONAL RESPONSE

+FACIAL AND VOCAL RESPONSE

+FULL BODY RESPONSE

REPEATED CYCLE OF ALL FOUR
RESPONSES, BOTH INTERNALLY
AND EXTERNALLY STIMULATED

—SMILE—

—GRIN—

—CHUCKLE—

—HOOT—

—SHAKE—

*Figure 5.10* Five modes of laughter.

Suggest to the client that they view the issue through the lens of tragi-comedy. Help them to describe it firstly as a tragedy, then as a comedy; or vice versa. Then ask:

- How do you think other people view this issue?
- Which of the three perspectives is most realistic?
- What alternative responses do you have?
- Which of those responses would be most effective in achieving the outcomes you want?

### Summary

Whatever the profession, the role or the situation, positive outcomes always come down to the question: "What's the conversation that needs to happen here?" Good conversations depend on connectedness – even a conversation with yourself requires you to be listening. Our world is increasingly connected electronically but this has done little or nothing to enhance our connectedness as humans. Perhaps this is the greatest challenge for us in adapting to evolving society.

## Notes

1   Kardas, M, Schroeder, J, & O'Brien, E (2021). Keep talking: (Mis)understanding the hedonic trajectory of conversation.
    *Journal of Personality and Social Psychology* https://doi.org/10.1037/pspi0000379
2   Young, E. (2021) *Supersenses,* John Murray, London.
3   Canning, EA, LaCosse, J, Kroeper, KM (2019) Feeling Like an Imposter: The Effect of Perceived Classroom Competition on the Daily Psychological Experiences of First-Generation College Students *Social Psychology and Personality Science* (Nov 19) Vol 11 Issue 5, 647–657.
    Cokley, K, Smith, L, Bernard, D, Hurst, A, Jackson, S, Stone, S, Awosogba, O, Saucer, C, Bailey, M, & Roberts, D (2017). Impostor feelings as a moderator and mediator of the relationship between perceived discrimination and mental health among racial/ethnic minority college students. *Journal of Counseling Psychology, 64*(2), 141–154.
    Muradoglu, M., Horne, Z., Hammond, M. D., Leslie, S.-J., & Cimpian, A. (2021). Women—particularly underrepresented minority women—and early-career academics feel like impostors in fields that value brilliance. *Journal of Educational Psychology*
4   Grant, A (2021) *Think Again*, Penguin Random House, London.
5   Clutterbuck, D and Kernaghan, S (1995) *The Power of Empowerment,* Kogan Page, London.
6   Clutterbuck, D (2003) *Managing Work-Life Balance*, CIPD, Wimbledon.
7   Diamond, J (2020) *Upheaval*, Penguin, London.
8   Stone Douglas, Heen Sheila & Patton Bruce, 1999, Penguin.
9   Guest, D and Conway, N (2002) *Pressure at work and the psychological contract* Chartered Institute of Personnel and Development.
    Guest, D and Conway, N (2001) *Public and private sector perspectives on the psychological contract* Chartered Institute of Personnel and Development.
    Kessler, I and Undy, R (1996) *The new employment relationship: examining the psychological contract* Chartered Institute of Personnel and Development.

Makin, P (1996) *Organizations and the psychological contract: managing people at work*, Greenwood Press, Conn 416pp.

10  Coaching, mentoring and psychology frequently generate relational triangles. There is probably a pattern to this pattern, but I haven't worked it out yet!

11  The Tales of Gribble the Goblin were published by Hodder and Stoughton, London in 1983.

12  I greatly enjoy tombstone humour – witty epitaphs such as Clement Freud's Born 1927; best before…" I have suggested a limerick for my own: *Under this slab lies Dave/ Who never quite learned to behave/ His great epitaph? Was he made people laugh/ And he's chuckling still in his grave!*

13  Baron-Cohen, Simon (2012) T*he Pattern Seekers: A new theory of human innovation.*

# 6  Coaching and mentoring culture

I've been lucky enough to follow the evolution of modern coaching and mentoring from close to their beginnings. In the late 1970s and early 1980s, both mentoring and coaching attracted academic attention, particularly in the United States. The evidence-based literature on coaching then was almost exclusively related to coaching as instruction. My first forays into the field explored the nature of the developmental conversation between line manager and team member. (Like many people, I now have an aversion I can't quite explain to the term "direct report.") Tim Gallwey's *Inner Game of Tennis* seemed at the time only marginally relevant to learning and performance in the world of work, where my interests lay. It was the aspect of conversation, from my work in communication, that focused my attention. The model of performance-related developmental conversation and the other frameworks I evolved at that time stemmed from delving into literature on motivational theory and simply asking line managers to describe situations where their conversations with team members either had or had not resulted in substantial performance improvements. My frame of reference at that time was that the line manager would coach team members – so, coaching took place within a power relationship. Over time I questioned that assumption and increasingly viewed coaching (and mentoring) as mutual learning, with the line manager being a role model for learning by inviting team members to coach him or her when appropriate. And that led to a perspective of coaching as an intervention that focused not just on the individual, nor on the coach-coachee dyad, but on the dyad within the context of organisational systems.

This progression was facilitated by researching aspects of professional, externally resourced coaching and, in particular, by the coach assessment centres that I and colleagues developed to help companies evaluate the competence of externally resourced coaches. One of the key elements of a coaching assignment for executives is often the sponsor. My curiosity was aroused by the near total absence of study of the influence of the sponsor on the dynamics of the coaching relationship. It was simply assumed that the sponsor was a passive stakeholder. I took the view that the sponsor was in fact a critical part of the system. He or she can facilitate the coachee's changes by, for example, recognising and acknowledging small but significant steps. What typically happens

DOI: 10.4324/9781003323990-7

*Table 6.1* My learning journey

| *My learning journey* | | |
| --- | --- | --- |
| Coaching as instruction | Coaching as personal development | Coaching as systemic development |
| Coaching as a line activity | Coaching as a profession | Coaching as an aspect of organisational culture |
| The line manager coaches team members | The line manager creates a coaching culture in the team | The line manager curates coaching between team members |

instead is that the sponsor is more likely to notice behaviours that reinforce the coachee's pre-coaching behaviours (because they fit the sponsor's existing assumptions and narrative about the person) and more likely to discount new behaviours as minor aberrations from the norm. I now see individual coaching as being vested in the wider system, where sponsors, peers and team members all have a role in supporting the individual in making desired changes stick.

The coaching system extends to the whole organisation. I've been told I coined the phrase "a coaching and mentoring culture," but I doubt it's true – I certainly don't remember doing so! The origins of the concept lie in the much broader term "learning culture," which in turn comes from the "learning organisation." The latter owes much to the work of Peter Senge and David Garvin in the 1990s. It is described in a seminal *Harvard Business Review* working paper as "a compelling vision of an organization made up of employees skilled at creating, acquiring, and transferring knowledge"[1]. A big difference between the learning organisation and the coaching/mentoring culture, however, is that learning and knowledge are only one part of development. It's possible to learn and know a great deal but not grow up! Coaching and mentoring imply additionally an evolution in identity and wisdom as well as competence.

I and my colleague David Megginson spent a lot of energy trying to define what *we* meant by the term. We concluded that neither coaching culture nor mentoring culture is an adequate enough term on its own. Sticking with the term "coaching culture," we concluded that it was "one where the beliefs, values and mindsets driving people's behavior are deeply rooted in the discipline of coaching." To this we added that "mentoring enlarges the scope of the coaching culture, so that it encompasses not just skills and performance, but the holistic development of the each individual and his or her career."

Peter Hawkins in 2012 defined a coaching culture in the following terms[2]:

A coaching culture exists in an organisation when a coaching approach is a key aspect of how the leaders, managers and staff engage and develop all their people and engage their stakeholders, in ways that create increased individual, team and organisational performance and shared value for all stakeholders.

The book David Megginson and I produced in 2005[3] was the result of several years of research with both companies and coaches helping those companies. Two key frameworks emerged from the analysis of our interviews: the **coaching energy field** and **the stages of development of a coaching culture**. The latter formed the basis of the **coaching culture diagnostic**, which has been widely used across the world to assess where an organisation is on its journey towards achieving a coaching culture. Building on this work, we were able to identify the building blocks of a **coaching and mentoring strategy** and to develop powerful strategies for **building coaching cultures inside teams**. I also introduce briefly the concepts of **coach assessment centres** and **coach development centres**.

This chapter is in two parts: the evolution of line manager coaching and creating a coaching culture. In the former, we look into **seven steps of traditional coaching** – a reminder of where modern coaching has come from. I also present **a situational model of line manager coaching**, along with **the questioning cycle for coaching** and **styles of line manager coaching**.

## The evolution of line manager coaching

As we explored in Chapter 4, coaching as we now know it, or developmental coaching as we might call it, is a very recent phenomenon. My earliest research and concept development focused on coaching by line managers. The models, frameworks, and tools in this section relate primarily to this period. In the late 1990s and early 2000s, the professional bodies got serious about setting standards for coaching, producing competence frameworks that continue to evolve. These frameworks were designed on the assumption that coaches would normally be externally resourced professionals. That's not how things have worked out. There are at least 150,000 people globally describing themselves as professional coaches, most of them working externally. However, the growth in coach numbers is increasingly internal and internal accredited coaches are expected to overtake external within the next five years.

It helps, therefore, to distinguish between line manager coaches, for whom accreditation is not normally seen as essential and internal professional coaches, for whom it is. Some key contextual differences lie in:

1. *The role of coaching.* In the work team, coaching is typically a continuous activity, stimulated by events and opportunities that happen in the delivery of the team task. It is therefore more of an everyday *process* than a discrete assignment. In executive coaching, the relationship is both bounded and defined by the number of sessions allocated.
2. *The breadth of issues covered.* Executive coaching tends to focus on one or two predetermined issues and to conclude with at least partial resolution of those issues. Line manager coaching tends to deal with a changing agenda related to changes in the work tasks and the coachee's role competence.

3. *The nature of the coaching.* Hawkins & Smith[4] refer to four types of coaching, with different perspectives and requirements of a coach – skills, performance, behavioural, and transformational. Generally speaking, line manager coaches do not focus on either end of this spectrum (skills coaching tends to be delegated to other team members or to subject experts outside the team) and transformational coaching is too long-term and requires a much more substantial set of coaching competences than most line managers would be able to provide. Line manager coaching therefore tends to concentrate on performance and on behaviour, insofar as it has a direct impact on performance.

4. *The contractual relationship.* Except where a team has a coaching culture, line manager coaching is essentially a duty, deriving from being effective in a leadership role. Executive coaching tends to be seen as more of a service. (This is quite distinct from mentoring, which is built more around a relationship.)

There are also a number of practical differences, as Table 6.2 identifies.

The revolution of leadership style towards distributed leadership is likely to accelerate the blurring of these distinctions. The more that coaching becomes regarded as an essential competence for managers and leaders, the more relevant

*Table 6.2* Line manager as coach v coach external to the team

| Line manager as coach v coach external to the team | |
| --- | --- |
| Line manager as coach | Coach from outside the team |
| Focus mainly on solving today's problems and meeting short-term needs | Focus on raising awareness and building capacity |
| Agenda driven by line manager | Agenda driven by client |
| Pace and timescales driven by line manager and/or needs of the team/organisation | Working at client's pace and timescales |
| Importance of consequences for the whole team | Emphasis on consequences for the client |
| Strong link with performance management – typically looking at multiple areas of improvement | Weak link with performance management – focused on small number of specific objectives |
| Responsibility for discipline | Responsibility to the client |
| Conformance with HR policy | Independent of HR policy |
| Embedded in the corporate culture and politics | Brings external view of the corporate culture and politics |
| Confidentiality is complex. Separating out what gets said in coaching from what gets addressed in performance management is a constant challenge. | Confidentiality is relatively simple, with the rules about when it can be broken enshrined in coaching ethics |

it becomes to achieve at least a basic level accreditation, to extend the range of coaching interventions and to create more of a service relationship.

Effective coaching by line managers integrates the skills and behaviours of the coach with those of the coachee. The core process involves several stages of integration, as shown in Figure 6.1.

Coach and coachee work in close partnership, sharing their feedback on each other's performance.

### The Coach

- helps the coachee plan, set up, and run a development activity
- observes them in action
- gives the coachee "external/extrinsic" feedback on what they have done

### The Coachee

- carries out the development activity
- assesses their own performance through "internal/intrinsic" feedback
- reviews their experience with the coach

## The seven steps of traditional coaching

The line manager as performance coach needs to apply a systematic approach to helping people achieve personal change. The framework below sets out the seven key steps to follow:

*Step 1: Identify the need to improve:*
- Where do the development priorities lie for the coachee?
- Where will a performance improvement have the biggest business impact?

*Step 2: Observe, and gather evidence:*
- Identify sources of evidence that will help the coachee understand the reality of their situation
- Wherever possible cross-check one source against another to make sure that the findings are accurate
- Determine the coachee's current level of performance as a baseline against which to measure their progress

*Step 3: Motivate to set and own personal improvement targets:*
- Help the coachee understand they have a development need, and that they can improve
- Help the coachee set achievable targets they can commit to
- Define and clarify what you are both trying to achieve

*Figure 6.1* The traditional coaching cycle.

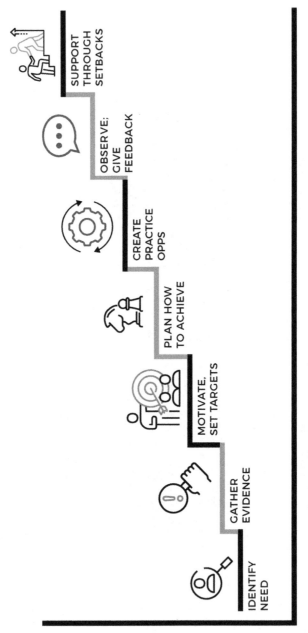

*Figure 6.2* Seven steps of traditional line manager coaching.

*Step 4: Help to plan how to achieve those targets:*
- Ensure that the target is broken into small enough steps to be able to track progress
- Listen to the coachee's ideas about development opportunities
- Identify potential development opportunities for the coachee
- Guide the coachee, helping them choose the opportunity right for their needs

*Step 5: Create opportunities to practise the desired skills:*
- Talk in detail with the coachee to identify the most effective development activities, targeted precisely at their needs
- Create opportunities, for example work based projects, to develop or practise the target skills

*Step 6: Observe in action and give objective feedback:*
- Review their performance
- The emphasis is on the coachee giving their assessment of their performance first to see what they've learned from the experience before the coach feeds back

*Step 7: Support and help to work through setbacks:*
- Identify further options to accelerate or reinforce the learning

This approach would undoubtedly be seen as old-fashioned by many coaching schools. But it still has high validity in circumstances where the intended outcome is an improvement in skills or basic behaviours. It's arguably still the most common approach in sports coaching. It is an important part of the legacy and history of coaching and, while it may not be as "sexy" as more modern methods, this "workhorse of coaching" is far from obsolete.

## A situational model of line manager coaching

Line manager coaching achieves most in situations where the coachee has a fair degree of motivation and ability to learn, and a belief in their ability to influence their performance – an attribute called *locus of control*.

An *outer locus of control* occurs when someone feels that what happens to them is in someone else's hands; by contrast, someone with an *inner locus of control* has great confidence in their ability to influence events. Seeking out opportunities to learn is closely associated with being a "high flyer."

*Narrow achievers* have a strong interest in their own development, but a low sense of their ability to influence their environment and/or performance. Typically, they are competent in a narrow range of tasks, but show low flexibility. Coaching for these people often needs to focus on motivating them to experiment more widely.

High achievers have both a strong sense of direction in terms of development, as well as a strong sense of their own worth. They are already good performers.

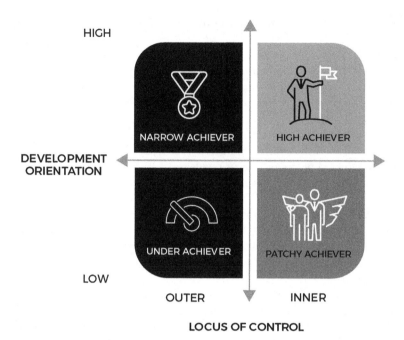

*Figure 6.3* Developmental orientation versus locus of control.

Preparation for them focuses on achieving even higher performance; it also helps them maintain their grip on reality and to focus on specific skills.

Patchy achievers are generally capable people who lack either the capacity or motivation to achieve the consistency of performance that characterises high achievers. Coaching helps them understand the need for consistency and plan how to address that need.

Underachievers are people who have both low development motivation and an outer locus of control; they may sometimes need remedial counselling before they can benefit fully from coaching. However, with patience, most can be helped to recognise that they have more potential than they admit to themselves.

## The questioning cycle for coaching

This model was my earliest foray into the use of questions by coaches and mentors. As in much other research, the starting point was observing coaches coaching. The effectiveness of the coaching was assessed on the basis that it was a purposeful conversation that resulted in useful insights on the part of the coachee. The coaching method or philosophy was not taken into account, to make the assessment of effectiveness as clean and with as little observer "noise" as possible. The four kinds of question are represented here as a cycle, but in practice coaches often extemporised in the order they followed.

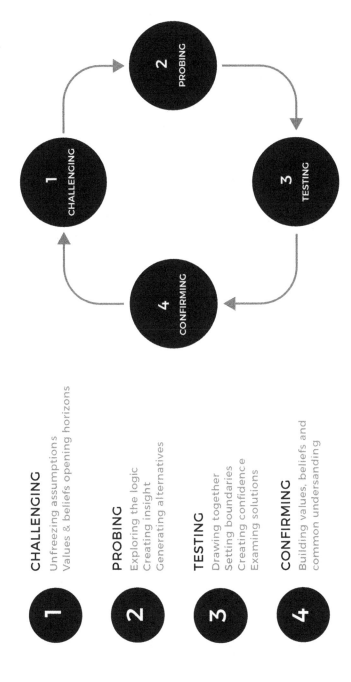

*Figure 6.4* The questioning cycle.

The cycle of questions can be entered or left at any point, but it provides a logical framework, by which the coach can ensure that the learner gains appropriate understanding and uses it to develop realistic plans of action.

Challenging questions are about causing the learner to take stock and reassess what they may have taken for granted. They are often discomforting. An example might be: "How much of the problem you are having with your colleague could be the result of your own behaviour?"

Probing questions dig deep into the logic and structure of problems, generate alternative ways of looking at things, and suggest new possibilities. For example: "What behaviours in you might stimulate a different reaction from your colleague?"

Testing questions aim to examine proposed solutions, to establish if they are really practical and appropriate. For example, "So, how do you think he would react if you asked for his advice at the beginning of the project rather than half-way through?" or "What are the potential benefits and risks of this approach?"

Confirming questions ensure that coach and learner both have the same understanding of the issue and the options for tackling it – or that they are clear where they don't agree. They often sound like statements: "So, we've agreed that this is probably a case of behaviour breeds behaviour and that you could break the negative cycle?"

## Styles of line manager coaching

The style line manager coaches adopt (according to situation if they are adept, or according to the approach that feels most comfortable to them, if they are less experienced) appears to depend on two dimensions:

1. The *directive – non-directive* dimension concerns the question of who is in charge of the relationship and its process. Who sets the learning goals? Who sets the pace? Who suggests the learning tasks or experiments? Who owns the feedback? In practice, a good coach will vary how directive he or she is according to the attitudes and behaviour of the learner.
2. The second dimension is the *intrinsic – extrinsic* perspective. This distinguishes between giving feedback and enabling the coachee to generate their own feedback.

The combination of these dimensions gives rise to four distinct coaching styles, which we can call "assessor," "tutor," "demonstrator," and "stimulator."

*Assessors* set task and learning goals for the individual. They give mainly extrinsic feedback. This style inevitably takes ownership of the learning away from the learner and, at the extreme, results in relatively narrow learning: employees learn only what they need to keep the manager off their back! This style sits broadly at the "tell" end of the coaching spectrum.

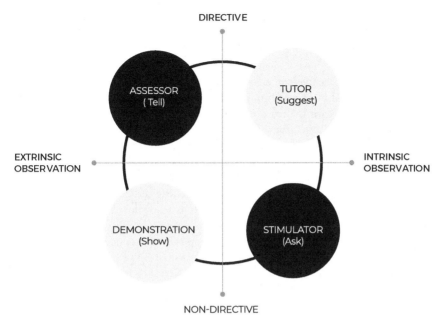

*Figure 6.5* Four styles of line manager coaching.

*Demonstrators* are most comfortable at the "show" stage of the coaching spectrum. They show the learner what could be achieved, either by doing it themselves, or by reference to other people's experiences. The emphasis on showing implies a "right" way of doing things, but learners are encouraged to adapt what they have seen and to experiment with their own approaches. At their most effective, they avoid phrases like "*Do it this way*" in favour of more inclusive wording, such as: "*What did you notice about the way I dealt with those side issues at the meeting?*"

*Tutors* set learning goals and negotiate with the learner about how to achieve them. They typically tell the learner what to observe intrinsically: "When you give this presentation, think about the degree of eye contact you achieve with the audience." The problem with this style is that by directing the learner's attention towards some observations, the tutor may cause them to tune out other, equally useful, ones. This style corresponds reasonably well with the "suggest" stage of the coaching spectrum.

*Stimulators* work with the learner's own goals. They operate at the "work it out yourself" end of the coaching spectrum, encouraging the learner to apply his or her own logic and experience to the situation. This style is much more demanding of the learner who takes considerable responsibility for the process and needs a certain maturity to cope with uncertainty about where the process is going.

Effective line manager coaches demonstrated a high ability to shift style according to the needs of the learner. The most common reason managers make poor coaches is that they always operate at the same point in the style spectrum – whatever the situation.

## Coming up to date

In the nearly three decades since I and colleagues generated these models, there has been a gradual shift away from line managers doing coaching to team members and towards creating a team climate and culture, where coaching behaviours are inherent in collective co-development. More recently, I observe that some leaders have evolved into roles where they curate the coaching conversations that happen between team members. This is not quite supervision (in the coaching sense) but it does have elements of supporting the growth of team members' coaching skills, role modelling coaching and being coached, and integrating coaching into team routines, such as team development planning, quality management, and decision-making.

One area that has not shown much progress is the concept of the skilled coachee. It's been a hobby-horse of mine for at least 20 years that, if coaching is a collaborative learning conversation, the coachee needs to understand what to expect and how to make the most of the coaching dialogue. Otherwise, it's like doing the tango when only one partner knows the steps! It is regrettable that so few organisations think to invest in coachee education.[5]

There is also much work to be done about the status of internal coaches. It's becoming more common for internal coaches to be accredited with one of the professional bodies in the field, but professional supervision is rare.

Not long after the turn of the century, I started asking participants on workshops what happened when their managers went on a line manager as coach course. Frequently, they described a sense of discomfort, in both the manager and themselves. Either the manager was self-conscious and plodding as he or she worked through the coaching model they had been taught, or they were relatively fluid, but didn't create the context where the coachee felt they were an equal partner in the process. Most of the time, everyone went back to their previous behaviours, which were more comfortable in their familiarity. From these insights, we experimented in a range of organisations with approaches that allowed everyone in the team to learn about coaching together and to collaborate in applying their learning to the way they worked as a team. Thus, the concept of a **team coaching culture** was born.

We had already been exploring the concept of coaching culture for some time, but the evidence that "sheep dip" approaches weren't working heightened our interest. Hence the specific investigation that David Megginson and I conducted into organisational coaching culture for *Making Coaching Work*.

## Creating a coaching culture

Looking back, I detect some naivety in our original perceptions of a coaching culture. Our vision was that it would be a way of organisational being

– a mindframe that permeated every aspect of the processes and relationships within an organisation. While many organisations gave lip service to this, in practice the underlying assumptions were much more related to creating an overlay that only connected to organisational systems at key points – a bit like pegs holding down a tent. In a recent study I conducted with The Conference Board, a major current challenge revealed was that many senior managers were unable to adapt to the requirements of post-Covid leadership. To cope with an environment that felt increasingly out of their control, they resorted to trying to control more and more – to less and less effect. A high proportion of these leaders have been through some form of coach training. What's lacking is support in the organisational systems to help them let go and embrace the roles of both coaching role model and curator of a coaching culture.

The coaching energy field and the coaching culture diagnostic are both useful tools to at least create some clarity about where the organisation is on its journey towards a coaching culture.

## The coaching energy field

A coaching culture doesn't happen in isolation. It is embedded in and influenced by the organisation's existing culture, structure and systems. We identified five critical factors that either provided positive energy to support the evolution of a coaching culture – or prevented it from taking root. These were:

1. Experience of coaching and being coached. One of the downsides of widespread training of line managers as coaches is that it produces a lot of people who coach badly. Formulaic coaching, rigidly following a prescribed model such as GROW, is uncomfortable for both the coach and the person coached. The situation is made worse when the focus is mostly on remedial coaching – a study by Phillip Ferrar found that employees actively avoided their managers to escape being coached![6] On the other hand, positive experiences of being coached can lead people to seek coaching, which helps to build the coaching culture.
2. Capability. The more confident people feel in their ability to coach well, the more they will coach. One of the practical ways organisations encourage this is to train people to be mentors – because they can practise in the mentoring relationship the developmental skills and conversations they might hesitate to employ with direct reports, where there is more personally at stake. We also found that capability could be enhanced with technology (for example, training people to coach remotely), infrastructure (are there quiet places people can meet away from the subtle influences surrounding the normal working space?) and the availability of opportunities for people to grow and enhance their coaching skills. It's now also possible for managers to gain accreditation as coaches and mentors, for example, from the European Mentoring and Coaching Council.

3. Beliefs and values. How switched-on people are to continuous learning and how well the organisation balances the importance of task achievement versus personal development.

4. Integration with HR and other key organisational systems. The strength of the link with business priorities, appraisal and development processes, and reward systems is also important.

5. Dialogue. The degree of psychological safety and honest conversation that is the norm in the organisation.

Measuring the energy field can be done very simply, through interviews, to provide a baseline that indicates the scale of the task ahead, if the organisation commits to creating a coaching culture.

## Stages of development of a coaching culture

Based on multiple case studies, we were able to identify four stages that organisations went through in creating a coaching culture. It's fair to say that we didn't find any organisations that had reached the final stage, where coaching was firmly embedded in the whole organisation – and it is very hard to find examples even now, 17 years later. What we did find was pockets of excellence within larger company structures. The four stages were:

*Nascent.* Here coaching happens but it is ad hoc, often either an executive privilege or a remedial intervention. Coaching is just another tool and there is little concept of what effective coaching looks like, nor measurement to see what the organisation is getting for its expenditure on external coaches and investment in line manager training. Top managers present poor role models for coaching behaviours and invest little in developing their own coaching skills. Coaching takes a back seat to other, more urgent, short-term demands in the workplace. When and whether people get coaching is only loosely related to needs and wants – so, the most difficult behavioural or ethical issues often don't get addressed.

*Tactical.* The organisation understands how establishing a coaching culture will add value, but little idea of how to realise that value. Top management are only loosely involved – this is an HR issue. Training for line managers is widely available, but post-training support is sparse. The link between HR systems such as succession planning and appraisal is at best tenuous. People recognise the need to tackle difficult issues but will only do so in environments where they feel very safe.

*Strategic.* People generally see the value of coaching and feel both competent and confidence to coach in a variety of situations. It's a lot more difficult to get promoted if you don't demonstrate coaching behaviours. Top management generally set an example by coaching others and being open about being coached. There is also some reciprocal coaching and mentoring (where junior employees coach or mentor more senior). The link between coaching and key business drivers is widely understood. However, while the formal coaching process works well (in part because it is measured), the informal process creaks at the joints. Coaching and mentoring are beginning to be integrated with the wider portfolio of HR systems.

*Embedded.* Both formal and informal coaching happen frequently and consistently across the organisation. Coaching and mentoring are so seamlessly built into the structure of HR systems that they occur automatically. People seek feedback and coaching from colleagues, irrespective of their relative position in the hierarchy. Coaching and mentoring are so seamlessly incorporated into the culture that they don't necessarily get referred to by name – it's simply a normal working conversation.

The questionnaire, which has been used widely both for assessing where an organisation is and for research, can be downloaded from *http://www.clutterbuck-cmi.com/* [WEBSITE] and is available for open research use, with acknowledgement.

## Creating a coaching culture

Ed Schein at the Sloan School of Management at MIT describes three aspects of culture. He defines culture as a process of social learning, based upon:

1. Basic assumptions – how the organisation relates to its environment; how it perceives the nature of reality, time and space, human nature, and the appropriateness of relationships. Basic assumptions are often taken for granted and are rarely expressed consciously.
2. Values – what people hold to be important (for example the relative importance of family versus work)
3. Artefacts and creations – technology, art, physical structures, visible and audible behavioural patterns. (For example, directors' parking spaces or separate staff entrances to retail premises.)

A significant issue is the degree to which the top management team understand what is involved in making culture change happen. They need to understand:

1. The complexity of changing the culture
2. Their role in doing so – it's very common for them to assume that everyone else needs to change but not them!
3. The time frame (what can reasonably be achieved in one, two, and three years) and scale of investment needed
4. The implications of succeeding. (Do they really want to lead an organisation where people constantly question and reflect, where continuous improvement of both people and processes is the norm?)

The table below describes one way I developed with organisations to put the culture change into context, so that it could be more closely linked with business outcomes. It is loosely based on the European Quality Model.

*Table 6.3* The coaching culture quality process

The coaching culture quality process

| | Purpose (goals) and policies | Systems and processes | People | Outcomes and measurement |
|---|---|---|---|---|
| Individual | Personal development plans | Performance management<br>Time management<br>Reflective space | Coaching/ mentoring skills<br>C & M support systems<br>Executive coaching resources | Quality of coaching<br>Achievement of developmental and career goals |
| Team | Team development plans<br>Resource allocation policies | Communication<br>Task management<br>Quality management<br>Decision-making | Team member's co-coaching skills | Achievement of team goals<br>Psychological safety |
| Organisation | Business development plans<br>HR policies and procedures | Strategic planning<br>Recruitment and retention<br>Talent management | Leadership role models<br>Culture change steering group | Measures of:<br><br>• Coaching culture<br>• Innovation and risk climate |

The items in each column are examples – each organisation will have its own perspectives and emphases. Detailing the various elements in this way provides a pragmatic and coherent method of culture change planning.

## Components of a coaching culture strategy

Multiple workshops with organisations around the world provided the basis for creating a simple framework to address all the key issues in a strategy for achieving a coaching culture. The 12 elements are:

1. *Quality and VFM in using external coaches.* It might be assumed that external coaches are generally more effective than internal, but there's no real evidence for that. Indeed, a study in 2015[7] concluded that internal coaches were more effective. Among reasons advanced are that internal coaches have a better understanding of the corporate culture and politics and are more likely to have good professional supervision. The problem is that coaching qualifications don't equate to coaching competence (accreditations are hygiene factors!), nor do fee levels, nor do claimed hours of coaching experience. Coach assessment centres are one way of evaluating an external coach's competence, but they are expensive to run. Interviews tend to favour coaches who are good at self-marketing, so rewards hype over substance. There really is no substitute for observing a coach actually coaching. It's therefore important to have:
   - A robust process for evaluating how external coaches coach and how they will fit the specific needs and culture of the organisation
   - A clear structure and policy for determining appropriate fee levels for different kinds of coaching. What is the change intended and what is the value of achieving that change? What corresponding level of skill or mastery does this require in a coach? So, for example, team coaching would normally attract a higher rate than individual coaching.

2. *Creating an internal cadre of experienced, semi-professional coaches.* Externally resourced coaching is relatively expensive. So, it's not surprising to see a major shift towards developing in-house coaches with similar levels of qualification to their external counterparts. It's normally assumed that these coaches should work with people below the C-suite, while externals coach the top team and most senior executives. That's a view I regularly question, by recommending that the organisation have a clear policy about when and why an external is needed. There are, of course, issues of relative power (though external coaches can also be over-awed by their clients) and confidentiality, but often the main reason for bringing in coaches from outside is to feed executives' egos. A creative solution can be to ensure executives have experience of both internal and external provision. If internal and external coaches can be seen as an integrated resource, as in the UK's National Health Service, it can be to everyone's benefit. It's now also increasingly common for team coaching pairs to

have one internal and one external coach. The different perspectives each brings enrich the coaching sessions.

3. *Supervision for coaches.* The main professional bodies all recommend that coaches have professional supervision and those bodies that originated in Europe all require it. Lack of evidence of regular supervision would rule out any executive coach in working for many of Europe's major organisations. Mentor-coaching, as recommended by the ICF, can be useful for business building and for gaining accreditation, but is not supervision, which requires extensive additional study and qualification. Within companies, group supervision for internal coaches is the most cost-effective form of provision in groups of up to eight, but some organisations also provide internal coaches with the opportunity to take urgent issues to individual supervision. Mixing internal and external coaches in supervision groups can also have positive outcomes in terms of co-learning.

4. *Developing the skills of line managers to use coaching behaviours and hold developmental conversations.* Mentoring programmes can be a "Trojan horse" here. Developmental conversations with someone outside of their reporting line have less at stake for a manager, so they can experiment more freely.

5. *Creating a coaching culture within the work team.* Educating employees in how to be coached and mentored and to take charge of their own careers and self-development is a strongly worthwhile investment.

6. *Team coaching.* Team coaching, explored in greater depth in Chapter 7, is many times more complex and more impactful than individual coaching. Team coaching is not team building, nor team facilitation, nor coaching all the members of a team individually, although it might encompass all of these. It is about enhancing the performance of the team now and creating the capability to perform even better in the future.

7. *Linking the coaching mindset to business objectives.* Given the similarity between coaching and mentoring, it is surprising that the norm of focusing mentoring around a business objective hasn't often carried over into coaching. For example, if retention of talent is a key business enabler, how can we employ coaching in support of that? Pretty much every corporate objective, from increasing sales to developing a more ethical climate, can be supported by coaching. Making explicit connections takes coaching from being a generalised behaviour focused on individual change to a mindset that has the potential to promote systemic, organisational change.

8. *IT and other supporting resources.* From coachbots to apps, technology is providing all sorts of enhancements that can increase the effectiveness of coaching. At the simplest level, having a pool of coaches who people can research and approach online reduces the admin burden for HR. Integrating coaching systems with general HR systems means that development needs identified through appraisal feedback or self-administered diagnostics can be addressed immediately through a combination of coaching and other learning resources.

9. *Continuous education for coaches.* A phenomenon that occurs frequently in corporations is that they train a cohort of internal coaches, who are enthusiastic at first, but gradually lose interest and drop out. From interviews with both coaches and HR responsible for them, it seems that they lose enthusiasm and tend to turn their attention to their own teams rather than the wider organisation. The key to retaining their interest is to provide opportunities for them to grow in their roles as coaches. This can be through coach development centres, ad hoc continuous education and/or creating a coaching career path for them. The latter is becoming more significant as independent coaching becomes a "normal" late career choice. Experience as an internal coach is motivating, because it links directly to their future career.

10. *Measurement.* The coaching culture questionnaire provides a general overview of progress towards a coaching culture. However, it's also valuable to target more specific issues, such as:

    1. The impact of coaching and mentoring on key business enablers, such as diversity and inclusion
    2. The coaching style and competence of line managers, as assessed by themselves and by their direct reports
    3. The quality of coaching by internal and external accredited coaches

11. *Top management sponsors and role models.* I've seen numerous examples of progress towards a coaching culture made or broken by the behaviour of the top team. The CEO of Barclay's Bank lost all credibility, in terms of insisting on the need for an open and ethical climate, when he was himself censored for demanding confidential details of a whistleblower and the company fined $15 million. This is one of the toughest challenges in creating a coaching culture. To be effective role models for coaching, executive leaders must be larger than life in demonstrating coaching behaviours and ways of thinking.

12. *Coaching and mentoring management.* The role of programme manager has grown in importance and stature as organisations focus on achieving greater value from their investments in coaching and mentoring. The formal qualification for programme managers introduced by the EMCC in recent years has also given status to the role, which is often seen as a career move that enables the role holder to acquire a breadth of knowledge about and build connections across the company.

## Building the coaching culture inside teams

In the early 2000s, I started to gather anecdotal evidence about the effectiveness of "sheep-dip" training for line managers as coaches. (Typically, this would be a two- or three-day line manager as coach workshop.) The results were even worse than I expected. Many managers went back to their teams and reverted to their old behaviours immediately. Others tried to behave as they had learned, but found that within a few days, they were back to normal.

What had gone wrong? As I listened to their stories – and in some cases also listened to their teams talking about their experience of the same events – it became clear that this failure was nigh-on inevitable. Line managers and their teams form a complex system. Over time, they develop patterns and habits of working together, and these can be hard to break. Once a system is established, it will react to any change from within or without by attempting to revert back to the way things were before – even if those ways were dysfunctional. Given that coaching, when done effectively, can be quite an uncomfortable experience, it is hardly surprising that the system sought to return to equilibrium. From these experiences, we captured a number of significant ground rules for embedding coaching within work teams:

## If you are going to change the system, you have to change the whole system

Change one part and the system will resist. Change the whole and you have a high chance of making the change stick. In the team context, it is critically important to engage the whole team – manager and all his or her direct reports – in understanding and supporting the change to a coaching culture. An analogy with just training the line manager is ballroom dancing. If only one partner knows how to tango, a couple is not going to do well! In a team with a coaching culture, everyone understands the basics of coaching and can coach everyone else. (That includes, on occasion, the line manager being coached by a direct report!) Equally, everyone needs to know how to *be* coached, so they can help the coach help them.

### Acquiring the coaching mindset takes time

Coaching is both a mindset and a skill set. A concentrated workshop can provide basic knowledge, skills, and some opportunities to practise in a safe environment outside the team. But the impact of coaching typically happens between coaching conversations, when the learner reflects on insights, ideas, issues, and intentions. It seems that learning to coach and be coached is most effective when broken up into relatively small chunks, with sufficient space (at least a couple of weeks) to reflect, absorb, and practice using what has been learned.

### The line manager and the team need to have clear expectations of each other

Research identifies a long list of potential barriers to effective coaching by line managers, from being seen to have their own agenda, to finding it hard break out of parent-child behaviours. All of these can be overcome, if the line manager and the team have clear expectations about the nature and purpose of coaching. One of the big mind shifts needed is from the assumption that the line manager will do coaching to team members, to the recognition that their role is to create the environment, where coaching happens. (The coach may be another team member or someone from outside, as well as the manager.)

### The change process needs to be supported

Within the team, developing an environment of psychological safety is closely correlated with speed of acquiring a coaching culture. At the same time, teams progress more confidently if they feel that their learning journey is supported from outside, for example, by senior management. External support may take the form of a specialist team coach or facilitator – an outsider with the skills to help the team deal with issues such as unsurfaced conflict or clarifying the team purpose.

### Learning needs to be related to current issues for the team

Teams focused on delivering demanding targets don't have a lot of time for the abstract and theoretical. They do want to know what the benefits of achieving a coaching culture will be (both individually and collectively), but, for the most part, they want to see how what they are learning can be applied to practical and relatively immediate issues the team faces in delivering what is expected of it.

We took our conclusions to a number of large UK and multinational employers and shared some ideas about how to design an approach that would address all the issues we had identified. The result was a series of experiments, in sectors from retail to higher education. The core of the experiment, in each case, was an on-line learning resource, consisting of podcasts, self-diagnostics, and background reading. The number of modules varies according to the depth of learning required and the logistics of learning management in each organisation. Each member of a team is expected to work through these materials (taking typically no more than one hour) before the team meets for a session, often attached to the end of a regular team meeting, where they explore their learning from the pre-work together and discuss how they will apply it in their own environment. They then contract with each other to practise skills and processes they have learned. Over the course of the modules, the team gradually becomes more confident and capable of using coaching processes and the coaching mindset becomes engrained in the way they think about work issues generally.

As I write, I and colleagues are revisiting the experiments with a revised and updated set of resources incorporating the extensive new knowledge that we have about team culture.

## Coach assessment and development centres

The idea of assessing coaches arose because various companies asked for help in determining whether they were getting value for money from the external coaches they were hiring. Part of the problem was that fees tended to be related more to marketing expertise than to competence. At the same time, formal qualifications didn't always reflect how effect a coach was – they were (and are) more of a hygiene factor than a comparison of value-added. In the next chapter, I explore our ongoing work in coach maturity, which was a direct outcome of the assessment centres we established with a number of large employers to observe how coaches actually coached.

The design of assessment centres varied, but the starting point was always an application form that covered basic factors such as initial and continuing coach education, philosophy of coaching, areas of specialisation, and so on. All of the organisations wanted coaches with considerable experience. The other elements were:

1. A psychological interview (included in early designs but dropped for cost reasons in most subsequent ones). This aimed to check that the person was safe to practice. We did find some coaches, for example, who were so caught up in their own problems that they could not help but project these onto clients. Over time, we realised that these traits would also be picked up in subsequent stages.
2. A panel interview, exploring the coach's journey, philosophy, and approach. A frequent concern here was when the coach exhibited no curiosity about the client in context. It didn't seem to matter to them what the client's role was, or the circumstances of the organisation and sector. Many also failed to exhibit any evidence of systemic thinking.
3. An observed real play, with a real client, provided by the organisation. Two observers sat at the back of the room with a checklist of basic attributes that amounted to *can they hold a purposeful learning conversation?*
4. Written evaluations of the real play by the coach and the coachee.

Scores were recalibrated at the end of each day, to ensure consistency.

The depressing realisation from these events was that consistently, two-thirds of coaches were unable to achieve event the basics. (I recall one, in an event for a European bank, who talked at the client for 45 minutes. When he finally asked a question, he answered it himself!) On the positive side, the coaches who really listened and posed insight-provoking questions were a joy to observe. One of the interesting facets was the difference in how coaches approached the assessment centres. Some saw it as a unique opportunity to get some feedback on how they coached; others saw it as an affront to their dignity and experience. There was a near perfect correlation between how they scored – the former were always amongst the most effective coaches and the latter amongst the worst!

The principles behind the assessment centre can be applied to coaches within organisations, as development centres. The same basic approach is supplemented with a much higher level of feedback, by both expert observers and peers, and an action learning set, in which they are supported by colleagues in following a detailed personal development plan as a coach.

## The role of a coaching and mentoring programme manager

The coaching/mentoring programme manager is key to the success of the programme. Their role and responsibilities are to:

1. Promote coaching and mentoring across the business and ensure that senior management are supportive
2. Manage and administer the programme – from defining the objectives and success criteria to recruitment, matching, training, and evaluation
3. Provide and maintain confidentiality
4. Be available to help relationships that are struggling
5. Managing expectations of all stakeholders and keep them informed
6. Ensure participants and HR have the support resources they need
7. Monitor relationships and evaluate the programme – constantly assessing the status of their programme and making adjustments to it
8. Maintain financial control over the programme
9. Set up and maintain administrative records for the programme. For example:
   1. Participant details
   2. Training attended
   3. Matching details
   4. Date of first meeting
   5. Waiting list of participants
   6. Relationship and programme outcomes
      A programme manager will ensure appropriate systems are put in place to track this data and will store and share this data safely.
10. Ensure their own succession so that the programme will not falter when they move on

## Summary and a look ahead

The concept of a coaching culture brings together many of the themes elsewhere in this volume. It requires leadership committed to personal change as well as organisational change. It requires recognition that the fulcrum for progressing through the phases of achieving of coaching culture is the work team. It is in the day-to-day work of the team that people make the choices whether or not to think and behave in a coaching manner. This in turn requires a high degree of connectedness and communications – so that all parts of the team and organisational systems become open and responsive to questioning and co-reflection. It requires the integration of coaching and mentoring as mutually supportive ways of supporting people's growth – in how people perform and how they become the persons they aspire to be.

I'm reminded of a question that arose out of my attempts to define systemic talent management. It was: "Why would anyone really talented want to work here?" In the great surge of post-Covid resignations, a factor driving people to move is their search for a working environment where they can feel valued, purposeful, and fulfilled. Creating coaching cultures is one of the most efficient – and potentially, the least costly – way I can think of to achieve that!

## Notes

1 Garvin, D.A., Edmondson, A.C., and Gino, F., 2008. Is yours a learning organization?. *Harvard Business Review, 86*(3), p.109.
2 Hawkins, P (2012) *Creating a Coaching Culture,* Open University Press, Maidenhead.
3 Clutterbuck, D and Megginson, D (2005) *Making Coaching Work: Creating a coaching culture*, CIPD, Wimbledon.
4 Hawkins, P. and Smith, N., 2010. Transformational coaching. *The complete handbook of coaching*, pp.231–244.
5 Aside from my e-books, *How to be a great coachee* and *The leader's guide to being coached*, there is very little literature. One notable exception is a paper by Paul Stokes (Stokes, P.K., 2015. *The skilled coachee: An alternative discourse on coaching*. Sheffield Hallam University (United Kingdom).
6 Ferrar, P. (2006). The paradox of manager as coach: Does being a manager inhibit effective coaching? Unpublished Master's dissertation, Oxford Brookes University, Oxford.
7 Jones et al (2015) The effectiveness of workplace coaching: A meta-analysis of learning and performance outcomes from coaching, *Journal of Occupational and Organizational Psychology,* March, pp20–21.

# 7    Coach practice and development

The history of coaching is relatively short. The word "coach" doesn't appear till 1849, according to the *Oxford English Dictionary*, where it referred to a tutor who helped students get through their exams. It then appears in 1851 in *Pendennis*, a novel by William Thackeray, where the coach was a dance instructor. From there, the concept of a coach spread to sport, first rowing, then tennis. It caused considerable debate. Was it unfair and unsportsmanlike for one person (who could afford it) to be coached, when a competitor was not? The word "coach" itself comes from a Hungarian design of luxurious horse-drawn transport – the analogy lies with taking the slog out of learning in the same way that a carriage was a lot easier than walking! There is also probably an influence of the word "coax," which morphed from "make a fool of" to persuade or influence.

For 120 years and more, coaching was primarily associated with instruction in sport, with coaches often being called "coachers." It also became absorbed into the world of work, where coach and instructor became synonymous. Coaches were expected to demonstrate how to do things, observe and give feedback, until the learner was able to do the task without supervision. Even today, this mode of coaching is heavily ingrained into corporate practice. It was only with the writings of Tim Gallwey, a US tennis coach, that the shift began towards the definitions of coaching generally accepted today. Gallwey's experiences as a disciple of an Indian guru convinced him that instruction was less effective than helping people access their internal resources. His book, *The Inner Game of Tennis* revolutionised tennis coaching and ultimately coaching in a wide range of contexts.

What Gallwey didn't access was the 3,000-year history of mentoring, which was built on the principles of helping people access and develop their own wisdom.

By the mid-1990s, the growing army of coaches was increasingly desperate to distance themselves from coaching's directive, instructional origins; and this was one of the drivers behind the creation of professional bodies. Of the half-dozen or so professional bodies, achieving the higher status that goes with a professional identity fuelled their rapid growth. The exception was the oldest of the bodies, the European Mentoring and Coaching Council, which started

DOI: 10.4324/9781003323990-8

*Table 7.1* My learning journey

| My learning journey | | |
| --- | --- | --- |
| Coaching is instruction | Coaching is a formal, structured process for learning | Coaching is a form of learning dialogue |
| Coaching and mentoring are competing for the same space | Mentoring is "coaching plus" | Coaching and mentoring integrate at the highest levels of effectiveness |
| The spoken conversation | The silent conversations in coaching | The coach–client–supervisor system |

life as the European Mentoring Centre. As the end of the twentieth century approached, this body (originally co-founded by David Megginson and me at Sheffield Hallam University) chose not to create artificial differences between coaching and mentoring, but to emphasise the similarities and invite coaches to join the party. We now know that coaching at its most effective includes many aspects of mentoring; and vice versa.

When modern coaching first started to make waves, one of the first things I attempted was to position it against other forms of helping to learn. Table 7.2 captures the essence of this.

When this table was first constructed in the mid-1990s, it was a fairly accurate depiction of the weight of literature at the time. By the turn of the century, coaching had significantly shifted. With professional coaches, who were outside the leader-follower relationship, the power distance diminished. The focus of feedback also shifted from mainly performance to a wider range of issues determined by the coachee, although the role of sponsors in decreeing what the coaching should concentrate on was still often strong.

In a more recent review (2019), I expanded the scope of helping roles and included some reflections on psychotherapeutic interventions. There are many roles in helping people make positive changes in their lives, relationships, careers, and well-being, so it's hardly surprising that even experts get confused as to how those roles relate to and intersect with each other. For the spectrum, in which coaching and mentoring are located, we can define several common threads:

- They all involve a greater or lesser degree of dialogue – conversation that opens minds to new perspectives and possibilities
- They all contain or imply a duty of care between the person helping and the person they help
- They all involve creating greater awareness, so that the learner can make better choices
- They all require some level of support to the learner in implementing choices

*Table 7.2* Comparison of methods of helping to learn (with some minor modifications to the original)

*Comparison of methods of helping to learn(with some minor modifications to the original)*

| | Teacher | Tutor | Coach | Mentor | Counsellor |
|---|---|---|---|---|---|
| Nature of transfer | Information with some knowledge Explicit | Knowledge Mainly explicit | Skill, some knowledge Mainly explicit | Wisdom Mainly implicit | Self-awareness, insight Making the implicit explicit |
| Direction of learning | Teacher to pupil | Mainly tutor to student, but sometimes moderately two-way | Coach to learner Stimulating learner's own reflections | Two-way reflective learning | Stimulating learner's own reflections |
| Power distance | High | Moderately high | Moderately high, depending on work relationship | Low | Low (but potential for abuse) |
| Nature of feedback | Impersonal – marks and scores Provided by teacher | Personal, questioning processes Provided mainly by tutor | Personal, questioning performance Provided mainly by coach | Personal, provided mainly by the learner | Avoids direct feedback but encourages learner to review own issues |
| Intensity of the personal relationship | Usually, low | Low to moderate | Moderate | Moderate to high Friendship likely to develop | Minimal |

Within this spectrum, roles we can identify include:

- Teacher
- Tutor
- Basic coach (relative amateur)
- Basic mentor (relative amateur)
- Sponsor
- Accredited coach/mentor
- Coach or mentor with strong grounding in behavioural science
- Counsellor
- Psychologist
- Psychiatrist (although there is some disagreement as to whether this role involves dialogue)

Some, but not all of these roles, are subject to a form of professional discipline, but these don't necessarily provide any great clarity between the roles, because they overlap and because a practitioner may practise in several roles. For example, the British Psychological Society has a substantial membership group of psychologists, who also act as coaches. Moreover, professional disciplines also impose a hierarchy of perceived competence, through standards and/or levels of professional accreditation. In coaching, the EMCC offers Foundation, Practitioner, Senior Practitioner, and Master Practitioner accreditation. The International Coach Federation offer Associate Certified Coach, Practitioner Certified Coach, and Master Certified Coach qualifications.

The role "coach or mentor with strong grounding in behavioural science" deserves particular mention. The more complex the client and their situation, the more important it is to recognise behavioural patterns and the psychology behind them. Having a psychological qualification isn't enough to be an effective coach (and vice versa) and it can be argued that psychologists tend to define their practice within quite narrow specialisms. "Coaching psychologists" – a relatively recent term – tend to emphasise the use of psychometrics and other diagnostics. Behavioural scientists, on the other hand, engage with a wide spectrum of human motivations and behaviours, including group processes and complex systems. This is a messy area, but a significant difference between basic coaches and coaches, whose practice is informed by behavioural science, seems to be that the latter place much greater emphasis on having a strong evidence base.

It is tempting to try to put these various roles into hierarchies on various characteristics, such as directiveness or level of intimacy, but all that would do is reinforce the particular prejudices that practitioners in one role employ to protect their identity from encroachment by other roles. So, for example, coaching organisations that peddle the idea that mentoring is directive and coaching non-directive choose to ignore the weight of history that suggests exactly the opposite!

Table 7.3 attempts to tease out some of the key similarities and differences between the roles above. It is important to emphasise that each of the statements

*Table 7.3* An updated comparison of helping roles

*An updated comparison of helping roles*

| Role | Purpose | Relationship(at core) | Focus of learning | Limitations |
|---|---|---|---|---|
| Teacher | To impart knowledge in a specific domain | Instructor-student learning is almost all in one direction | Enabling students to demonstrate retention of information and knowledge (e.g. in exam conditions) within a curriculum. Linear perspective (focused within the subject area). | Great teachers generate enthusiasm for learning outside the curriculum. In particular, they aim to grow well-rounded individuals. However, administrative duties and large class sizes often restrict this aspect of the role. |
| Tutor | To stimulate understanding and creative thinking beyond the regurgitable information and knowledge | Challenging and supporting the student in the learning process. Helping the student overcome roadblocks to their learning and/ or problems with self-management of their studies. | Sense-making. Divergent perspective (encourages connections with other relevant sources of knowledge). | While some tutor roles explicitly include responsibility for the general welfare of the student, this is not always the case. Tutoring seems to be an aspect of other educational professions, such as teacher or lecturer. |
| Basic coach | To support a learner (who may be a direct report) in acquiring or improving a required skill or improving a narrow area of performance | Largely transactional While a certain amount of rapport contributes to effectiveness, it is not necessary that coach and coachee like each other. Much coaching is short-term in duration – indeed, long-term relationships may generate dependency. | Progress towards clearly defined, SMART performance goals | Coach is typically unaware of just how directive they are being. (For example, by sticking to a simplistic model, such as GROW; or simply in choosing the line of questioning to follow.) |

| | Purpose | Relationship | Benefits | Risks |
|---|---|---|---|---|
| Basic mentor | To support a learner in making good career choices and developing networks | Quality of the relationship is essential to effectiveness. The mentor offers friendship and much greater insight into themselves than a coach. So there is typically a much higher level of intimacy. | Opening new horizons. Significant shifts in learner's identity and contextual awareness facilitate career self-management and ownership of personal development. | Mentor's experience and contextual knowledge may lead them to "unload" on the mentee rather than use these to craft insight-provoking questions |
| Sponsor | To provide hands-on career management | Social exchange of access to sponsor's power and influence and loyalty to the sponsor by the junior partner | Supporting the learner in finding projects and roles which will stretch them and/or give them greater visibility. Exposing the learner to influence networks. Advocacy. | Can be highly disempowering May emphasise the sponsor's agenda (or the organisation's) rather than the learner's. Can be coercive. |
| Accredited coach | To support a learner in achieving their potential in a specific area | Professional support in resolving problems and pursuing defined goals | Learning relevant to a specific context or goal | Focus is mainly linear – client and their issue – when the context requires a systemic perspective |
| Accredited mentor | To support a learner in becoming more mature (wiser) | Balance of nurturing and challenging Role modelling Professional friendship | Transition in identity | Effectiveness dependent on the mentor's own level of socio-emotional and cognitive maturity |

*(Continued)*

Table 7.3 Continued

*An updated comparison of helping roles*

| Role | Purpose | Relationship (at core) | Focus of learning | Limitations |
|---|---|---|---|---|
| Coach or mentor with strong grounding in behavioural science | To enhance the quality of the learner's thinking | High level of mutual personal disclosure<br>Systemic perspective | Transformation | Operating at the boundaries between coaching-mentoring and therapy requires constant self-monitoring |
| Counsellor | To help a client cope with a specific problem | May range from relatively transactional (e.g. career counselling) to one of high trust and emotional connection | Improving capability to cope (for example, in situations of stress). Becoming more resourceful. | Contracting tends to be less formal than other roles, leading to potential lack of role clarity |
| Psychologist | To help a functional individual understand the drivers of their thinking and behaviour, in order to make better choices | Trust is important Maintaining an appropriate level of professional detachment | Self-efficacy | Multiple schools of psychology set different rules and promote lack of role clarity |
| Psychiatrist | To diagnose a disorder. To raise client awareness of their dysfunctional mental processes and work with them to change those processes, making the person more functional. | Expert<br>Trust is important<br>High level of professional detachment | Recovery | Professional regulation and oversight limit the ways, in which the practitioner can legitimately help |

is a generalisation and that individuals may choose to combine roles in unique ways. For example, my best teachers at school were also my first mentors.

*N.B. These distinctions are not intended to be definitive. They represent an attempt to reflect and speculate where differences and similarities may lie. The table might look very different from the perspectives of people, within the roles described!*

Even if widely accepted very clear distinctions between these roles were possible, they may not be desirable. Overlap between roles may be a significant factor in efficacy, through avoiding overly narrow perspectives. What we can extrapolate, however, is that the more complex the context in which change is desired, the more important it is that the practitioner has an appropriate level of understanding of human motivational and behavioural dynamics.

There are now dozens, possibly hundreds of different schools of thought about coaching – a diversity I welcome. Coaching has borrowed from many other disciplines and philosophies, ranging from psychology to Sufism to dance, all with different perspectives to offer. (I draw the line at astrological coaching and I have had a lot of fun with my annual April Fool's blogs, such as the one on hot stone coaching!)[1]

The downside of this diversity is that it is very difficult to determine what "good" coaching looks like. Tatiana Bachkirova's experiments with getting coaches to evaluate other coaches' performance in observed sessions demonstrated that they made judgements based primarily on "do they do it the way I do?". Tatiana and I designed together Europe's first coach assessment centres (described in more detail in chapter 6), designed to rise above any specific methodology and simply focus on three factors:

- Were they safe to practice? (For example, did they come with so much psychological baggage of their own that they projected this upon the client?)
- Did they have a coherent philosophy of coaching practice?
- Could they hold a purposeful and attentive learning conversation with the client?

Coaches in the assessment centres were all either existing suppliers to the client organisation or had passed a paper screening that explored experience and credentials. Yet consistently 60%–70% proved inadequate. Neither the number of hours they had coached, nor the fees charged showed any significant correlation with coaching competence. The level of accreditation achieved was no more than a general indicator – some coaches with high levels of accreditation from some professional associations and training institutions were amongst the worst performers.

On the other hand, the "good" coaches were often outstanding. The more assessment centres we ran, the clearer it became that the coaches we interviewed and observed exhibited several different ways of thinking about themselves (their identity) and their practice (the relationship to their clients). Over time, these coalesced into a model of **coach maturity**. The idea also arose of a coach development centre, also discussed briefly in Chapter 6, which built on the assessment framework but with the objective of helping coaches create evidence-based personal development plans for their coaching practice.

In parallel with this activity, both I and David Megginson from different directions started to question the prevailing wisdom on **goals in coaching**. The concept that coaching conversations need to start with a clear and preferably SMART goal is a very Western one and only weakly supported by evidence.

**Supervision** has played a major role for me, both in my own development and in supporting the development of other coaches and mentors. In the mid-1990s, a group of six of us, all very experienced coaches and most of us prolific researchers and writers in the field, came together to form one of the first and perhaps the first peer supervision group. Every six months or so, we rotated roles, so everyone was supervised by everyone else over time. We also held regular sessions, where we would explore common issues in supervision or share specific expertise. The latter was my first introduction to Gestalt, for example – each of us brought domains of experience and knowledge the others didn't have. When Oxford Brookes University launched its first coach supervisor course, I had the option, as visiting professor, of being faculty or participant. I chose participant because I wanted to find out what I didn't know. Nowadays, I supervise coaches from all over the world, both individually and in groups. These include a pro bono programme to supervise coaches from developing economies in Africa, who would not otherwise be able to access supervision.

I've also supported numerous programmes to provide supervision for mentors. All the coaching professional bodies in Europe and many bodies in other continents require coaches to have supervision. Few corporate buyers of coaching in Europe would hire a coach, who did not have a high level of formal qualification and regular, professional supervision. So why isn't the same expected of mentors?

The traditional response has been to point to the amateur/professional distinction. Executive coaches are typically seen as being professionals, and compared with other professions, such as therapy and counselling, where supervision has long been an essential part of continuous professional development, quality management and the maintenance of boundaries, especially in terms of client protection. Mentors, by contrast, have typically been seen as amateurs – less well-trained, operating in an unpaid capacity.

That assumption is increasingly questionable, for several reasons:

* The emergence of professional mentors, who have equal levels of training compared to their coach counterparts (plus substantial and relevant experience to the client's role). When the European Mentoring and Coaching Council established the first competency framework for the field over a decade ago, it referred to coaches and mentors equally, recognising that both coaches and mentors could take on professional roles and that this required supervision. This prescience provides a ready platform for mentor

supervision, at least in Europe. Now we see, especially in Northern Europe, a growing movement for retiring executives, who might previously have considered becoming coaches, preferring instead to become professional mentors. The main reasons given for this shift are firstly, that the coach market is crowded and secondly, that they want to be valued for and able to use their experience.

- Mentoring programme managers in several countries, including the UK and Denmark, have offered group supervision to "ordinary" mentors, on the basis that they want to perform well in the role. These sessions provide an opportunity to surface problems within the mentoring programme, to create a sense of camaraderie amongst the mentors, and to support the mentors in gaining higher levels of knowledge and skills.

- Most executive coaching takes place in the context of achieving specific short-term skills or performance goals. A much smaller proportion addresses medium-term behavioural issues, and even less aims to achieve personal transformation. Mentoring, however, tends to be a longer-term relationship involving relatively high levels of disclosure and intimacy. It focuses on helping the mentee *become* rather than on what they *do*. The potential for boundary and other issues that need supervision to arise is therefore very similar to that for coaches working on deep behavioural and transformational issues.

- Mentors and mentees within the same organisation may be exposed to all sorts of pressures, from which they need to stand back. For example, the mentor's knowledge of the system and its politics can be a great benefit; but it can also bring with it a lot of baggage. Supervision helps the mentor determine when and how to use their knowledge to beneficial effect; when to "park" their own knowledge; and how to separate their values, ambitions, and career needs from those of their mentees.

- Executive coaching, by and large, is primarily an *assignment* – a finite contractual arrangement. Mentoring is primarily a *relationship* – and, like all relationships, complex and difficult to understand from within. While international standards for mentoring recommend that mentor and mentee regularly review their relationship, supervision can help the mentor reflect more deeply on the relationship dynamics and how they and the mentee can achieve, for example, greater trust, openness, and sense of purpose. One of the most common occurrences in mentoring is "relationship droop" – the sogginess that comes after six months or so, when the easy, surface issues have been dealt with. Through supervision, the mentor can work with the mentee to delve into deeper issues, with much greater potential impact on the mentee's career. Similarly, the ending of a mentoring relationship can be difficult for both mentor and mentee. If the relationship simply fades away, both parties feel that they have in some way failed or been abandoned. This is almost never the case when the mentor has a supervisor to discuss these emotions with and to help plan how to achieve a positive, fulfilling, formal ending.

Britain's National Health Service and the Danish trade union Djøf are two strong examples of organisations which have embraced supervision as integral to the effectiveness of their mentoring programmes. But a handful of examples don't make a trend. What is clear is that the professional bodies that incorporate mentoring, and the mentoring academies now springing up around the world, are all taking the topic seriously.

More recently, I and a group of colleagues (Lise Lewis, Craig McKenzie, Michelle Chan, and Tony Dickel) brought together in 2021 some of the world's most experienced supervisors, with expertise in supervising team coaches, to develop a framework for this extension of supervision practice. This is another whole area of supervision that is opening up rapidly. In this chapter, I review **the seven conversations of coaching,** a framework developed to help coaches and their supervisors explore the coaching conversation from seven perspectives; and a systemic framework for supervision.

## Coach maturity

The issue of coach maturity evolved from observation of dozens initially and hundreds ultimately of coaches attending coach assessment centres. The coaching conversations observed ranged from the painful and laborious that achieved little to the deft and inspirational that brought wonderful insights with far less expenditure of energy. David Megginson and I published the conclusions from these observations in both journals and coaching handbooks.[2] They have now been presented to tens of thousands of coaches worldwide and appear to have at the minimum strong face validity. Never satisfied that a topic has truly been nailed, however, I and a group of scholars and practitioners are currently going back to square one. Our first intention was to retest the four-phase model of coach maturity already developed. However, we abandoned that in favour of an approach that would not be influenced by the original work. In the *Becoming of a coach* project, we have interviewed highly experienced coaches in several countries to capture the learning journey of how they became the coaches they are today. The data provide broad support for the original model, plus a number of additional deep insights. The latter, when fully validated, will be the subject of another book – we are not yet ready to make definitive statements about the study.

From the original observations and reflections, four coaching mindsets emerged, which do appear to represent a progression for many, if not all coaches. The four levels are models-based, process-based, philosophy or discipline-based, and systemic eclectic (Table 7.4).

Models-based coaching is typically where new coaches start. They need the re-assurance of a closely defined approach that they can take into any situation they might meet – such as GROW (Goal, Reality, Options, Will), or one of its derivatives. If the conversation doesn't achieve what's intended, they assume they are not following the model properly and become even more rigid in their application of it. Following the model becomes more important than exploring the client's world. It is about doing coaching *to* the client. The driving need to find a solution within the coaching session often rests more with the coach than the client. The dangerous myth that a good coach can coach anyone in any situation appears to stem from this very narrow perception of coaching. Often, they fail to see the irony between aspiring to a person-centred approach, yet controlling the conversation …

Process-based approaches happen when the coach finally realises that their rigid approach is ineffective in situations that aren't about simple skills-based issues. They seek a solution in adding a wider variety of tools, techniques, and models. Rather than control the conversation entirely, they are relaxed enough to allow some "power-sharing" with the client. For example, they may ask for permission to experiment. We talk about this stage as doing coaching *with* the client – though it's still mainly doing and not being. At this stage, coaches often incorporate into their practice one or more diagnostic tools that they apply routinely. While intended to help the client's understanding, the effect is often to slip back into a more subtle form of control – the conversation is now confined not by a model but by the assumptions in the diagnostic.

Over time, with greater confidence and a much bigger portfolio of resources to call upon, coaches let go of the focus on doing and shift to *being*. They integrate what they do with who they are. They now operate within a broad set of assumptions about helping and human development. They demonstrate a much higher level of reflective practice and a greater use of self, as in, for example, Gestalt. Their own self-awareness is instrumental in helping clients

*Table 7.4* A comparison of the four levels of coaching maturity in coaching conversations

*A comparison of the four levels of coaching maturity in coaching conversations*

| Coaching approach | Style | Critical questions |
|---|---|---|
| Models-based | Control | How do I take them where I think they need to go? |
| | | How do I adapt my technique or model to this circumstance? |
| Process-based | Contain | How do I give enough control to the client and still retain a purposeful conversation? |
| | | What's the best way to apply my process in this instance? |
| Philosophy-based | Facilitate | What can I do to help the client do this for themselves? |
| | | How do I contextualise the client's issue within the perspective of my philosophy or discipline? |
| Systemic eclectic | Enable | Are we both relaxed enough to allow the issue and the solution to emerge in whatever way they will? |
| | | Do I need to apply any techniques or processes at all? If I do, what does the client context tell me about how to select from the wide choice available to me? |

understand themselves and their situation. Although their toolkit is bigger, they use fewer tools, much more selectively.

As they continue to mature, they absorb more complex ways of thinking, especially in developing greater awareness of and comfort with systems. Systemic eclectic coaches, as we described them, demonstrate great calm and presence. They speak far less than coaches at earlier stages on the journey. They integrate the skills of coaching with the wisdom of mentoring. They experiment in the moment more than use existing tools. They ask fewer questions, but these are often insightful and thought-provoking. (At one point, I counted the impactful and original questions asked by coaches in assessment centres. With very few exceptions, they all came from coaches in the latter two stages of maturity.)

## Why is coach maturity an issue?

### Coaching is becoming much more complex and demanding

In the earliest days of modern coaching in the 1970s, coaching was about enabling someone to become more skilled in a specific task, such as golf or tennis. Over the decades to the turn of the century, the scope of coaching expanded to cover behavioural change and personal transformation. In the past two decades, it has incorporated systemic perspectives The playground of coaching can now be seen as nested complexities, for example:

* Skills coaching for an individual
* Helping an individual work with the systems, of which they are a part
* Helping an individual leader create a coaching culture in their team
* Coaching the team and the leader together
* Coaching teams of teams
* Coaching organisations

In the world of team coaching, recommended good practice is for coaches to work in pairs, role modelling effective teaming. At each level of complexity, the coach requires greater levels of maturity to work with complexity, messiness, and disorder.

### Basic level coaching is under increasing threat

Coachbots and artificial intelligence are already encroaching on traditional one-to-one coaching at the skills and basic behaviour change levels. Current neural networking computers can simulate any predictable conversation. Coaching platforms with recordings of millions of coaching conversations are close to the point where the AI will be able to hold a more purposeful, more responsive conversation than any coach still basing their practice on simplistic models.

At the same time, the world of education is beginning to recognise the value of the fourth R (Reading, Writing, 'Rithmetic, and now Reflection). Millions of schoolchildren are learning the basics of coaching and mentoring and this trend is set to grow. Take the analogy of the third R, arithmetic. It takes a lot more study for someone to build on their basic arithmetical skills to become an accountant or an astronomer. Coaches similarly need to acquire and demonstrate skills well beyond the basic.

### Accreditation inflation

The increasing emphasis by coaching professional organisations on continuous development has to be a good thing, if it leads to coaches devoting more attention to improving their practice. However, a side effect is that accreditation has become a marketing tool – "I have more credibility as a coach than you do, because I have a higher level of accreditation." The evidence linking accreditation level with efficacy – except perhaps at master's degree level, which is not the equivalent of "master" in the language of the professional bodies – is thin at best. It's easy for coaches to assume that their level of accreditation defines how effective they are as a coach, but that correlation is far from proven. The magpie effect is a commonly observed phenomenon in supervision – coaches amassing more and more qualifications but failing to do the work on themselves that leads to genuine transitions to maturity.

## The vexed issue of goals

Shortly before he died, Sir John Whitmore, in an interview for our book, *Beyond Goals*[3], discussed the origins of the GROW model. It should have been VROW (with the V for Vision) but that wasn't catchy enough.

Setting and pursing goals helps people to focus on what's important, to establish and stick to schedules, and feel that they are (to some extent at least) in control. But over-concentration on goals comes at a price. Research[4] shows that it leads to:

- Failure to see the larger picture – so we don't notice other opportunities or threats
- Short-term thinking
- Ethical failures (if people are within sight of achieving a goal, but can't quite get there, they tend to cheat!)
- Inhibited learning, especially when goal is for someone else's benefit, so the motivation is extrinsic rather than extrinsic

What makes things even more complex is that the word "goal" has a range of different meanings. These range from "an objective to aspire to," to the Oxford English Dictionary's "a boundary or limit" (which contrasts strongly with the idea of coaching as liberating people's imagination and spirit!).

Particularly in the coaching literature of the 1990s, there is an emphasis on the need for goals to be SMART – specific, measurable, achievable, realistic, time-bound – but not much on what goals are. Much of the general literature on goals in coaching is simplistic, if not misleading. For example, it makes little distinction between the relationship between goals as desired outcomes and goals as relatively short-term stepping stones towards a desired outcome. It also takes a linear perspective that fails to take into account the influence of the client's systems on their potential to achieve goals.

Received wisdom about the setting and pursuit of goals within coaching and mentoring emphasises specificity and focus. However, the evidence base we accumulated from academic and practitioner studies suggests that this is a simplistic perspective – that effective coaching often works with messy, unclear, emergent, and evolving goals. Indeed, it can be argued that coaching and mentoring are more about the process of *achieving* goal clarity and goal commitment than about starting with these characteristics.

The role of the coach is to help the coachee examine their purpose (what they want to achieve on a larger scale) and to explore various ways in which they might achieve that. Any original goals the coachee or mentee brings into the conversations frequently evolve into something different as they gain a greater understanding of themselves and the external situation. My definition of the distinction between purpose and goals is included in the table.

Whether at the individual, team, organisation, or societal level, a healthy system is one where purpose and goals are aligned. When coaching starts with goals, the potential for pursuing the wrong objective is high. Even starting with purpose may be too soon. Time after time coaches tell me that their clients struggle to define purpose in any meaningful way. People can only get their heads around personal purpose after deep reflection – and so many coaching clients are too busy doing "stuff" to think about something so abstract. Much more effective is to start with exploring the three areas of Identity, Values, and Resources. These also can be quite challenging for people with low skills in self-reflection, but we have to start somewhere!

*Table 7.5* Purpose v goals

| Purpose v goals | |
| --- | --- |
| Purpose | Goals |
| Envisaging the world we want to live in and our role in bringing it about | The actions, decisions and intermediate steps that will help to create that world |

### Identity

- Who are you?
- Who do you want to become?
- How does what you do now align with who you aspire to be?
- What prevents you from being the person you aspire to be?
- Who/what supports you in becoming the person you aspire to be?

### Values

- What do you care about?
- Why is that important to you?
- What difference do you want to make and why?

### Resources

- How well supported are you?
- Who is in your developmental network?
- How does this affect your sense of the possible?
- What resources could enable you to be more effective in your work and non-work roles?

### Purpose

- What do you want to contribute?
- What do you want to achieve for yourself?
- What's the point of these?
- What achievements will give you greatest satisfaction to look back on in ten or 20 years' time?
- What's wrong with the status quo?

When people set goals too early, there is often a strong urge to hang on to them, even when it is obvious it's no longer what they want. In decision-making, it's called the "sunk cost trap." So, coaches should avoid pushing clients into setting clear goals and simply let the goals emerge. Useful questions to ask when the coachee brings a goal to the conversation include:

- Why *this* goal? Why now?
- Is it truly your goal or someone else's?
- Is it a subset of a larger goal, or a number of connected goals?
- How does this goal align with your values?
- What will achieving this goal replace? (i.e. what will you have to stop doing to achieve it?)

### Assessing commitment to goals

Once a goal is agreed, it doesn't follow that the client will give it the priority it needs. When people come to coaching and mentoring, they often do so with goals they have only part thought through. They may also come with goals imposed on them by others. Or they jump at a goal because they want to please the coach or mentor. In these circumstances, it's important to review with them just how committed to the goal they are. Just asking if they are committed won't necessarily lead to an honest or considered answer, especially if they feel obliged to pursue the goal.

My practical work with coaches and mentors led to two frameworks that have met the test of time. One is a simple test of commitment, in which we ask the client to rate the level of their commitment against a spectrum of ten statements.

10) I am totally determined to achieve this
 9) I'm prepared to make major sacrifices to do this
 8) I will make this my number one priority
 7) This will be one of my key priorities
 6) It's very important to me
 5) It's quite important to me
 4) I feel obligated to do this
 3) I'm not sure this is what I really want
 2) I'm quite reluctant
 1) Over my dead body!

Anything below 6 is unlikely to happen!

The second model (Figure 7.1) came about from simply asking people in workshops to tell the story of an important change they had undertaken successfully, and one that they hadn't been able to stick with – for example, giving up smoking. *Awareness* is the initial state of dissatisfaction or recognition of the desirability of change. In some cases, this may not be self-generated – it might be feedback from others, which we can choose to ignore or accept. *Understanding* is a deeper level of awareness, in which the consequences of not changing become clearer and the pressure to make a decision increases.

*Acceptance* happens when we finally admit to ourselves that we must do something. However, the gap between thinking and doing can be huge. Acceptance is primarily an intellectual process. *Commitment* integrates intellect and emotion. It also typically requires someone to commit to. Hence the role of coaches and mentors as consciences. Falling down on a commitment becomes associated with diminished self-respect, if we feel we are letting someone else down.

To build upon commitment, we need a practical way of *implementing* the change – a plan that can be started before the enthusiasm wears off. The plan has to be easy to articulate and clear about the first steps. Finally, to keep going and retain commitment, we need to have positive reinforcement, which may be intrinsic (e.g., I feel so much better) or extrinsic (e.g., positive feedback from colleagues).

Having set a goal and started on the path to achieve it, progress can be affected by a number of factors. Among them:

- Motivation (How important is it to us and to others? Does it generate energy or apathy? How well can we vision the difference it will make?)
- Contextual awareness (How grounded is your picture of what is going on? What other perspectives have you considered?)
- Ownership (Did you choose the goal or was it chosen for you? Who shares this goal with you and has a stake in its outcome?)
- Clarity (What will it look like and feel like when you achieve it? Can you envision the outcome?)
- Measurability (How will you know you are making progress?)
- Stability (Is it a fixed or moving target? What is changing around you that might make the goal either obsolete or even more important to you?)
- Personal values (What deep-seated needs and beliefs does achieving this address for you?)
- Previous experience of goal pursuit (How confident are you in your ability to achieve this? Do you have the habit of success?)

### Emergent goals

In a survey of 200 US coaches by Kaufmann and Coutu (2009), it emerged that all but eight said that goals often changed as a coaching assignment progressed, adjusting to clients' new insights about what they really needed and wanted. This aligns with the contextual model of coaching and mentoring in Chapter 4. The clearer we understand our internal context and external context, the easier it becomes to put them together to generate new insights that will inevitably lead to different goals.

In the research for our book on goals, David Megginson and I asked lots of coaches and managers where the goals they now had had originated. What we found has strong echoes of the emergent process described by Herminia Ibarra in her work on career transitions.[5] We identified three stages of "goal attentiveness" or emergence, for self-generated goals. In the first stage, itch, there are many minor dissatisfactions in our general awareness. Most of the time, we accept them as passing irritations and expect them to go away. In bodily terms, it's only when irritations become persistent or activate our pain circuits that we start to really attend to them. Then we typically ask ourselves, consciously or unconsciously, "Is this important enough to divert my attention from other tasks?" We might decide upon an interim fix – for example to create some time to think about it – but we now have a heightened awareness that an issue needs to be addressed. How we will address it, however, requires time and reflection. It might be assumed that the goal is what stimulates thinking about how to achieve it, but the narratives from our interviews suggested it is much more complicated and iterative than that. For example, it's often important to discover the why before determining the what. When a clear goal emerges, it is this hinterland of previous reflection that provides roots for motivating us towards goal achievement. We experiment, learn from failure, and recover

*Table 7.6* How goals emerge

| How goals emerge | | |
| --- | --- | --- |
| *Stimulus* | *Response* | *Process* |
| Goal | Score | Keep going until you have a result |
| Question | Better question | You can stop at any point; pick up again at any time |
| Itch | Scratch | Decide whether to acknowledge or ignore it |

from setbacks, because we have already asked the questions that link the goal with our values and future identity.

As I explored goals more deeply, however, I realised that the emergence model didn't capture the complexity of goal setting and goal management. Like all my other areas of interest, it turned out to be a lot messier than I thought and standard goal theory implies.

Once again, I listened to the stories coaches and leaders recounted about how goals emerged and how they went about achieving them. The reality from these narratives was not consistent and didn't conform to a predictable, linear process. Figure 7.1 captures one, common narrative. Were the exercise repeated with a different set of people, in a different culture and circumstances, the pattern might well be different. When I use this model, therefore, I do so to stimulate the coachee or mentee to reflect upon and build their own goal achievement narrative.

As in the simpler model above, the starting point for any intentional journey of change has to be a *stimulus*, either generated internally or externally. That stimulus produces a reactive response (for example, "I made a mess of that presentation. Next time, I'll research my audience better") that develops into an intention for change, which we can describe as a *reactive goal* that is instinctive and relatively ill-defined at this stage. It may also be more motivated by avoidance of an undesirable outcome rather than moving towards a desirable outcome and involve some instinctive steps towards achieving the reactive goal.

Once the initial, instinctive reaction is past, our slow brain (as described by Daniel Kahneman) can take a calmer, more rational look at the goal. *Reflection and contextualisation* allow us to step back from the goal, put it into a wider context, and check against our values and longer-term purpose. We can also review how it fits with other goals we are pursuing. Frequently, this results in substantial amendments to the goal. It becomes *adapted* when we own it and are able to put it into a rational context. The process of goal commitment kicks in here. We have a clear plan of how to pursue the goal and why we are doing so. The goal feels more considered and we have greater confidence in our ability to achieve it, in whole or part. We have an *impetus for action*.

AWARENESS

UNDERSTANDING

ACCEPTANCE

COMMITMENT

PLAN OF ACTION

IMPLEMENTATION

SUPPORT / POSITIVE FEEDBACK

*Figure 7.1* Commitment to change.

With a clear sense of direction and the motivation to pursue it, *application* is about getting on with it. Setbacks cause us to go back around the circle, reflecting on the goal itself, reconnecting it with purpose and experimenting. If the goal is a changed behaviour, by now a new habit is being established. In order to keep the momentum, however, we need to recognise that we are making progress – it's about sustaining self-efficacy, which appears in much of the academic literature on motivation studies. If that recognition is both internally and externally derived, it is likely to be stronger and lead to fewer relapses than either alone. One of the differences between coaches and business leaders in their accounts was that the coaches were more likely to emphasise the value of looking back and reflecting on the whole journey of goalsetting and goal pursuit. And the more experienced the coaches were, the more importance they placed on this process. Additionally, the most experienced coaches perceived that a key part of their role was helping clients develop the same skills and habits of reflecting on the goal-driven developmental journeys.

The general messiness of goals in coaching is exacerbated by the fact that goals can have very different natures. Common dimensions include whether they are:

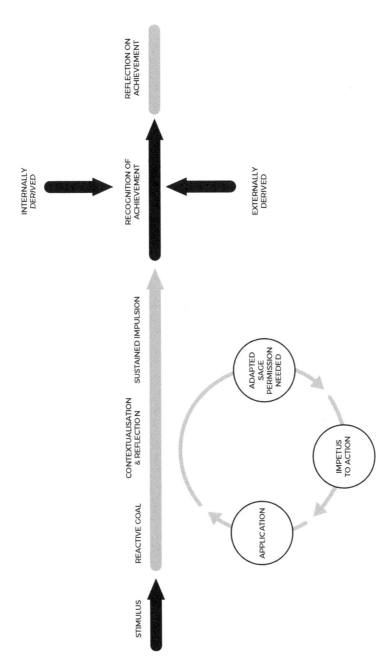

*Figure 7.2* The messy story of goal pursuit and achievement.

- Convex – focusing in, narrowing choices; or concave – focusing out, enlarging choices
- Self-driven or other-driven (i.e., internally or externally generated)
- Approach or withdrawal (moving away from or moving towards)
- Short-term, medium-term, or long-term
- Specific or general
- Self-contained (ends in themselves) or stepping stones to other, large, perhaps less well-defined goals

For the coach or mentor, therefore, the process of helping a client set and follow through goals is significantly more complex than it may appear. For a start, it is important to establish the point to which the goal has evolved, to select an appropriate intervention strategy. It's also important to be clear about the kind of goal, as both the coach/mentor and the client will need different strategies to tackle different goal types. And finally, the coach/mentor needs to understand – and help the client understand – the context, in which the goal is set and which may help or hinder its achievement.

## Supervision

### *Using the seven coaching conversations in supervision*

When does a coaching or mentoring conversation start? The obvious answer is when the client enters the room (actual or virtual). But by then it's too late to prepare mentally. Similarly, the conversation doesn't end when the client leaves. On the contrary, in effective coaching and mentoring it continues long after. Whether they plan it or not, in practice both coach and client carry out reflective dialogues in their minds before, during, and after the spoken conversation. Each of these additional dialogues has an important role to play in the nature and the effectiveness of the coaching conversation (Figure 7.3).

The seven conversations of coaching were originally conceived after realising that coaches frequently became "stuck." They had a general sense that a coaching relationship was not working properly, or that they were not delivering sufficient value to the client, but couldn't pin down why. What became obvious through interviews, observation, and supervision was that the issue frequently lay not with how they were engaging with the client within the coaching session, but in the silent conversations that did or didn't happen surrounding that spoken conversation. Two of these conversations happen in the head of the client before and after the coaching session; two in their respective heads during the spoken conversation and two afterwards. Expanding perspective to seven conversations has proven highly valuable both in self-reflection and in supervision. It shifts the emphasis of reflection and analyses away from what the coach said or did, and towards the dialogue between the coach and the client – and hence permits more of a systems approach to understanding the conversational dynamics.

The seven conversations are:

1. The coach's reflection before dialogue (their preparatory thinking before the coaching conversation)
2. The client's reflection/ preparatory thinking before the dialogue
3. The coach's internal, unspoken reflections during the dialogue
4. The spoken dialogue
5. The client's internal, unspoken reflections during the dialogue
6. The coach's reflections after the conversation
7. The client's reflections after the dialogue

While there is a massive literature on the spoken conversation, with lots of tools and models to draw upon,[6] and some on the coach's post-session reflections,

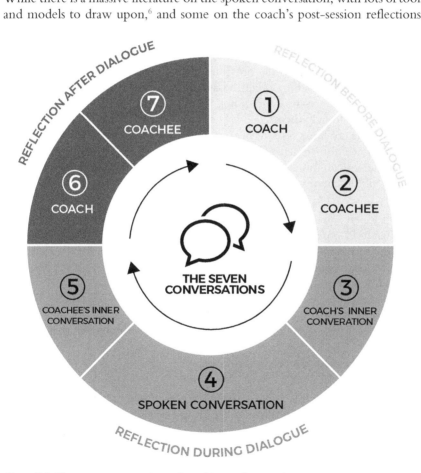

*Figure 7.3* The seven conversations of coaching and mentoring.

sources of guidance on coach reflection before sessions are meagre and there are even less relating to the client's pre- and post-session reflections. Yet, if coaching is a collaborative endeavour, both parties' internal conversations are equally important.

The aim of the coach's inner dialogue before the session is to prepare mentally. Three aspects are particularly relevant here:

- *Context*: What is going on in the client's world that might support or hinder them in engaging with the coaching conversation?
- *Avoidance*. What issues or emotions is this client avoiding? What issues is the coach avoiding? What collusion may be happening between coach and client?
- *Attitude*. How does the coach feel about the client? How does the level of liking or dislike affect the relationship?

Preparation by the coachee is equally important. The coach can prompt (and expect) them to spend some preparation time reviewing what they have done and not done as a result of the previous session, what they want to bring for exploration, and what they might be avoiding. Equally, is the client looking forward to the conversation and, if not, why not? They have a responsibility to help the coach to help them.

Within the coaching session, the coach inevitably carries on an internal dialogue or "reflection-in-action" (Schon, 1983). It takes skill to both participate fully in the conversation and observe it as dispassionately as possible.

Some of the questions experienced coaches ask themselves include:

- What is the quality of my listening?
- What am I observing/hearing? And not observing?
- Is my intuition turned on?
- What assumptions am I making? How might these be acting as a filter on my listening and my understanding?
- Am I spending too much attention on crafting the next question?
- What is the client not saying?
- How am I feeling in the moment? If I feel uncomfortable, what is making me so?
- How is the client feeling at this moment?

All the while during this silent conversation, the spoken conversation carries on, interrupted by occasional pauses. It's important for the coach to be aware of the structure, flavour, pace, and context of the conversation. For example, who is doing most of the talking? Is the conversation purposeful?

While they may be less conscious of it, there is also a silent conversation going on in the mind of the client. At some level they will be making choices about what they say, how honest they will be with the coach, and how much attention they are paying to their own words and emotions. Part of the coach's role is to act as a mirror on this inner conversation, helping to surface unspoken thoughts, and to heighten the client's self-awareness. In this way, the coach helps the client become more skilled at self-observation.

"Reflection-on-action" happens after the coaching session. While the meeting is still fresh in his or her memory, the coach should review the five previous conversations. The five questions below provide a practical framework for this:

- How did I help?
- What choices did I make and why?
- What did I learn?
- What concerns do I have?
- What do I want to take to supervision?

Finally, it's beneficial to agree with the client where, when, and how they will find reflective space to review the coaching conversation and what they want to do as a result. For example, who else do they want to discuss the issue with? As part of this reflection, of course, they may consider what they want to bring to the next coaching session – and thus create a virtuous circle!

Among the most common issues that the seven conversations help to unpack are:

- When the coach feels they have "failed" the client
- When the client keeps procrastinating, without apparent cause
- When the coach senses the presence or influence of parties outside of the room
- When conversations go round in circles and there is little sense of progress
- When intuition says that the coach is missing something important in the conversation or the relationship

I find it helpful for both my understanding and that of the coach to extract as much detail as is possible and relevant about each of these conversations. How might each conversation have influenced the coaching session and its outcomes? Where appropriate, I will encourage the coach to relive the conversation, asking them to attend to different aspects (for example, the content of the conversation, their feelings, their perception of the client's feelings, their sense of purpose from the dialogue). Questions I have found helpful in enhancing attentiveness include:

- What am I seeing/experiencing?
- What am I not seeing/experiencing (but is there)? [e.g., who else is in the room?]
- What am I not seeing/experiencing (and isn't there)?
- What knowledge/previous experience am I connecting to / not connecting to?

We often also explore the "texture" of the conversation from different perspectives:

- Atmosphere: temperature, bright/dull, colour
- Flow: pace, energy, direction, purposefulness
- Efficacy: what changed or what foundations were laid for change?
- Openness: self-honesty, instinctive responses, body language
- Identity: self-awareness, authenticity, awareness of perceptions by others
- Ownership: coach-directed, client-directed, jointly owned, jointly disowned
- Creative thinking: multi-perspective, constrained/unconstrained
- Attentiveness: awareness of nuance, unspoken meaning, unspoken communication, being "with" or "holding" the client
- Focus: convex or concave (i.e., were we focusing in on a very specific theme or widening out and more discursive; or moving backwards and forwards between these foci?)

Most of the time, this analysis reveals unnoticed connections and patterns. The coach recognises that, for example, the client's unwillingness to be self-honest in their reflections before sessions is causing them to be defensive in the spoken conversation and resistant to committing to change afterwards – and that apparent agreement in the session is more about compliance and "helping" the coach than about engaging with an issue. The big lesson from these supervision sessions is that the coaching conversation is a small part of the coaching relationship. So, coaches need to work with all the seven conversations to achieve maximum benefit for the client.

## A systemic model of coaching supervision

When we think of systems in coach supervision, the seven-eyes model from Peter Hawkins and Robin Shohet[7] immediately comes to mind. This valuable approach provides multiple perspectives to look into and out from the coach–coachee relationship. However, there is more than one way to look at a system and the postgraduate diploma programme I took at Oxford Brookes encouraged me to put flesh on a module that had been percolating in my mind for some time.

My systemic view of both coaching and coaching supervision was influenced by Feldman and Lankau[8] (2005), who state: "The coach assumes that the executive's behavior is not only the result of intrapsychic forces, but is also a response to the multiple work demands (often inconsistent, unrealistic, or vague in nature) put on executives by various stakeholder groups ... behaviour can only be understood in the context of organizational dynamics."

In this model (Figure 7.4), the client, the coach, and the supervisor all bring a different perspective, because of who they are and sometimes, who they aim to become. This inevitably stimulates a different world view – expressed in the supervisor as a philosophy of supervision – in the coach as a philosophy of

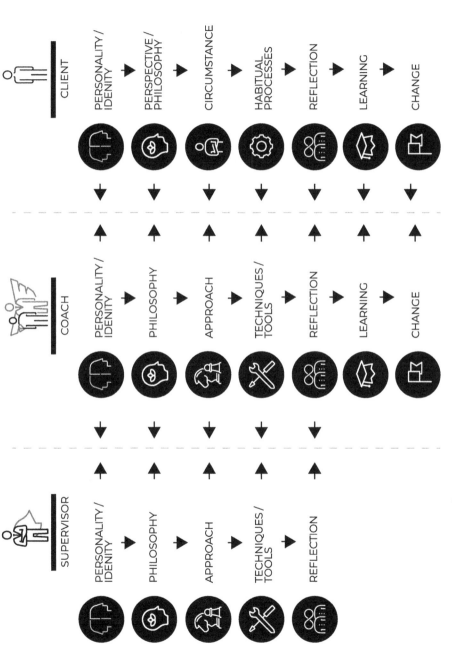

*Figure 7.4* A systemic view of supervision.

coaching and in the client as a set of assumptions about how the world is and how it should be. It can be argued that, while a client can operate and progress without a defined and articulated philosophy, a coach will find the absence of a philosophy a barrier to self-understanding and a supervisor will struggle to contextualise the complexity of the supervision system.

From a philosophy or personal perspective, the client selects a means of making sense of their circumstances.[9] He or she also consciously or unconsciously decides what they pay attention to and what they ignore. The coach selects a methodology, based on an approach (e.g., solutions-focus), which they feel comfortable with. The supervisor may do the same but needs to be aware of and able to work within the coach's approach as well as their own.

The client's approach to their circumstances leads them to apply heuristics which have worked before. The coach selects tools or techniques, compatible with their chosen approach, which help the client to address the issue in different ways (i.e., using unfamiliar heuristics or thinking patterns). The supervisor helps the coach consider, where appropriate, an even wider range of techniques; or helps them analyse what happened in applying techniques.

The aim of using techniques is to stimulate reflective and reflexive thinking. The client's reflections should lead to insight (learning) about themselves and or their issue; the coach's reflections should lead to improvement in their coaching practice, with self-knowledge being part of the process; and the supervisor's reflection should lead to improvements in their supervision practice. Finally, reflection leads to learning and change in the coach, the client and the supervisor – and in the relationships between them.

Feedback from coaches is that this framework gives another, useful way of preparing for supervision and that it can be applied in parallel with the seven-eyes model.

## Summary

The story of coaching and mentoring is one of multiple and evolving tensions. It can be challenging to avoid being drawn towards extreme points of view, yet the great power of these approaches is their ability to integrate and co-learn – to role model what we expect of our coachees and mentees.

In the next chapter, I explore what is arguably the fastest growing area of coaching, team coaching, which takes everything coaches do to a significantly higher level of complexity that requires commensurate maturity.

## Notes

1 See the appendices.
2 Clutterbuck, D. and Megginson, D., (2011). Coach maturity: An emerging concept. *The handbook of knowledge-based coaching: From theory to practice*, pp.299–313.

3 David, S, Clutterbuck, D and Megginson, D (2013) *Beyond Goals: Effective Strategies for Coaching and Mentoring*, Gower, Farnham.

4 Ordo Ordonez, LD, Schweitzer, ME, Galinsky, AE & Bazerman, MH (2009) Goals gone wild: The systematic side effects of overprescribing goal setting, *Academy of Management Perspectives*, 23(1), 6–16.

5 Ibarra, H., (2004). *Working identity: Unconventional strategies for reinventing your career*. Harvard Business Press.

6 It should be noted that when people talk of coaching models, such as GROW, they mean models of a coaching conversation. They do not mean how the coaching relationship evolves.

7 Hawkins and Shohet (2006) *Supervision in the helping professions*. Open University Press, McGrow-Hill Education.

8 Feldman, DC & Lankau, MJ (2005) Executive Coaching: A Review and Agenda for Future Research, *Journal of Management*, 31 pp 829–848.

9 Weick, K. E. (1995). *Sensemaking in organizations*. Thousand Oaks, CA: Sage.

# 8   Team coaching

One of the few things I heartedly disliked at school was team sports. A combination of mild dyspraxia, being born late in the school year, and being already resistant to the herd mentality, meant I was much more attracted to individual sports. I didn't (and still don't) "get" being competitive for its own sake. I preferred to compare against myself, not against others.

It was through my kids that I began to appreciate team sports, 30+ years ago. Watching them play rugby instilled an appreciation of the skills required for effective teaming. More recently, I became friendly with Maurizio Sarri, then manager of Chelsea Football Club. Taking my two eldest grandsons to watch a match, I sat analysing the patterns of play. "I wonder if they realise it's all about overlapping triangles," I asked myself. (Of course, they did – it's a standard part of football theory.)

My fascination with dialogue and with boards both prepped me for an increasing attention to teams. (Boards, of course, are not teams – they exercise "collaborative independence.") The mentor–mentee relationship is a form of team. I had been involved with group facilitation for several decades – the result of being introduced to action learning and its progenitor "grumpy" Reg Revans. Then in the mid-1990s I got a research contract from the European Union to investigate the concept of team learning. The project involved interviewing teams in several organisations and countries about how they managed the learning process.

First, we had to define what was meant by a "team." Then as now people used the word "team" to describe a wide variety of groups. Nowadays, I can state with clarity that a team is not defined by an organisation chart of people in the same reporting line. That's a group. It only becomes a team when the individuals within the group agree to act together in a teaming manner. The section below on **team types and roles** derives from this research.

Most of my work with teams until this time had been in the context of improving the quality of dialogue. I now started to explore more deeply other aspects of team dynamics, function, and dysfunction. My eclectic reading had ensured that I retained over the years an interest in systems, chaos theory, and complex adaptive systems and I started the laborious process of making connections, from the perspective of a team as a complex adaptive system

DOI: 10.4324/9781003323990-9

*Table 8.1* My learning journey

| My learning journey | | |
| --- | --- | --- |
| Coaching the team leader | Coaching the team | Coaching the system in which the team resides |
| Teams as systems | Teams as systems of systems | Teams as complex, adaptive systems |

nested within other complex adaptive systems. Over several years at the turn of the century, I gathered evidence from wherever I could about team function and performance, then about team coaching as the term became more widely used within the world of employment, rather than a phenomenon reserved for sport. An early disappointment was to discover that hardly any of the websites promoting team coaching services were actually offering team coaching. Instead, they were using the term to describe a mish-mash of existing services, ranging from team building to coaching separately individuals in the same team. Relatively few met the criteria of a) using coaching approaches and b) working with the whole team collectively.

When the first edition of *Coaching the Team at Work* was published in 2007, it brought an evidence-based approach to the subject. Interviews with team coaches around the world provided a broad description of what a team coaching assignment looked like, reflected below in the section on the **stages of team coaching** framework.

The next decade or so was spent partly in continued scrutiny of the evidence surrounding widely promoted approaches to working with teams and refining the concept of the team as a complex, adaptive system. Much of the groundwork in academic studies of teams had been laid in the late 1990s and early 2000s, by great scholars such as Richard Hackman and Jon Katzenbach, followed up by their collaborators, including Ruth Wageman and Amy Edmondson.[1] But pygmies stand on the shoulders of giants and team coaching is full of examples which fail what I call the "reflexology test" of validity.[2]

- Does it derive from or build upon existing theory with a valid evidence base?
- Is it replicable when tested in a controlled environment?
- Is there a volume of independent evidence to support the primary assertions?
- Does it differentiate appropriately between linear and systemic effects?
- Does it ask you to accept some things on faith?

If the answer to the first four questions is "yes" and to the fifth question is "no," then that's a good starting point for credibility. On this basis, reflexology fails on all five elements. Draw your own conclusions about various models of team function and dysfunction – but remember that labelling any commercial product "scientifically proven" is often a sign that raises the suspicion of the wary!

I and colleagues were deep into an analysis of the literature on team performance when one of the world's largest technology corporations invited us to carry out focus groups with their highest performing teams globally, with a view to identifying characteristics that could be used in supporting less effective teams. This project gave rise to the concept of the secure leader, described in Chapter 3. It also accelerated our project to map the factors that multiple research studies had identified as being relevant to team performance and how teams add value. Depending on how you classify factors, there is evidence for between 100 and 200 factors, ranging from diversity of membership to ownership and accountability of roles. All previous studies had focused on identifying the key factors – which inevitably meant that a lot of influences on team performance got left out. That's the classic approach to creating requisite simplicity – a framework people can get their heads around. Our approach was very different. We wanted to ensure that **all** the influences on performance were taken into account. A key principle was that, while classic studies identified the most common significant factors, when it comes to individual teams some of the statistically less important factors may have high significance in their dynamics. In other words, we were less concerned with generalisations and more concerned with the specific circumstances of each team.

Several stages of condensing topics into clusters brought the number of factors down to around 20, then to just six, which encompass every factor we had been able to identify. These six – now known by the acronym PERILL[3] – formed the first **complex adaptive systems model of team function and dysfunction**. The core principle is that most problems identified in the context of teams are only symptoms of interactions between the six factors – or to be more precise, between subfactors of the overarching six acting with subfactors of each other.

In the 1990s, I coined the term "simplexity," to describe the act of making complex things simple but not simplistic. The PERILL framework does just that. It allows us to hold and work with both the simplicity and the complexity at the same time.

In recent years, the establishment of the Global Team Coaching Institute, in partnership with Peter Hawkins, has given a boost to team coaching generally, with over 1000 students on the first programme. The faculty are drawn from more than 20 countries.

Inevitably, what we have learned about teams and teaming (the latter a word coined by Amy Edmondson) has focused my attention on the next big stage in the world of team coaching – working with **teams of teams**. It's also led me to gather data from the literature and multiple interviews about what *really* happens when **new teams form** – and hence to map out a much more credible description than the popular but poorly supported forming, storming, norming to performing model.

## Team types and roles

The Learning Teams project, funded by the European Union at the turn of the century, gave me an opportunity to conduct focus groups around how teams managed their learning. There was a loose correlation with performance, in that the participating companies selected teams that were both high performing and perceived to be effective at continuous learning. The focus group questions were aimed at gathering team members' perceptions of:

* How often they participated in or how familiar they were with each type of team
* Good and bad experience of learning in each type of team
* How much learning is planned, rather than accidental
* How each type of team captures and shares learning within the team and with other teams

The project started from a very small base of assumptions:

* Teams can learn
* Teams are not all the same
* A team is more than a group of people who work together

The first assumption is that teams can, indeed, learn. Individuals obviously do so; and we are increasingly assured that organisations – from small companies to whole societies, do learn. It could be said that a team is simply a small organisation – which is in many respects true – but the team occupies a very special role as part of the fabric of an organisation. If the individuals are bricks, the team provides the wall; structure and strategy are the roof; while organisational culture provides the furniture.

Learning involves the acquisition of data, information, knowledge, and ultimately, wisdom. Information is structured data; knowledge is structured information; wisdom is ability to apply knowledge in different, often unfamiliar circumstances. By these definitions, all teams have to learn if they are to manage and increase their contribution to the organisation.

Learning can also be defined as adaptation to new circumstances. The teams in our study all referred to change as a constant in their environments; in particular, change in task requirements, organisational goals, and people.

The second assumption is that teams are not all the same. This may seem an obvious statement, but what is less obvious is *how* are they different? And more importantly, *what are the significant differences* between teams? One of the first issues we encountered was that teams had very different structures and dynamics. We classified the teams in the study on a matrix of stability of task and stability of membership, a concept derived a few years earlier.[4]

The six types of teams we identified were:

- *Stable teams*, which have relatively consistent membership doing a relatively unchanging task
- *Cabin crew teams,* where the task is relatively stable but the team membership keeps changing – for example, an aircraft crew or a "scratch" sports team
- *"Hit"* or *project teams*, which are set up to deal with short term, usually one-off tasks, with members typically drawn from several other teams
- *Virtual teams*, which typically have no formal recognition, yet whose members work together for mutually understood goals, on an ad hoc basis – in effect, a network with strong ties and influence, often including people outside the organisation, such as suppliers or key customers
- *Development alliances*, composed of two or more people not linked within a normal team, who agree to share learning – for example, off-line mentoring or an action learning set
- *Evolutionary teams,* which tackle longer term developmental projects, such as the design and launch of a major new product or the establishment of a greenfield factory site. Their membership is relatively fluid, with members entering and leaving according to the stage the project has reached.

Each type of team has its own strengths and weaknesses, from a learning perspective. Those identified within UK-wide workshops on team learning are as follows (Figure 8.1):

- Stable teams easily fall into routines, where there is little stimulus to question how things are done. Only under crisis, normally externally generated, do they put great effort into learning, and sometimes not even then.
- Hit teams exist for such short periods that, by the time they have gone through the learned how to work closely together as a high performing team, they are disbanded and the learning acquired is scattered. The need for speed in resolving problems or making things happen leaves little time for reflection and review of learning.
- Evolutionary teams suffer from the same learning difficulties as hit teams, but usually have the breathing space to reach maturity. They then meet a second set of learning problems in how they deal with newcomers. The original members have coalesced into a functioning team, they have a strong shared experience and understanding of the values, principles and reasoning behind the way the project is being run. Newcomers find it difficult to join the club. All too often, there are two teams – insiders and outsiders, because the newcomers cannot catch up with the learning the originals have undergone.

- Virtual teams, being mainly informal, rely on intuitive systems to ensure that learning takes place. Indeed, knowledge can be seen as the currency of the virtual team, so people with low levels of influence and experience may not be invited in. (This possibly explains why so few people at lower levels in organisations in our research had experience of working in virtual teams.)
- Development alliances have fewer inherent learning problems than other types of team, in part because their focus is already learning. The primary problems tend to revolve around *what* people learn in this mode. The attitudes, habits, and behaviours of the more experienced partner will inevitably rub off, and not all of them may be helpful. Another frequently reported problem is insufficient frequency of interaction to make a significant difference.
- Cabin crew teams have lots of people to learn from, but must do so rapidly

The third assumption is that a team is more than a group of people who work together. Teams are different from groups in that they: share a common purpose; are relatively adaptable in the roles members play; share information, understanding, and expertise; support each other; and accept personal discomfort or disadvantage for the greater good of the team as a whole.

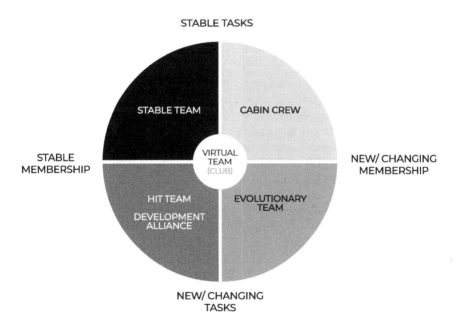

*Figure 8.1* Types of Learning Team.

*Table 8.2* Team learning: drivers and barriers

| Team learning: drivers and barriers | | |
|---|---|---|
| *Team type* | *Barriers* | *Drivers* |
| Stable team | • Conflict avoidance<br>• Time and opportunity for internal politics to take a hold | • People have time and space to build working relationships<br>• Quality processes and procedures easier to embed |
| Project ("hit") team | • By the time the group establishes trust and rapport, it may be dissolved<br>• Members' first loyalty likely to be with their stable team | • Usually focused on clear goals<br>• People have a relatively strong personal stake in success<br>• Sense of urgency |
| Evolutionary team | • Changing membership (and sometimes changing leadership) make relationship building more difficult | • Usually focused on clear goals<br>• People have a relatively strong personal stake in success<br>• Sense of urgency |
| Cabin crew | • Lack of time/opportunity to build relationships | • New faces often stimulate spontaneous creativity<br>• Processes *have* to be simple and well-practiced |
| Learning alliance | • May not have clear outcomes | • Can focus on specific learning goals for the group and the individual |
| Virtual team | • More difficult to maintain cohesion of purpose | • Able to function with minimum bureaucracy |

By these definitions, all teams are learning teams. However, there is a major difference between the ad hoc, haphazard learning that occurs in most teams and *planned team learning*, which involves a conscious effort to: define the learning needs of the team and its members; plan both formal and informal learning; create the maximum opportunities for unplanned learning; establish and maintain continuous systems for reviewing and sharing learning both within the team and with other teams.

Having a common sense of purpose is achieved when team members share a clear set of goals. Ideally, these have very clear outputs, a link with organisational goals and a common understanding of what the team as a whole needs to do to achieve the task. Goal clarity informs the teams members about what they need to learn and why.

A *common sense of priorities* follows on from shared goals. Knowing what is important and why enables people to make decisions about what learning needs are most urgent.

*Willingness to speak openly* is critical to creating genuine dialogue. The longer and more closely a team has worked together, typically, the less willing they

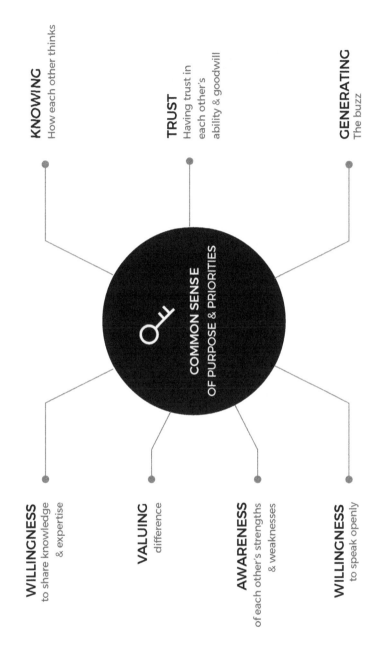

*Figure 8.2* Nine Key Behavioural Drivers of a Learning Team.

are to be constructively confrontational towards each other. Overcoming this reluctance – giving honest feedback to each other – supports continuous learning.

*Awareness of each other's strengths and weaknesses* provides a platform for mutual assistance and co-coaching. *Valuing difference* establishes the mutual respect that oils the giving and receiving of learning between peers. It also helps build *willingness to share knowledge and expertise* – there is no room in the learning team for the concept that "knowledge is power."

Members of effective learning teams tend rapidly to develop an instinctive *understanding of how each other thinks*. They are able to substitute for each other across a wide range of tasks or decisions. In part, this ability derives from *having trust in each other's ability and goodwill* – they have worked at establishing mutual confidence.

Finally, all the most successful teams in our study – and all the respondents who recalled teams that had been significant learning experiences for them – talked about *generating the buzz*. In fact, there are two elements here: buzz is the enjoyment that comes from the social environment, from working with others from whom you can learn. Fizz is the enjoyment that comes from the work itself. When combined, fizz and buzz become powerful motivational vehicles for both learning and task achievement.

Effective learning teams more or less instinctively established and maintained a routine of learning management, in which all members participated.

They set goals for learning that were both individual and shared. A critical element here was some form of team development plan – an amalgamation of individual learning needs and goals with each other and with the overall learning needs of the team as a whole. Key questions included (Figure 8.3):

- What does this team need to do better in 12 months' time?
- What new skills do we need?
- Which development needs apply to all of us and which to only some?
- What resources for learning do we have within the team and what will we have to bring in from outside?

### The learning roles team members can play

From the experiences of the research participants, it was clear that they or people who had helped them had played several different developmental roles, expressed in Figures 8.4 and 8.5.

The development process is made up of two dimensions: challenging versus nurturing; doing versus reflection. These dimensions give rise to four roles: motivator – providing the vision and the enthusiasm from which shared learning goals arise; coach – helping other team members acquire skills and knowledge; reviewer – ensuring the team does take time to reflect and engage in learning dialogue; question-raiser – ensuring that issues, which need to be the subject of discussion and dialogue, are raised at appropriate times.

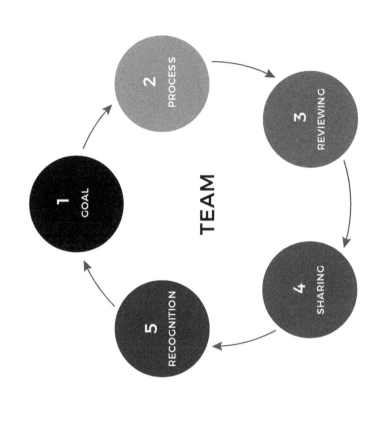

*Figure 8.3* Key Processes for Team Learning.

**LEARNING ROLES**

*Figure 8.4* Developmental roles for team learning.

The same principles apply to the process of gathering knowledge, from which learning is derived. The dimensions here are: external versus internal; formal versus informal. The four resultant roles can be described as: gateway to permission/ information – gaining the organisation's agreement to experiment, spend money on training and so on; plus access to formally held information, which may or may not be generally available; gateway to knowledge – using informal networks to access other people's expertise and experience; specialist – becoming a knowledge resource in one or more areas; recorder – capturing and recording knowledge acquired by the team and/or its members.

These various roles were surprisingly common and consistent amongst the more learning oriented teams we investigated.

### Characteristics of high learning teams

1.  Fun

Just how important is it for people to enjoy their work? Decades of research into motivation indicates that people put more mental energy, more creativity,

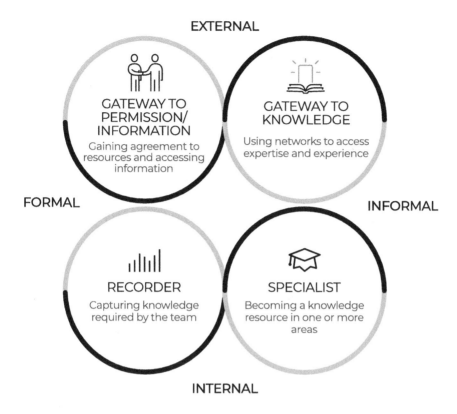

*Figure 8.5* Roles for knowledge gathering.

and higher levels of performance into tasks they feel good about. Such tasks typically have a number of core characteristics, which may include some or all of the following:

- They involve some sense of stretching of the employee's capabilities, of being opportunities to learn
- The employee feels supported in trying new ideas and approaches
- They are perceived by the employee as essentially worthwhile and beneficial
- They will enhance (or at least not damage) the employee's status and self-esteem
- They provide an opportunity for working with other people, whose company the employee enjoys

Put simply, such tasks capture both fizz and buzz. To recap on these

*Fizz = the enjoyment that comes from the task itself*
*Buzz = the enjoyment that comes from socialising with others, who share the same interest*

To the question *why do we need fun at work?*, one can respond *why do we come to work if it's not fun?*

## 2. Knowing how each other thinks

Very close-knit teams develop an instinct that allows each member to make accurate guesses about how others will think and behave in various circumstances. This is not just a characteristic of teams that have worked together for a long time. Some "Barbarian" rugby teams, or players in national sports teams who spend most of their time playing for a specific club, rapidly settle down into routines that seem almost telepathic.

How do they do it? Among other things, they:

- Spend a lot of time observing and listening to each other
- Try to understand how other members approach different situations
- Explain why they tackled a particular situation in the way they did (i.e., make their thinking processes transparent)
- Adopt an open attitude to feedback from colleagues and demonstrate a willingness to learn from them
- Recognise the importance of making other members look good to the outside world

## 3. Recognise each other's strengths and weaknesses

It is often assumed that recognising the strengths and weaknesses of colleagues is relatively easy. After all, you feel the impact of their behaviours fairly directly much of the time and you may have lots of opportunity to observe them. In reality, however, what we see and experience is often only part of the picture. We tend to be blind to some of their greatest strengths and weaknesses; and over-conscious of others.

Moreover, what constitutes a strength or weakness varies according to the situation. For example, having a good eye for detail can be a great strength, when accuracy and considered analysis is important – for example, in checking out a contract. Equally, being enmeshed in the detail isn't very helpful when trying to design a broad strategy. In general, strengths become weaknesses when we over-rely upon them, or when we try to use them in inappropriate situations.

Some of the actions people can take to raise accurate awareness of their own and other people's strengths and weaknesses include:

- Sharing them openly within the team and discussing them
- Asking for and receiving honest feedback from colleagues (ideally 360 degree, but at least from peers and superiors)
- Building a skills inventory
- Examine together tasks that have gone very well/very badly. What patterns can you discern about people's behaviours?

Helping a colleague address an area of weakness is a valuable developmental opportunity for the person, for whom this characteristic is a strength.

3. Valuing difference

The social psychology of human beings is based in very large part on the concepts of *similarity* and *belonging*. By and large, people like and prefer to be with others who have similar values, backgrounds, experience, and so on. The more different someone else is from ourselves, the more difficult most people find it to establish rapport. (Leave aside the fact that, genetically, people differ from each other by less than 0.1% – our social brain is trained to recognise and act upon small differences, originally as a survival mechanism, but increasingly also as means of determining who is in or out of the "tribe.")

At the same time, most people find their identity by virtue of the group with which they associate (or want to associate). Sometimes this can be synonymous with the job they do, but not always. How the group responds to you determines in large part the strength of your feeling of belonging. In general, the more your team emphasises the value it places on each member's mix of experience, personality, and interests, the greater the sense of belonging; and vice versa.

Hence the difficulties many multicultural teams experience in working together. The main problem is not normally language. It is typically the inability of members to understand what values others are applying and how.

The core skill of learning to value difference is being able to accept and recognise the importance and validity of perceptions other than our own. One way of doing this is to use psychometrics or other diagnostics, which explore the personality or preferred styles of each member of the team. Some teams have made significant improvements in the way they operate, by recognising that they have too many people with the same personality profile and none with counterbalancing behaviours and thinking patterns. For example, using a Learning Styles diagnostic, one board found that most of its members were activists (people who prefer to learn by doing) and none were reflectors (people who like to step back and think about the process). Consciously bringing someone with this style onto the board made discussions deeper and more deliberative. By contrast, another top team, which did have a single reflector amongst six activists, failed to appreciate the importance of this counterbalance and constantly ignored or side-lined his comments. When things went wrong and he said "I told you so," they resented and ignored him even more and eventually he left.

4. A common sense of purpose

In a study I led for the International Association of Business Communicators Group in the early 1990s, we identified several characteristics that linked communication activity with business performance. First among these was having clarity of purpose:

- Did everyone share the same understanding of what the organisation was trying to achieve?
- Could they relate that to their own role in making things happen?

The same principles appear to apply to the team, as an organisation within the organisation. The greater the sense of shared purpose, the easier it is for the team to work, learn, and achieve together.

### 5.  A common sense of priorities

It's easy to assume that everyone in a team is working to the same set of priorities. Only when the team fails to perform, does it become apparent that this assumption was unjustified.

How we prioritise is affected to a considerable extent by the values we apply. For example, managers in the United States often perceive immigrants from Latin America as lazy, because they are reluctant to work all hours. The Latin Americans, on the other hand, perceive the white managers as workaholic and failing in their responsibilities to their families. Both groups recognise the value of work-life balance, but they apply different priorities.

Priorities typically come in two types: immediate and underlying. Immediate priorities relate to decisions and activities today. For example, "unless we get that proposal out today, we will lose a really important order." Underlying priorities relate to the key things, which the team has to achieve over the longer term – for example, keeping the customer informed and involved in the progress of their project.

### 6.  Willingness to speak openly

Nowadays, we automatically refer to this as "psychological safety." Many managers spend a large proportion of their time avoiding confrontation. In general, that makes sense. Continuous conflict doesn't provide a solid basis for teamwork. Equally, however, continuous avoidance of confrontation isn't very good for teamwork, either. Groups become increasingly dysfunctional as they accumulate what the author Daniel Goleman calls *lacunas* – issues they agree by silent consensus to leave well alone, because they are too difficult or painful to deal with. Take the example of a highly assertive, driven manager in an IT company. She had a reputation for getting things done, fast, and for never letting anything get in her way. The downside of her behaviour was that she showed little patience for people who didn't share her sense of urgency, riding roughshod over them. Her brusqueness and, occasionally, sheer bad temper alienated staff; she had the highest staff turnover of any manager in the company. The CEO tolerated this behaviour because she got results. Rather than discuss what the impact on the top team was, he and the rest of her colleagues spent a lot of time trying to work around the problem. The turning point came when the team was encouraged to share openly how they felt about each other, in terms of mutual respect and supportiveness. Suddenly aware of how much of a problem she was causing her colleagues, the manager for the first time put some of her energy and determination into changing her behaviour. Asking for and receiving continuous feedback from her colleagues, about her progress, helped her sustain the effort.

## Seven golden rules for a learning dialogue in teams

One of the first things to do in a team coaching environment is to enable the team to establish new norms that will encourage psychological safety, open dialogue, and co-learning. Typically, I encourage them to set their own – but I always have a ready-made set available!

- We will not make assumptions about each other's motives or perspectives
- We will listen with courtesy and respect
- We will take joint ownership for the team's successes and failures
- We will each present as our "best person"
- We will be generous towards each other
- We will give each other the space to speak and ourselves the space to reflect
- We will replace judgement with curiosity

## From systems to complex adaptive systems

The first edition of *Coaching the Team at Work*[5] pioneered evidence-based studies of team coaching. At the time, the volume of academically sound studies of teams and team function was rapidly growing, but the role of coaching in supporting teams was not clearly articulated. It was until a year later that Ruth Wageman and her colleagues published *Senior Leadership Teams,*[6] which established the connection between top team performance and coaching. Peter Hawkins' focused attention on the systemic aspects of teams in 2011[7] and my attention was drawn towards teams as complex, adaptive systems nested within other complex adaptive systems. I had some years earlier in the learning teams project established a model, in which effective teams maintained a constant focus on three core areas – Task, Behaviour, and Learning – supported by interacting processes. The analysis of my interviews with teams suggested that high performing teams constantly shifted their attention between these foci, so that they did not let the emphasis on one dominate the others.

The opportunity to conduct focus group interviews with the highest performing teams of one the largest global high technology companies allowed us to test an emerging model of team dynamics, taking a complex, adaptive systems perspective. To develop this model, we analysed hundreds of papers, both academic- and experience-based, to extract factors that were cited as affecting a team's performance. We went through several stages of categorising clustering them until we identified six recurrent themes that incorporated all the evidence-based factors and many of the opinion-based ones. In taking a complex, adaptive systems perspective, we recognised that the probability of

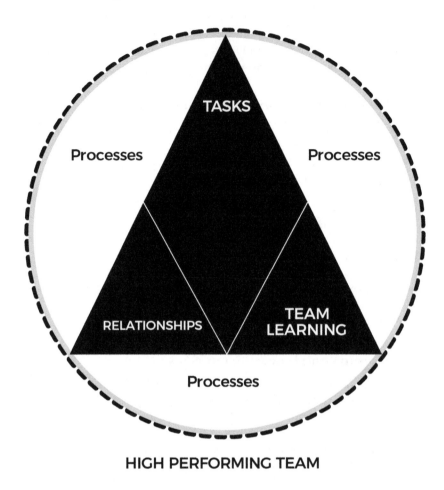

**HIGH PERFORMING TEAM**

*Figure 8.6* Where high-performing teams focus.

finding a neat, packaged and universal model of team function and dysfunction was low – and so it proved. Subsequent experience with hundreds of teams and coaches tells us that the patterns of interactions that enable teams to perform and add value – or prevent them from doing so – are unique, often transitory, and downright messy. Complex, adaptive systems theory and particularly the Cynefin concept created by Dave Snowden (after 15 years of working with his model, I still can't pronounce it!) tell us that trying to bring order and structure to a system that is chaotic is largely a waste of time. Working with the patterns within chaos, however, allows us to develop solutions and ways of working that are flexible enough to respond to the system as it changes.

A key principle here is that the issue a team or a sponsor identifies as "the problem" is rarely that. A bit like the human body, one of the most complex adaptive systems we know, where we feel a pain is not necessarily where it originates. If the presented issue is conflict between team members, that is typically a symptom of other forces at work.

The six factors we identified were:

1. *Purpose and motivation*

Purpose is about what the team is there to do. It is the mission in Hawkins' commissioning. The team purpose may be a subset of a wider organisational purpose or one generated from within. From purpose flows the collective energy that makes "the whole greater than the sum of the parts." Indicators include clarity of shared vision, goals, and priorities.

2. *External processes, systems, and structures*

These are about how the team interrelates with its multiple stakeholders – customers, suppliers, shareholders, other teams within the organisation, more senior levels of management, and so on. Indicators include reputation, performance against targets, environmental awareness (evolving markets, technology, competition etc). They also cover the team's access to resources, such as information and finance.

3. *Relationships*

These are about how people work together – whether they enjoy each other's company, respect each other's ability, are honest towards each other, and so on. Indicators include the level of psychological safety.

4. *Internal processes, systems, and structures*

This is the internal mirror to the external and includes how the team manages workflow, supports each other, and maintains high quality of communication (both task-related and affective). Indicators include role clarity and decision-making quality.

5. *Learning*

This relates to the team's ability to respond to its changing environment and maintain continuous improvement and growth. Indicators include whether it is ahead or behind the curve in terms of change in its environment and the clarity and relevance of members' learning objectives.

6. *Leadership*

The literature on leadership is vast and often contradictory (see Chapter 3). The GLOBE (Global Leadership and Organizational Effectiveness Studies – globe.com) demonstrate that perceptions and expectations of leaders vary extensively between cultures. The link between what leaders do and how the team performs is very hard to pin down, because it is not just about the leader and what he or she does. It is about the system of which the team and the leader are part. So, models that rely solely on a set of leader competencies miss the point. One of the most powerful exercises in team coaching is to ask the team (with the leader's agreement) to specify what kind of leadership behaviours they need to be able to perform at their best, both individually and collectively. (The two lists are not necessarily the same!) Then the team discusses with the leader their responsibilities in helping him or her become the leader they need.

The six sections of the PERILL questionnaire mirror the six elements of the PERILL model. Examples of the questions are:

## Purpose

- We can collectively and clearly articulate our shared purpose
- We review our goals and priorities regularly (every few months) to test them against changes in our environment
- We believe that our job roles allow us to contribute something special to the world

## External processes, systems and structures

- We are very clear who our stakeholders are and the priority we attach to them
- We build long-term plans and ambitions around our those of our stakeholders
- The language we use to describe our customers and suppliers is respectful

## Relationships

- I believe my team colleagues want me to succeed
- If we were starting this team today, these are the people I would choose as my colleagues
- It's OK to admit and discuss our mistakes

## Internal processes, systems and structures

- We know exactly what we are dependent on each other for
- We quickly recognise and respond supportively to an overload on any colleague
- We look forward to our regular meetings

## Learning

* We include learning goals as well as task goals on our regular meeting agenda
* We allocate time for collective learning and reflection
* We value honest feedback

## Leadership

* The leader's style is less about managing people and more about enabling them to manage themselves
* The leader promotes the achievement and reputation of the team and its members, rather than his or her own
* The leader is a role model for the team values

However, it's not necessary always to use the questionnaire (which is now available as an app). The most common use is for the team (with or without the support of a team coach) to explore together a number of instances, where things have gone well or less well, using a matrix that compares each factor with the others. The leadership qualities and behaviours moderate each of these comparisons. Table 8.7 Illustrates the kind of issues that emerge in this exercise. The items above the diagonal LQB (Leadership Qualities and Behaviours) line are all positive interactions; those below are all negative ones. Repeated clusters of interactions usually occur. So, for example, a high level of psychological safety correlates with strong collaborative relations with stakeholders and together these lead to rapid and effective responses to quality issues. That in turn leads to product and service innovation … and so the virtuous cycle proceeds. Patterns of dysfunction emerge in the same way.

Significant insights and lessons can be learned from comparing the patterns that arise from analysing different cases. What is it that we can do more consistently from the positive patterns to address the negative ones?

For more detail on the PERILL model and the theories of team dynamics from a complex, adaptive systems perspective, see the second edition of *Coaching the Team at Work*.[8]

The past 15 years have spawned a constant stream of concepts and frameworks relating to teams. Some of those that I have contributed to and find fascinating include:

* Team energy – the forces that lead to collective motivation and demotivation, when fix and buzz are optimised
* Temporal orientation – the timeframe in which a team's thinking and awareness is grounded (past, present, near future, or future)
* Team personality – its collective identity
* Team narrative – the stories it tells itself about itself, its world, and others
* Distribution of power and status
* Making diversity a positive driver of team function rather than a source of conflict
* Team maturity – both collective and in the context of different levels of personal maturity among team members

*Table 8.3* The PERILL matrix – examples of interactions between factors

| LQB | Purpose & Motivation | Externally facing processes | Relationships | Internally facing processes | Learning |
|---|---|---|---|---|---|
| **Purpose & Motivation** | LQB | Alignment of values between the team and its key stakeholders | Working enthusiastically together towards shared goals | Clarity of priorities; putting collective priorities before personal | Actively seeking ways to leverage and expand team strengths |
| **Externally facing processes** | Stakeholders unclear what you stand for | LQB | Strong collaborative relationships with stakeholders | Rapid and effective response to quality issues | Rapid product and service innovation |
| **Relationships** | People pursue their own agendas | Conflict with stakeholders; disrespect for stakeholders | LQB | High level of psychological safety leads to constant questioning of what we do | People take active responsibility for supporting each other's development |
| **Internally facing processes** | Duplication and waste of effort | Quality issues not acknowledged or addressed | People avoid "interfering" in each other's territory. Large "elephants in the room". | LQB | Culture of continuous process improvement |
| **Learning** | Learning focused on the individual not the collective | Slow to innovate | People "hoard" knowledge and expertise | Resistance to change | LQB |

Team coaching is not team building, which is largely about enabling team members to get on together. The impact of team building fades as team members move on – it's hard to leave a legacy. It's not consultancy, which is about providing solutions rather than helping the team develop its own solutions and better habits of solution generation. It's not facilitation, which is staying with a process, while team coaching is staying with the conversation. It's not coaching the members of the team individually, although that is a common add-on. Team coaching is a longer-term, more deeply impactful intervention.

The objective of team coaching is only partly about helping the team solve a current problem or achieve a current opportunity (a performance issue). It is equally about helping the team build its capability to continue to achieve in the future (a capability issue). And it's about how it achieves more with less (a capacity issue). Team coaches help the team to learn and incorporate teaming behaviours and thinking patterns that in effect make the coach obsolete. They do this in a number of ways, but especially through:

- Role modelling teaming as a pair of coaches. The larger the team, the more important it is to have two coaches working in partnership.
- Observing the team in its meetings and helping the team become more aware of its dynamics, processes and habits, so that it can change those that aren't achieving the value-add the team wants. Feedback-giving is part of this, but the emphasis is on enabling the team to generate its own observation and feedback.
- Challenging the team to develop the habits of systemic and complex adaptive systems thinking. For example:
  - Seeing purpose through multiple perspectives
  - Bringing stakeholders into the room
  - Building psychological safety
  - Equipping the team with the mental tools to engage in continuous upgrade of all its internal systems and processes
  - Helping the team create and pursue its Team Development Plan – a process to integrate individual and collective learning and link both with the business goal and team purpose
  - Helping the team achieve a mode of distributed leadership that works for it

In 2019, Peter Hawkins and I launched the Global Team Coaching Institute with what is now Coaching.com. Our first course for beginner team coaches had 1350 students. Our experience since then has reinforced our belief that team coaching is a key part of the future for coaching generally, for several reasons:

- The market for professional coaches appears to be moving towards saturation and commoditisation

- This situation will get worse as coachbots become more effective, taking over much of the basic, rote coaching (see Chapter 10). To stay ahead, coaches need to establish new ways of adding value – and team coaching is one of the most obvious ways to do that.
- Employer organisations are shifting emphasis from the individual to the team, as we explored briefly in Chapter 3
- The main professional bodies in coaching have developed standards and other methods of recognising team coaching quality, so coaches now have a clear route map for professional development in working with teams

However, the complexity of team coaching is much greater than with individual coaching, the demands are higher and the required toolkit much larger. Stepping up several gears to become a team coach will not be right for every individual coach. However, the good news is that, without exception, every coach we have interviewed, who has completed team coaching, from any of a growing number of systemic team coaching providers, reports that there has been a major positive impact on their coaching one to one. In particular, their ability to see the client in his or her systems is greatly expanded.

One of the earliest and most significant innovations I introduced in the world of teams was the Team Development Plan. In retrospect, it seems so obvious. We have personal development plans and business development plans, but rarely anything to link them.

The Team Development Plan is a road map for a team's learning journey, to enable it to be resilient to and responsive to change. Its key components are:

1. *An overview of the current strengths and weaknesses of the team.* This can be achieved using a simple SWOT analysis but the team needs to carry out some pre-work with stakeholders and influencers:
   a. What do they see in the team now?
   b. How prepared do they think the team is for the future?
2. *An overview of likely scenarios for the next 12–36 months,* bearing in mind:
   a. Likely developments in the needs of stakeholders and influencers
   b. Developments in the general environment (e.g., the market, technology, pressure to achieve more with fewer resources)
   c. Availability of resources to respond to these changes
   d. Again, it's important to gain perspectives from key stakeholders and influencers. If the team has not done sufficient groundwork on this aspect, a practical approach is to develop three scenarios, each based on a significant disruption to "business as usual" – for example, a major technology shift, entry of a new significant player, and a shift in the economic environment. These scenarios, along with how the team intends to meet them, can subsequently be explored with stakeholders and influencers, for validation and/or amendment outside of the team coaching session.

3. *An overview of the learning that needs to take place in the team collectively to meet the challenges of these scenarios, with timelines.* The learning does not all have to take place within the team. In many cases, it will be sufficient to secure access to specialist knowledge and expertise as it is needed. In this case, the plan includes how to integrate this learning rapidly into the team's thinking and ways of working as the relevant scenario looks increasingly likely to occur, or on a just-in-time basis.

4. *A breakdown of that learning into individual development needs and personal development plans.* Here each team member takes personal responsibility for key aspects of the learning. This may be either to support colleagues or to develop a competence the team needs them to have. It is important that everyone understands both their own learning plan and that of their team colleagues.

5. *Agreement on how team members will support each other's personal development.* At this stage, team members request and offer support to colleagues in making learning happen.

6. *Agreement on how team members will collaborate in supporting the collective development.* For example, they may agree coalitions, where two or more work together on a specific area of learning on behalf of the whole team.

7. *Agreement on how to measure and review progress against individual and collective development plans.* Key questions here include:
   a. When (how often) will we review the team and individual development plans?
   b. What will the review process look like?
   c. What measures will we use? (How would each person individually recognise their progress? How would team colleagues recognise it? How would stakeholders recognise it?)

## Teams of teams

Just as focusing on individual performance doesn't necessarily lead to improved collective (team) performance, high-performing teams don't necessarily work together to deliver a high-performing organisation. In his book *Team of Teams*,[9] retired US general Stanley McChrystal offers a number of examples of how functional silos within organisations or even within departments can undermine performance overall. Every increase in the efficiency of a narrow slice of the organisational system can reduce the effectiveness of the whole.

These insights are not completely new, of course, but it is only now, as team coaching becomes increasingly entrenched in organisations, that the focus is beginning to shift to the wider system beyond the team. The emerging challenge is: how do we apply what we have learned about coaching teams to coaching multiple, interdependent teams? To date, there is a severe lack of both empirical research and theoretical models relating to the concept of teams of teams.

### What is a Team of Teams (TOT)?

Traditional organisational structures have a hierarchy of teams, with leaders of individual teams linked within a team of managers, who in turn are linked into more senior manager and leader teams. Communication happens up and down through these managerial "linking pins." A team of teams may or may not have formal leaders for each team but communicates through about multiple points of connection between teams horizontally, vertically, and transversally. While traditional structures aim to produce greater efficiency, TOTs aim to increase effectiveness and agility.

### How can teams of teams build shared purpose and motivation?

MIT's Strategic Agility Project[10] provides a disturbing review of strategic awareness amongst leaders and middle managers. It reveals that strategic alignment amongst executives and managers is consistently overestimated, with only slightly more than half of top teams agreed on the highest three strategic priorities and only 22% of their direct reports able to name the top three priorities.

Among practical approaches team coaches can initiate are:

- Encouraging every team to create and share a narrative about what the organisational purpose looks like from their perspective and what they can best (and or uniquely) contribute to achieving the purpose. Sharing these stories with other teams in the TOT structure allows them better to understand and appreciate each other – but also to develop a clearer consensus about what they need from each other to achieve their part of the purpose and what they can do to support each other.
- Identify in each team the tasks its members find most and least energising. This gives birth to opportunities for creative swapping – redesign of tasks and roles that make more flexible use of the energy within the whole TOT system.
- Explore the concept of interconnected responsibility. Just as individually based reward systems undermine teamwork, so teams can develop an internal focus on their responsibilities. Making at least one third of each team's key performance indicators (KPIs) reflect contribution to *the system* changes attitudes and behaviours, so that teams take partial responsibility and ownership for other connected teams' performance, capability, and capacity in respect of achieving the collective purpose.

### How can teams of teams enhance how they interface with stakeholders and the external world generally?

The external interfaces of each team will have some similarities with those of other teams in the system and some unique connections. In many cases, this will mean interacting with the same external system of systems, but at different points. So, for example, while the executive team might be connected with its counterpart in a major customer, teams at lower levels might be connected with users of the products or services. In a typical organisation, data from these interactions passes up and down functional silos. In a genuine TOT, information is shared equally horizontally, vertically, and transversely.

As a team coach, we might facilitate a team in developing better ways of listening to and capturing information from its stakeholders. With a TOT, it's important to be aware of and capture information relevant to other internal teams as well. Critical questions include:

- How is this information relevant to achieving our collective purpose as a TOT, as well as for our team on its own?
- How do we listen to stakeholders with the ears of other TOTs?

Stakeholder mapping is usually carried out at either an organisational or a team level. In a TOT, these two levels of mapping can be integrated in an intermediary level, which shows the overlaps between individual teams and connects directly to both team and organisational purpose.

### How can teams of teams build more effective, collaborative relationships?

Psychological safety and the trust that it builds are fundamental to the performance of individual teams. Achieving similar levels of trust *between* teams is challenging. Our tribal instincts kick in very easily, leading us to view "outsiders," who we should be collaborating with, as rivals for, for example, resources, attention, or reputation. Building inter-team trust is not greatly different from building trust within teams. Practical approaches include:

- Sharing personal histories and team histories. In a merger situation, rapid integration can often be achieved when two teams share with each other "How we became the team we are now."
- Sharing each team's values. There is usually a great deal of commonality, which may have been downplayed in an atmosphere of rivalry. Rediscovering the connectedness between them promotes understanding. Where there are differences of values, rather than engage in "right and wrong" mindsets, the two teams can explore how the diversity of values can enhance how they work together to support the shared purpose. (One outcome can be redefining work roles, so that aspects of the task that don't energise people in team A, are seized with enthusiasm by people in team B.)
- Having swift and respectful processes for resolving inter-team conflict. Existing conflict/predicting future conflict. Clarity about behaviours that build and undermine trust and reviewing what happens in reality.
- Physical location – having a desk in the other team's work area, to encourage regular human interaction
- Having an agreed *trust recovery process*. This recognises that trust does get broken from time to time and that, rather than let to fester, both teams have a responsibility to repair the damage as quickly as possible. Two key

principles underlie an effective trust recovery process. One is that this is a learning opportunity. The other is that with humility and a continued focus on collective purpose, trust may be strengthened by the experience.

### How can teams of teams develop better shared systems?

Team coaching can help with two key systems:

*   How do we communicate and coordinate across TOTs?
*   How do we make fast and accurate decisions that involve several TOTs?

A knee-jerk response is to make everyone aware of everything, which is likely to result in vital data being buried in an overwhelming mass of trivia and irrelevant data from every other TOT. McCrystal recommends pushing decision-making to the lowest practical level. For this to be effective, however, teams need shared communication and decision-making protocols and – over and above this – an instinctive understanding of what other teams need to know.

Artificial intelligence has much to offer in terms of learning when and where to route information of this kind, but a great deal can be achieved by old-fashioned conversation. Regular and ad hoc inter-team reviews of cases – both ones that went well and ones that didn't – can build collective instinctive understanding of what needs to be transmitted along with the level of urgency. They also reinforce shared accountability. The systems that genuinely enhance collaboration between TOTs are rarely imposed top-down – they are a continuous, emergent learning process that constitutes collective, adaptive intelligence.

A pragmatic set of coaching questions to explore communication between teams is:

*   What information that we could provide would be most helpful to you in making good decisions?
*   When will it be most helpful?
*   How can we provide it in the most helpful way?

To facilitate these conversations, team coaches can work at the interface between teams, supporting them when they come together to determine what decisions require or will benefit from input from more than one team. Among questions that are helpful here are:

*   Who is best positioned to make this decision (e.g. from a position of timeliness, and having sufficient information to assess the situation)?
*   Who should input into the decision, how, and when?

Although there may be some argument and give and take, recasting decision-making as a collaborative activity between teams helps to break down the "them and us" boundaries even further.

### *How can teams of teams better learn together?*

Much of what has been described above is in essence about co-learning across team boundaries. When coaching individual teams, a *team development plan*, which links personal development with team development and the business plan is an increasingly common and practical approach, now standard for all coaches, who have trained through Coaching and Mentoring International.

It is much more difficult to identify and manage learning that is needed across and by the system, but the same principles apply. Team development plans can be amalgamated into TOT development plans that link directly to the organisational purpose. An outcome of doing so may be the identification of hidden centres of excellence – small but valuable caches of experience and skill that can be enhanced and made more widely accessible, if other teams know about and value them.

The TOT development plan plays a vital role in regular (at least annual) reviews of learning by the system. Team coaching focuses on helping teams improve performance (what they do), capability (what it will be able to do in the future, if it acquires the knowledge, processes, and resources), and capacity (how it will do more with less). TOT development plans address the same issues and help teams think beyond their own horizons, expanding the collective consciousness, and reinforcing responsibilities to the system rather than just to a team or an individual job description.

### *How can teams of teams use leadership to greatest effect?*

Leadership is not the same as being a leader. Traditional hierarchies focus on the role of the leader, who is expected to be in control of everything, but increasingly can't. Effective team coaching clarifies the functions of leadership and enables the team to explore together how these might best be delivered. A typical outcome is that the appointed leader knows how best to add value and that they are valued by the team. It also frees them up to focus on tasks that are more important to building future capability and capacity.

Within a TOT, leadership may need to be expressed differently within teams that have different roles in relation to the organisation purpose. As in an individual team, this diversity within a TOT has potential to be both a strength and a weakness. Looking through the lens of leadership functions helps us to understand the leadership system in a much more perceptive way. It requires a mental shift in managers at all levels from seeking to control the TOT to facilitating it.

Collective coaching conversations enable the formal and informal leadership structures to listening to what the system needs. For example, where is it oscillating in ways that will interfere with performance and where are patterns emerging that should be encouraged and reinforced? Functions of leadership.

### Streams of connectedness

The thorniest question in terms of building teams and teams is "With what do we replace the obsolete *linking pin* theory of organisations?" Originally propounded by Rensis Likert[11] (1967), this theory assumes that each team is led by a manager, who takes primary responsibility for communicating upwards and downwards. If it is a management team, each member has the same responsibility, but at one level below. Communication therefore happens mainly vertically, in silos.

Teams of teams can't wait for this long-winded and easily interrupted chain of events to occur. They require rapid, instinctive reactions akin to those that enable a flock of birds or school of fish to shift radically in unison. For this to happen, there must be *multiple* connections operating not only vertically, but horizontally and diagonally as well. This is too big an ask for a team leader to undertake on his or her own. It requires the engagement of the team as a whole – a collective responsibility for connection.

I have been able to identify so far six streams of connectedness – categories of activity that contribute to the collective intelligence and agility of the organisational system as a whole. There are almost certainly more to be found. The six are:

*   Collective vision – the shared purpose that unites all the teams' efforts in pursuit of a commonly desired outcome
*   Information or collective intelligence – what is happening within the internal and external environments of one team that is relevant to the decision-making and functioning of others. Sometimes referred to as collective intelligence.
*   Resources – how people, technology, and other resources can willingly and rapidly be moved between teams to where they will have the greatest positive impact on achieving the team mission. (The opposite to the hoarding of resources that typifies most team structures.)
*   Invention – how rapidly new ideas are disseminated
*   Voice – how people with dissenting views can come together to express a collective view and exert collective, cross-team influence
*   Regrouping – changing structures to create instantaneous new teams to tackle short term crises or opportunities

These streams influence the organisation's behaviours and activities and hence its performance. They also influence what my Italian colleague Roberto Degli Esposti describes as intangible assets, which include corporate brand and reputation, collective memory, and collective identity. The internal aspects of these intangibles are almost impossible to manage in a top-down, hierarchical approach.

### Understanding each stream of connectedness

#### The collective vision stream

When the concept of collective vision was promoted strongly in the 1980s and 1990s, the underlying assumption was that it would be created by the leadership team and "sold" to employees. It gradually became clear that, if people were to take joint ownership of the vision, they had to have some say not just in interpreting it, but in shaping it. In a VUCA world, the context, in which organisational purpose exists, is constantly shifting. The words may stay the same, but the meaning behind them may change. So, for example, an oil company may continue to describe its mission as providing energy but refocus on how it delivers that mission using renewable resources.

The sense of purpose that binds people together and creates the emotional connection between who they are and what they do is therefore not as fixed and stable as people imagine. It is constantly shifting in subtle ways and people at the top may be the *last* to become aware of changes. The problem may become even worse, if the organisation has an entrenched and reactionary middle management hierarchy, which filters information both upwards and downwards.[12] Maintaining a constant dialogue – vertical, horizontal, and transverse – is the only known antidote (other than being taken over by an organisation with a different vision).

### The information stream

This stream is all about the right information to the right people at the right time. Most organisations have no shortage of data, but getting it to the people, who need it most, is a constant challenge. Each team and its members need information about:

- What needs to happen, when?
- What clouds are on the horizon (or just over it) that may interfere with our mission? (Early warning signs are often easier to see by someone outside the team.)
- What's interesting?
- What's intuitively significant?

Teams therefore need to include in their regular meetings discussion around these two questions:

- What do we need to know from other teams in order to respond swiftly and effectively to what's happening around us?
- What do other teams need to know from us to respond swiftly and effectively to their environment?

### The resources stream

A systemic perspective on resources provides a visible manifestation of systemic collaboration. Rather than wait for instructions from above to share resources or redistribute tasks, teams recognise when other teams are under pressure and try to help wherever they can. This empathetic approach – close to what we might see between colleagues in a single high-performing team – allows for much faster than normal responses to issues and events. It is broadly a horizontal rather than vertical phenomenon.

Questions that might be asked at meetings between teams include:

- What are the unique skills each team brings to the process?
- What resources and skills can we make available to other teams to enhance the overall system?
- If teams have peaks and troughs of workflow, how might they collaborate to support each other and smoothen the process?
- Where do things slow down at the interfaces between teams?
- What would enable each team to spend more of its time and effort on tasks directly related to the organisational purpose?

### The invention stream

"Not invented here" is a killer attitude for systemic collaboration. One of the simple ways to overcome it is to hold an *ideas fair*. This is an opportunity for every team to present innovations it has created and to seek collaborations on emerging ideas, bringing together the inventiveness of more than one team.

### The voice stream

This is about enabling the collective courage to speak up and dissent. When people who share similar perspectives and concerns link with others elsewhere in the organisation, there occurs an emergent clarity about these concerns. Iterative conversations enable them to challenge assumptions and confront taboo topics with a collective voice. A key factor in a powerful stream of voice is that conversations are not just between members of teams at the same hierarchical level, but also take place across levels. The result is that the voice stream surfaces issues that prevent individuals and teams performing at their full potential and creates an opportunity and responsibility for the system as a whole to address them.

### The restructuring stream

This stream is the organisational organism's way of filling the gaps between team responsibilities and fields of action. Key questions here include:

- What issues are not being addressed by any team?
- What issues are distributed (in terms of task and/or responsibility) amongst several teams, but are not dealt with as well as they should be?
- What issues interest people spread across the organisation, but have no formal assignment of responsibility?

The benefit of regular review of these questions is that informal groups can cohere from members of multiple teams, often addressing issues without the need for formal authority from above. Only when they need the formal assignment of resources do these teams become part of the recognised structure. The function of these groups can be likened to the lymphatic fluid that circulates between cells in a human body – constantly moving and responding in its make up to changes in both the internal and external environment.

### *Making the six streams flow*

In a traditional organisation, all these six streams are managed from above. For example, the targets for innovation are set at the top and budgets assigned according to the leaders' perspective of the urgency and difficulty of achieving them. One of the disadvantages of this approach is that innovations have to be of a significant size and impact to attract the attention of the leaders. Yet, as Amy Edmondson (Edmondson, 2012) explores in her book *Teaming*, it is the constant flow of small innovations, achieved through learning from small failures, which underpin organisational innovation in a modern corporate environment.

When the flow of all six streams is multi-directional, the leaders become just one of many influences. Rather than focus on *being leaders* they must focus on promotion of *leadership*, wherever and however it is needed. This is a central message of McChrystal's book. Within each team, the same principle applies – leadership must be distributed, if only because it is impossible for a team leader to maintain all the strings if connectedness within and outside the team single-handed.

Hence, contrary to the normal leadership treatise, this discussion starts anywhere but from the top. We can select any point in the complex system and examine it from there. So, let's start with an individual team of, say, eight people. When the team has its regular weekly or monthly meeting, it discusses each of the six streams in relation to its internal functioning. This can only happen in an environment that combines high psychological safety with future orientation and a coaching style of co-working. The team also explores, to the extent that it can, the implications for other teams, to which it is connected, either horizontally, vertically, or further away in the formal structure. (The traditional hierarchy chart is an impediment here – a much more accurate model might be a container of coloured balls, constantly shifting in relation to each other, as in a children's play area.)

If the team knows in advance that a topic on the agenda has implications for other teams in one of the six streams, it can invite representatives of those teams to attend its meeting. Conversely, it can send a representative to the next meeting of a team it identifies a need to liaise with. A crucial aspect of the team meetings is that, while everyone takes responsibility for *discussing* all of the streams, individuals and pairs are accountable for *linking* with other teams.

### The role of the team coach in supporting teams of teams

The challenge for the team is to move from its normal internally focused ways of working to more flexible, multi-perspective routines and behaviours. The team coach assists each team in achieving the clarity to understand how it works now, compared with how it wants to work, and how it will bring about the changes it and the system as a whole need. A core element here is overcoming the learned behaviour of putting the team's own tasks and priorities first, ahead of those of the wider team of teams.

The role of the team coach is also to assist at any point within the larger system of teams, where there is potential for improved connectedness. This can be, for example, where two or more teams need to build more effective task collaboration. It is not necessary in all cases for everyone in these teams to be present for these coaching sessions – if representatives are genuinely representative of the collective perspective of their team (rather than their own perspective or that of a subgroup within it), the smaller numbers can be much more efficient and effective.

## New team formation

Whatever stage of development a team is at, how it evolves is a complex and largely unpredictable dynamic of internal and external forces. Yet the most commonly cited model of new team development – Tuckman's[13] forming, storming, norming to performing – assumes a completely internal locus of control within a linear system. The Tuckman model was based on a macro-study of groups (not teams), most of them groups of people in therapy. One of the few academic studies to test the model found that only 2% of teams followed the prescribed pattern.[14] The anecdotal evidence we have from the experience of coaches trying to apply this model to the development of new teams suggests that it actually *slows down* development. In particular, effective coaching removes the need for a "storming" period.

The model below draws on the PERILL model of team functioning, on the empirical literature on teams and team coaching, and on the reported experience of team coaches. It provides a logical, pragmatic framework for ensuring the right conversations happen at the right time. There are five stages:

All elements of the PERILL model are represented in this sequence. In real world situations, there is always some overlap between stages.

The Tuckman model is based on what typically happens in therapy groups without intervention. It describes the gradual emergence of order out of chaos. Team coaching helps to cut through early chaos in new teams by providing structure to the team's dialogue. In existing teams, coaching provides a "return to basics," whenever a significant change occurs. For example, when:

- A new member joins
- A new leader arrives
- Stakeholders' expectations shift
- There are fewer resources available
- The technology changes

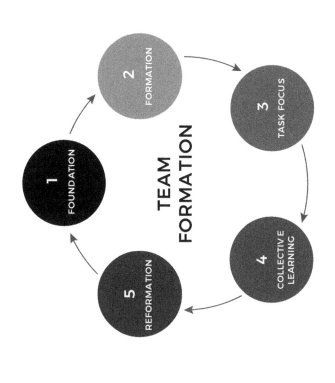

**FOUNDATION**
· Sponsorship/ Permission to operate
· Resourcing:
· Right people
· Right equipment, finances etc

**FORMATION**
· Shared purpose
· Relationship building

**TASK FOCUS**
· Shared processes
· Shared knowledge
· Distribution of authority,
  accountability and leadership

**COLLECTIVE LEARNING
AND ADAPTATION**
· Developing deeper processes,
  knowledge and relationships
· Realigning with stakeholders
· Managing successes and setbacks

**REFORMATION**
· Re-joining the cycle at any point

*Figure 8.7* Stages of new team formation.

*Detailed questions for team coaching*

The following questions provide a starting point for coaches to help newly formed teams and teams in formation to develop the mutual understanding and interdependencies that will assist their performance.

### Foundation

- Who are the sponsors of this project or business need?
- What is the business rationale?
- What is the (political) context?
- How important is it that this team delivers?
- Who decides who should be on the team and how? (On what basis were members selected?)
- Is there appropriate diversity?
- What resources will be needed to do the job? How sure are we of the predictions for this?
- Will additional resources be available, if needed?
- What previous experience do team members have of working together?
- (If relevant), what experience do they have of working in project teams?

### Formation

*Shared purpose*

- What makes achieving this purpose important to our stakeholders?
- What makes it important to us?
- How do we each interpret the given team purpose in terms of:
  o   Explicit and implicit values
  o   What achieving the purpose would look like to us?
  o   What it would look like to our stakeholders
- What is the main contribution you would like to make?
- How will we make sure we don't lose sight of the purpose?
- What identity do we want for this team?
- What hopes, aspirations and fears do we have for this team?

*Building relationships*

- How do we affirm that everyone belongs here and is a valued and equal member of the team?
- How do we ensure mutual trust and psychological safety?
- Understanding each other's story
- How will we care for each other?
- How will we build and maintain good relationships with each of our stakeholders?

## Task focus

### Shared processes

- What tasks need to be done, in what order?
- Who has primary, secondary, and general responsibility for each task?
- What tasks are reliant on people outside the team? How will we make sure these are delivered? (How will we manage the process boundaries?)
- How will we monitor and review?
- How will we benchmark?
- What needs collective decisions and how will we manage that process?
- How will we prevent "groupthink"?

### Shared knowledge

- What expertise do we each bring?
- Where are the overlaps and gaps?
- What new knowledge and expertise do we need to acquire? Who will have responsibility for each of these areas?
- How will we question our assumptions?
- How will we maintain a healthy level of naivety?

### Distribution of leadership

- What leadership functions does this team need?
- Who will be responsible for each?
- In what circumstances shall we pass functions to other team members?

## Collective learning and adaption

- How are we managing and learning from setbacks? Are we capturing that learning effectively?
- Do we genuinely believe our forecasts?
- Are we stretching and challenging ourselves enough?
- What support do we need from each other?
- Are we making full use of the resources available to us? (Are there resources we could use but aren't using?)
- How well are we managing the politics outside the team, insofar as they affect us?
- Which areas of the PERILL model most need our attention currently?
- Is what we are doing still the best way to achieve the team purpose?
- Could a different team deliver the purpose better than we can?

*Reformation*

- When did we last recalibrate against our purpose?
- What has changed in our team membership?
- What new challenges do we need to face up to?

## Agile processes for stable teams

One of the biggest criticisms of agile methodology is that it is very difficult to transfer from a project team environment to teams engaged in "business as usual" (BAU). In the latter, there is no definable end to the process. Instead of experimenting and making continuous improvements, in pursuit of frequently changing priorities, stable team environments seek to optimise and achieve consistency in workflow and other processes against long-term, relatively stable goals and priorities. Members of BAU teams may take part in a cross-team project using agile principles, or a sub-group within the team may take an agile approach to specific improvement projects. However, trying to run a BAU team as if it were a project team is like asking a marathon runner to fence. Performance for the former comes from consistent pace in pursuit of a fixed goal; for the latter, it comes from constantly adapting how they respond to new and evolving challenges.

So how can BAU teams make effective use of agile thinking? The answer is BEAU – Business *Evolving* As Usual. The starting point for this approach is that the team recognises that it must evolve in tune with and at least as fast as its environment (and particularly its stakeholders and influencers) require it to. The *purpose* of the team provides a relatively fixed point that indicates a required general direction of travel. A BEAU team works on the principle that it will have to make frequent changes to the actual course, to take into account perturbations, changes in wind direction, and other predictable or unpredictable events. Periodic recalibrations create the impetus for these course changes and these must be frequent enough to permit rapid, relatively small corrections but not so frequent that members find it impossible to plan.

The annual strategy binge so beloved of many organisations is far too long a cycle to achieve this balance. Like the mother bear's porridge, quarterly cycles seem to be "just right," not least because they integrate seamlessly with cycles of appraisal, as we will explore below.

Key components of a BEAU team approach include:

1. *Integration of individual and team development plans.* Critical questions here are:
   - What new or improved skills, knowledge, and capabilities does our purpose demand of us?
   - What skills, knowledge, and capabilities can we reasonable evolve over the next period?
   - What areas of process can and should we improve?

- What aspects of relationships and collaboration can we improve within the team?
- What can we do to enhance relationships and interactions with our stakeholders and influencers?
- What accountabilities and responsibilities do we need to clarify in order to fully support each other?

2. *Employee-led appraisal and performance management.* One of the problems with traditional performance appraisals is that there is little credible evidence that they actually improve performance. On the contrary, even positive appraisals can be demotivating. A much more effective approach shifts the control and ownership of the appraisal process from the manager to the employee, roughly on a six-week cycle. (So twice every quarter.) The process begins with the employee asking each of his or her team colleagues and some stakeholders outside the team what the employee has done to support them in delivering their part of the team purpose; and what more they would have liked him or her to have done. Based on this data, the employee creates a performance and learning plan, which details what they aim to achieve over the next six-week period. The manager – and, if appropriate, other team members – coach them and provide constructive challenge. At the end of the six-week period, the employee seeks colleague feedback once more, with the additional focus of how well they met their performance and learning targets and what they have learned as a result of their successes and failures. At the quarterly review session, the team members seek and offer each other help. They also identify recurring patterns preventing improvements and determine how to address these in the next quarterly cycle.

3. *PERILL reviews.* It's not surprising that the questions underpinning the development planning process above parallel the six elements of the PERILL complex, adaptive systems model. At least twice a year, the BEAU team reviews what happened when the whole team was performing at its best; and when this was not the case. Key questions here include:
- What has changed (or is changing) in the wider systems, of which we are a part?
- How does this affect our ability to deliver against our purpose?
- How can we calibrate or actual pace of evolution against the pace the system needs of us?
- If we are changing at an appropriate speed, is it in the right direction?
- Who are we listening to most? And who should we be listening to?

4. *Experimentation as a performance indicator.* Experimentation is the bridge between performance focus and learning focus. Quarterly reviews and PERILL reviews generate areas of focus, linked to the question "How can we faster and/or more surely along our direction of travel?" From these areas of focus spin out multiple opportunities for experiments at

individual, sub-group, and team level. The team agrees which of these it has sufficient capacity, resources, and energy for, building them into the personal and team development plans. Subsequent reviews decide whether to continue, develop, or drop each experiment, capturing learning for the next cycle. The key here is that experimenting and learning from failure are built into business as usual, rather than seen as an additional task; and that the team can self-evaluate on the level, scope, quality, and quantity of its innovation.

5. *The leader as curator.* A major challenge for designated leaders is to keep out of the way, supporting each of these processes but not attempting to control them. As curator, the leader ensures the team has the resources it needs and protects its boundaries – limiting interference from outside that might sap team energy or divert its attention from value-creation. Part of this shift involves letting go of their role as sole coach to members of the team and instead facilitating co-coaching and a coaching style of conversation in team meetings.

These five key principles are different in many aspects to project-based agile methodology, but they are far better adapted to the needs of mainstream teams in organisations. Like agile teams, however, BEAU teams require significant support to learn these new ways of working. Effective team coaching from accredited team coaches can be part of the solution. But the biggest impact comes from step-by-step experimentation, gradually learning how to apply the principles until they become ingrained in the team culture.

## Summary

The journey into coaching with teams has been one of expanding complexity and increasing systems awareness, both for me and for the coaching profession. Sometimes it feels as if every time we open the door into one level of complexity, another lies behind it. The challenge for coaches is to be at least one door ahead of client leaders and their teams.

## Notes

1 Hackman, J.R. and Wageman, R., (2005) A theory of team coaching. *Academy of management review*, 30(2), pp.269–287.
Katzenbach, J.R. and Smith, D.K., (1992) Why teams matter. *The McKinsey Quarterly*, (3), pp.3–28.
Edmondson, A., (1999) Psychological safety and learning behavior in work teams. *Administrative science quarterly*, 44(2), pp.350–383.
2 Does it all fall apart when you take a critical, evidence-based look at it?
3 Purpose and motivation, External systems and processes (stakeholders), Relationships, Internal Systems and Processes. Learning and Leadership.
4 Clutterbuck, D *Developing learning teams* Training Officer, July/August 1996.
5 Clutterbuck, D (2007) *Coaching the Team at Work*, Nicholas Brealey International, London.

6  Wageman, R, Nunes, DA, Burruss, JA and Hackman, JR (2008) *Senior Leadership Teams*, Harvard Business School Press, Harvard.

7  Hawkins, P (2011) *Leadership Team Coaching,* Kogan Page, London.

8  Clutterbuck, David (2021) *Coaching the Team at Work*, Nicholas Brealey International, London 2nd edition.

9  McChrystal, S (2015) *Team of teams*, Penguin, London.

10  Sull D, Sull, S and Yoder J (2018) No One Knows Your Strategy – Not Even Your Top Leaders, Sloan Management Review, (Research Highlight online February 12).

11  Likert, Rensis (1967). *The Human Organization: Its Management and Value*. New York: McGraw-Hill.

12  Oshwry, Barry (2007) *Seeing Systems,* Berrett-Koehler, SF.

13  Tuckman, B.W. and Jensen, M.A.C., 1977. Stages of small-group development revisited. *Group & organization studies*, 2(4), pp.419–427.

14  Knight, PJ (2007) Acquisition Community Team Dynamics: The Tuckman Model vs. the DAU Model. Paper to the 4th Annual Acquisition Research Symposium of the Naval Postgraduate School.

# 9 Ethics, the coaching profession, and the looming presence of artificial intelligence

The link between fairness and ethics may be tenuous, but it's probably why my interest was taken with the topic of corporate deviance. A flurry of books and studies in the late 1980s and early 1990s examined how organisations "went bad." Though few of them referred to systems theory, these studies pointed to a phenomenon, where people, who in other parts of their lives maintained ethical behaviour and values, somehow lost sight of these in a corporate context. Lack of work-life balance was one factor – too little contact with other contexts and value systems blinded them to what they were doing, whether that was an active role, or simply standing by.[1] It often starts with small breaches and gradually grows in scope and scale. So, for example, a group of employees who see that they are going to miss an important target, with adverse effects to their bonuses, may be tempted to cheat "just a little bit." The group effect gradually takes over – if "everyone is doing it" or if "my boss knows and turns a blind eye," the misbehaviour is increasingly seen as the norm and therefore acceptable.

Other factors that make unethical or illegal behaviour more likely include:

- Group loyalty – for example, when health professionals cover up the failings of a colleague whose incompetence is killing patients. Especially when services are under pressure, group solidarity tends to take precedence over patient care.
- Self-delusion. Most people think they are above averagely ethical. They also think they are above average as a driver. Our need to think well of ourselves leads us to rationalise away behaviours that dent our positive self-image. Apparently, creative people are more likely to self-delude, because they are better at making up narratives to explain away behaviour that doesn't fit with their espoused values.

I put my learning on corporate deviance together with the research I had carried out a decade before into whistleblowing. One of the lessons I took was that *ethics is not (only) an individual issue – it is a systemic issue.* In that simple statement lies the reason that so many organisations have failed to change cultures in which unethical behaviour is rife. I started to include discussions on ethical

DOI: 10.4324/9781003323990-10

*Table 9.1* My learning journey

| My learning journey | | |
| --- | --- | --- |
| *Ethics are individual* | *Ethics are systemic* | *Ethics are systemic and contextual* |
| Professional organisations in coaching and mentoring are there for the coaches | Professional organisations in coaching and mentoring are there for the coach/client or mentor/mentee system and their immediate stakeholders | Coaching and mentoring are irrelevant if they don't address the wider social issues of our time |

decision-making in my workshops for directors, my assignments with boards, and, of course, in my day-to-day coaching.

Then came the financial crisis of the early 2000s. The ICAEW (Institute of Chartered Accountants in England and Wales) saw an opportunity to raise the profile of senior corporate finance professionals by giving them the skills to challenge unethical practice in organisations, by being ethical mentors. An ethical mentor is someone who provides a safe space for a potential whistle-blower, or anyone who thinks they have an ethical dilemma, to work it through. I and colleagues have trained hundreds of ethical mentors, often in partnership with Celia Moore, a renowned professor of business ethics. There are more than 200 in the UK National Health Service alone.

## Ethical mentors

Ethical mentors focus on helping people think through situations where they have recognised the potential for conflict of values, or ethical lapses. They also help people develop their ethical awareness, so that they are better able to foresee and avoid ethical dilemmas, and provide a resource through which business leaders, who are concerned about ethicality, can shape more ethically aware cultures in their organisations.

Ethical mentors also help potential whistle-blowers to consider their actions and the potential consequences. Whistle-blowing processes in large organisations suffer from both reluctance of some people to use them, for fear that matters will escalate out of their control; and conversely from malicious usage, for example by staff who have been justifiably fired, or precipitate use, where the whistle-blower's actions undermine due procedure with regard to an issue already being investigated. The ethical mentor helps people think through when and how to ensure that their concerns are being addressed in an open and appropriate manner, and how to mitigate any negative personal consequences.

I am unsure how the ethical mentoring framework I use came about. I think I adopted or adapted it from my wide reading, but despite considerable effort I cannot find a source.[2] The six stages of the conversation are:

- Articulate the problem
  - Who does it affect, how, and why?
  - What is the nature of the conflict of interest?
  - What specific personal, organisational, and/or societal values are involved?
- Consider the context
  - Who is involved, directly and indirectly?
  - Is this a new issue, or an old one in a new guise?
  - What are your specific and general responsibilities?
  - Who has been consulted?
  - Who needs to be consulted?
  - Is there a relevant code of conduct or guideline?
  - What is the general ethical climate here?
- Consider the implications
  - What risks are involved? (Safety, financial, reputational etc)
  - What precedents may be set by this decision?
  - What would be the impact if this were done on a much larger scale?
  - Would the implications be different if this were played out publicly v privately?
- What other opinions/ perspectives may be relevant?
  - What might you be avoiding acknowledging?
  - Who might provide a robust challenge to your thinking?
  - How can you make other people feel more comfortable about speaking up?
  - Have we genuinely sought and listened to dissenting views?
- Balance the arguments
  - What would an impartial adviser see as fair?
  - What priorities should we apply to conflicting objectives and values?
  - What are the "zones of ethical acceptability" and what lies outside them?
- The final check
  - What decision-making biases might you be applying without realising?
  - How honest are you being with yourself? (How pure are your motives?)
  - Do you truly feel this is the right thing to do?
  - If we were to give this issue more time, would we come to a different conclusion?

Long before I made the transition from journalist to pracademic, I conducted an experiment, in which I asked people in various countries to rank what was acceptable business practice. I chose a handful of topics and offered a cascade of options. So, for example, one started with using a client's telephone gratis to accepting a suitcase full of used notes. What I wanted to know was, where did the line between what was and wasn't ethically acceptable occur? The conclusion I came to from the data was that national culture had little or no impact on the areas I explored. The variation occurred in the context of functional culture – so marketing and sales were typically more ethically relaxed than HR or finance. This wasn't a piece of research that would remotely meet the rigour of my later studies and I cannot label it more than an interesting set of data. But it caused me to confront my prejudices and cultural stereotypes and to begin to view ethics from a systemic perspective.

More recently, I have engaged with the complex issue of coaching ethics in relation to new technology. The two main ethical codes of practice in coaching both have basic statements on the need to keep abreast with technology and day-to-day housekeeping issues such as complying with data privacy legislation. However, there are several substantial ethical issues arising. Is it ethical, for example, for a coaching platform to record and data analyse the conversation between a coach and client? In what circumstances will it be acceptable for a coach's artificial intelligence assistant to communicate with that of a client or coaching supervisor? Supervisors at least will need training as ethicists in the not too distant future!

In this chapter, I explore three aspects of ethics: the **democratisation of coaching**, the **decolonisation of coaching**, and the role of coaches in **raising client awareness of ethical issues** such as climate change. I also take a brief look at the growing challenges arising for coaching from coachbots and artificial intelligence.

## The democratisation of coaching

If ethics is as much about the choices of the system, rather than just about the choices of individuals, this poses some interesting challenges for the coaching profession. I first started referring to the **democratisation of coaching** in the mid-noughties, concerned that the people who tended to receive coaching were generally those who were already privileged and likely to succeed. How ethical, I asked, was it for a coach to help yet another over-educated narcissist up the corporate ladder, yet ignore the needs of people who might make better leaders, but who couldn't afford the costs of coaching? I have been thrilled by the extent to which coaches around the world and, particularly within the EMCC, have taken on board the importance of balancing their commercial portfolio with pro-bono coaching for people who can't afford it. One of the projects I am especially pleased to be associated with was *Ethical Coach*, sponsored by the entrepreneur Ben Croft. Ethiopia was a country with very little coaching presence and a big need on the part of charities operating in the country. The project, for which I was chief coach, involved supporting aspiring coaches in the country to develop their skills, which they would then apply to help the executive teams of NGOs. Each local coach was supported by a volunteer experienced international coach, who worked alongside them with the NGO. Each pair of coaches was also supported by volunteer supervisors from the Global Supervisors Network.

I have also chosen to focus on the coaches of the future. Employers across the world struggle to convince managers at all levels to behave in a coaching manner. The system is self-perpetuating – people model their managerial and leadership behaviour on the leaders they had when they first entered the workforce. One way to break that cycle is to ensure that young people enter the workforce with coaching skills and mindset ready formed. Schools in several countries have experimented with the programme I've designed to create teenage coaches and mentors. The workbook even has a chapter on how to mentor your parents!

Several technology-based companies have recognised the potential to reduce the costs of coaching, making it affordable to a wider audience – and described this as democratisation. It's certainly part of the solution, although a potential downside is that it commoditises coaching. What it can't do is meet the needs of people too poor to afford the "affordable" – like those in rural African villages. Nor does it provide an easy answer for developing the coaching skills of people in those communities. In 2020 I issued a challenge to the coaching professional bodies: "What could we do together to meet a target to bring coaching to 100 million of the world's most underprivileged within the next 10 years?"

## Decolonisation of coaching

I do lay claim to coining the phrase the decolonisation of coaching.[3]
    Here are three statements:

*   Clear goals are essential in a coaching assignment
*   Modern coaching originated in the United States
*   Mentors give advice; coaches don't

If you agreed with any of these statements, you have been acculturalised into the dominant North American coaching culture. You have bought into a narrative that is specific to a specific culture at a specific time. And one that may blind you to fact that other cultural narratives see goals as emergent (see Chapter 8) or have a different perception of time, or relationships. We can in many cultures look back through thousands of years of person-centred, question-based dialogue.

The process of cultural colonisation in coaching has been rapid and insidious. But across the world coaches are pushing back, reasserting the validity of coaching from the perspective of their own cultural identity and history.

If I try to coach or mentor someone from another culture through my cultural lens, I deny the legitimacy of theirs. If I attempt to coach them through their cultural lens, I am in danger of inauthenticity. A mature, culturally aware coach creates a co-learning space with the client, where both perspectives enrich and enhance the learning dialogue.

The evolving challenge is to educate coaches everywhere to understand the limitations of their own cultural assumptions about coaching and the value of others. For coaches who have bought into an "imported" coaching culture, the challenge is how to reassert their own cultural identity. My own cultural blindness was brought home to me recently when a coach in supervision challenged the use of the word "decolonisation." In her culture, she explained, bringing in simplistic, formulaic, standard methods of coaching was important in addressing a business culture of rampant corruption. What we learned together was that, while decolonisation was an appropriate language and intent for the developed world, in other countries a more culturally appropriate term would be "contextualisation."

Whatever we call it, there is an ethical dilemma inherent in the conflict between creating universal standards and at the same time nurturing diversity and respecting different cultural perspectives. For the professional bodies, there is room for deep reflection on what the words "international" or "global" mean in this context. What is it about our coaching that is truly universal and what is simply an assumption derived from a particular culture?

## Raising client awareness of ethical issues

Helping clients recognise that there is an ethical issue in play is all in a day's work for experienced coaches and mentors. We raise their awareness by helping them reconnect with their values and compare what they are doing, or intend to do, against those values. It's a lot easier when what's at stake is personal and in their immediate sphere of influence. But some issues are too wide and too disconnected from the impact one person can have, or at least may seem so. They are also likely to be more difficult to connect directly to issue the client brings for discussion. Amongst the most common of these is climate change

Most coaches I supervise are alert to new ways of reducing their own carbon footprint. We've shared small actions we can take – like composting and condensing air travel into fewer, longer trips. But a recurring question is: *How far can I go in encouraging my clients (and through them their organisations) in being more environmentally conscientious?*

On the one hand, most coaching assignments are for a specific purpose. No-one in my practice has yet reported an assignment that was focused on climate change. Will clients and sponsors see attempts to introduce these issues into coaching as a distraction and misuse of coaching time? Said one coach: "It feels a bit like bringing out a religious pamphlet. I'm a coach, not a climate missionary."

On the other hand, it's unethical to collude with behaviours that are themselves unethical. Depending on our point of view, outright climate change denial or deliberating ignoring climate impact of corporate decisions would fall into this category. Often coaches have brought to supervision or workshops examples of turning down or resigning from clients who fell into this category.

It's the messy middle – as usual – where the confusion lies. When and how do we bring climate issues into the conversation without them seeming off the point? One very practical solution that works most of the time is to take a systemic perspective. Simplistic coaching follows a pattern of problem > exploration > solution. More mature coaches help the client understand the systems they are part of, and how these interact, before defining the issue. Most of the time, the issue looks very different from a systemic perspective and solutions that address the system are much more effective and sustainable.

Introducing climate change as an element of the system evolves naturally from exploring the leader's systems from the perspectives of multiple stakeholders. What frequently emerges at this point is that clients' myopia with regard to climate change is not wilful. Rather, it is because they don't appreciate the power they have to influence, even in small ways. When someone develops a picture of their ideal self as a leader, the big social and environmental issues become integrated. My experience is that, once leaders accept the relevance of the wider context to their coaching conversations, they are open to periodic reviews of these aspects of their leadership identity.

A question I have learned to drop at appropriate times is: "What of all the priorities you have right now is anyone going to look back on in five years' time and say *That made one hell of a difference!?*" A major part of our role as coaches is to enable our clients to take a different perspective that opens up different choices. A high proportion of the leaders I work with in their 50s and 60s are concerned about their legacy, but feel constrained from discussing it. As coaches, we are one of the few people to whom they can open up.

In short, most of the anxieties coaches feel about introducing climate change to client conversations are exaggerated. All we need to do is to create the right context for the client to explore their own climate guilt. What they seek from their coaches is compassion, creating clarity, and an absence of judgement – the very core of connected coaching.

### *An optimistic view*

The recent first global conference on ethics in coaching achieved more than double the expected audience. Only a few years ago, most coaches I supervise regarded ethics as a code you turned to if you ran into difficulties. Now it's more common for them to see ethics as an important part of their regular reflections on themselves and their practice. If we can be more effective at that, it bodes well for our ability to have a positive impact on the ethics of our clients and the systems, of which they are a part.

## The challenge of artificial intelligence

### *Coaching and mentoring have traditionally been low tech activities*

The issue of coach versus AI became one of the hot topics in coaching around 2017. As yet, there is little evidence that existing coaches have been given the

*Table 9.2* Modes of learning

| Modes of learning | | |
| --- | --- | --- |
| Mode | Coach-mentor | AI |
| Information | Limited depth, high breadth | High depth, limited breadth |
| Knowledge | Limited depth, high breadth | Moderate depth and breadth, depending on what databases linked to |
| Skills | Observation and feedback, plus motivation | Potentially higher levels of observation (faster and more comprehensive, including micro-movements and tonal analysis) |
| Wisdom | Mentor draw on narratives and values important – the parable as source of learning | Currently beyond the scope of AI |

sack and replaced by a bot; nor of coaches working closely with bots in an integrated practice. This is likely to change soon, with increased investment and greater coach familiarity with using new technologies, such as Zoom or Teams. Virtual reality coaching, until recently the province of a few tech-savvy enthusiasts is likely to become a client-led requirement. Table 9.2 offers a snapshot comparison of human coaches and mentors with AI, from a general perspective.

So, are coaches under threat from technology? A best guess is that, while simplistic coaching is likely to be under threat, truly developmental coaching can be greatly enhanced by partnerships between coaches and AI. Indeed, we can go further and say that it is in the coaching profession's best interests actively to encourage such integration.

Table 9.3 below provides what we hope are practical descriptions of the strengths of human and AI coaching, both separately and combined. The first table looks at the coach/AI issue from the perspective of the four modes of learning: information, knowledge, skills, and wisdom. The second explores the same issue from the perspective of what coaches do and how they do it.

The first part of the table below is based on coaching at its simplest – an expanded view of the GROW model. The more complex the relationship and the nature of the change intended, the less effective an AI will be. However, the AI can continue to add value in partnership with a coach at each level of complexity.

The rest of the table looks at the required skills and qualities of coach working alone and with AI.

## The coach–AI partnership

If coaches are to benefit from the rise of artificial intelligence, then they will need to embrace the new technology and integrate it with their practice. But what does that mean?

Table 9.3 Tasks, skills, and qualities of a coach

| Tasks | Coach | AI | Coach & AI together |
|---|---|---|---|
| Establish purpose and goals | Effective coaches work with context and values before agreeing goals | Focus on the goal and routes to achieving it. Unable to work easily with evolving goals | Deeper exploration of context and purpose. Able to look beyond initial goals |
| Building client self-awareness | Uses diagnostics alongside intuition to guide the client towards self-insight. Builds on insights to shape new horizons | Uses standard tools and questions to help the client become more self-aware. Stops at the point of potential insight. Unable to check how deep the insight has been. | Identify new avenues to explore. When bot brings the client to an insight, it creates the platform for the client to explore it more deeply with the coach. |
| Decision-making & critical thinking | More creative, but more susceptible to failures of reasoning and decision-making traps | Follows logic and decision-making processes more closely. Unable to include tacit knowledge or "unknown knowns." | Better at finding solutions that are both/ and rather than either/or |
| Generating options | Intuitive understanding of client of possibilities in light of cultural variables and values; and of what does and doesn't work | Offers both "iner thinking" (obvious) options and "way out" options | Coach can moderate and add to AI suggestions to create a wider palette of options. Capacity to be genuinely innovative. |
| Motivating | The Pygmalion Effect – motivating power of one person's belief in what another can achieve | Client has to generate own motivation | Combining intrinsic and extrinsic motivation |
| Follow-up | Coach acts as a conscience to the client. Difficult to keep reminding the client without appearing to nag and taking responsibility from the client to the coach. | More rigorous at reminding | Easier to monitor progress and give continued support without seeming intrusive |

| Skills | Coach | AI | Coach & AI together |
|---|---|---|---|
| Listening | Has wider store of mental associations to aid sense-making. May filter out important data. | Has large, but narrow store of associated algorithms and data to draw upon. May pay too much attention to irrelevant data. | Shifts focus more towards how the client makes sense of their issue |
| Questioning | Intuitive recognition of the "right" question. Intuitive understanding of when *not* to ask a question. | Able to draw upon a large database of questions from previous conversations. Difficulty in deviating from the "script." | Coach spends less time worrying about the next question, knowing that, if they don't have one, they can fall back on the AI |
| Rapport building | Building deep trust enables the client to delve further into issues and face their fears | AI can seem less judgemental, but can only build "transactional trust" | A big unknown! However, rapport with a coach may be undermined if the client suspects "collusion" between coach and AI. Transparency is vital. |
| Giving feedback | Coach gives feedback both on aspects previously agreed and on other things they notice | AI gives feedback only on what it is programmed to do. Can make comparisons with other people in its database, to provide a sense of proportion. (E.g. 83% of people fall into this category …) | Automating multirater feedback and analysis can put ownership of the process firmly in the client's hands and suggest topics to discuss in coaching |
| Use of self | In Gestalt mode, the coach is able to use their own feelings and associations to generate new avenues of enquiry | AI lacks a sense of self and can only draw upon observation or comparison with other similar conversations | Coach can use AI's observations to check their intuitions. (E.g. when the coach a sense of discomfort, does the AI observe relevant changes in the client's tone or micro-expressions?) |
| Being a role model | More an aspect of being a mentor than a coach | N?A | N/A |

*(Continued)*

Table 9.3 Continued

| Qualities | Coach | AI | Coach and AI together |
|---|---|---|---|
| Credibility | Combination of who the coach is and the experience they bring – leads the client to place more weight on their guidance | The Wikipedia effect – generally helpful but not to be trusted! | Likely to increase client confidence – but needs research to verify |
| Compassion | Feeling for the client and understanding their perspective | Rudimentary understanding of the emotions people generally in this situation may feel | May help the coach avoid over-sympathising and losing their objectivity |
| Curiosity | The instinctive desire to learn more and to follow a conversational path wherever it may lead | Algorithms require AI to follow the mist logical path | May make explorations more thorough. High potential to ensure that the conversation comes back to "parked" issues that might otherwise be forgotten. |
| Courage | The instinct to do or say what feels right | N/A | AI could potentially act as the coach's own conscience, prompting them to reflect on their own motivations both during coaching sessions or in reflection afterwards |

The coach–AI partnership fulfils several functions:

- It provides real-time information about what is going on in the conversation, in the client and in the coach
- It allows instant access to other sources of relevant and potentially relevant information
- The AI can suggest questions and lines of enquiry (meaning that you as coach have to spend less time thinking about what you are going to ask next)
- You can check your intuitions for confirming or disconfirming evidence
- It creates opportunities for in-depth review of each coaching session, from the perspective of alternative approaches (for example, "You chose not to follow this clue, but how might the conversation have gone, if you did?") or better wording of questions. Of course, this is a learning process for both the coach and the AI.

## Making the coach–AI partnership work

The key to successful partnerships will lie in questions such as the following:

- What am I not noticing? For example:
    - The client avoids questions that address a particular area
    - The micropauses, skin temperature changes, posture shifts, and so on that indicate discomfort or other emotions: for example, an AI can learn to recognise the physical patterns that indicate when a client is lying to themselves
    - How I am reacting to the client
- What patterns are emerging? For example:
    - Linguistic: for example, repeated words or phrase that appear to have a particular meaning or emotive undertone
    - Narrative: for example, a tendency to self-sabotage or a set of limiting assumptions in the client about themselves or others
    - Conversational: for example, is it going round in large circles? (The structure of conversation is usually too complex for humans to follow in the moment.) What can I as a coach learn from the patterns of this conversation that will improve my practice?
- What other bodies of knowledge might be relevant? For example:
    - If I am feeling manipulated by the client, what are the signs of sociopathy that I might look out for? (And the AI can, of course, compare the conversation with those signs.)
    - What do we know generally about people in the client's situation?
    - What strategic planning models might be helpful here?
    - What's too complex for me to analyse? For example, where the client is faced with multiple, complicated choices, you will be able to ask the AI to turn these into a decision-tree, which you and the client can work through together.

- How can I test my intuition? The AI can either provide data relevant to the client in front of you, or a general overview of similar situations.

### The dangers of an AI-coach partnership

Three main dangers stand out, though there may be many more that emerge with practice.

The first is that coach and AI may become such a strong partnership that the client is left out and feels both under scrutiny and manipulated. It will be essential, therefore, to develop a *three-way* partnership in which the client is also able to access the AI. The process of pausing and reviewing during coaching conversations will become even more important than at present, as both coach and client take the opportunity to review not just the conversation as they have experienced it, but also to request observations from the AI. As yet, we have no protocols for this situation, but there will need to be an understanding of whether it is most beneficial to the client to have constant data feed from the AI, or periodic-pause interactions with the AI, or a mixture of the two.

Another related danger is that the coach (or the client, if they are also AI-enabled) becomes distracted by the flow of information that the quality of their listening and attentiveness suffers.

Thirdly, humans instinctively respond to complexity-in-the-moment by focusing on process. The journey towards coach maturity is one that starts with models and processes and gradually lets go of them as we become more confident in letting the client and the conversation follow their own path. If we become overwhelmed with information, we may revert to mechanistic, plodding conversations. If that happens, it is we as coaches, who have become the robots!

### Summary

There is a delicious irony in how coaches sometimes cling to the past when their espoused role is to support clients in creating the future. We help clients identify what they need to let go of and what they can embrace going forward. Can we be effective role models for doing the same in our own practices? To do so will require wholesale jettisoning of limited cultural assumptions and developed world privilege; along with a willingness to use technology in support of great causes, such as decolonisation, democratisation, social enrichment, and climate change.

### Notes

1  A good insight into this comes from an articles by Saul Gellerman: Why good managers make bad ethical choices, *Harvard Business Review*, July–August 1986 pp 85–90.
2  Wouldn't it be ironic to be unethical about an ethical framework!
3  ...but I'm always open to correction!

# Just enough about me ...

When I conceived the idea for this book, I was determined that it would *not* be an autobiography. It's not that I am a particularly private person – far from it – but I have a deep aversion to self-promotion and self-aggrandisement. It's the ideas that are important, not the person behind them.

I'm grateful to the colleagues around the world, who read the draft manuscript and commented. One of their comments was that I had taken myself too much out of the text, to the extent that there was insufficient narrative about the person. So, here's a brief summary that I hope will suffice.

I was born in 1947. My mother was a shop assistant and my father a clerk. He had been repatriated from Japan at the end of the Great War – one of a handful of starved and emaciated survivors out of some 2000 prisoners working as slaves on the docks at Hokkaido. I never really got to know this traumatised man, but I have no bad memories of him. Most of those I do have revolve around his beloved allotment, a rented patch of land where we grew vegetables and fruit. He died of cancer when I was 22.

My mother and one of her sisters worked in the Women's Auxiliary Air Force during the War. Still alive and alert at 101 this year (though she did get a bit confused and think she must be 200) she kept the family – me and a younger sister – together, encouraging our independence and sense of adventure.

My secondary school was a strange mixture of pupils in a strange time bubble. The students were 50/50 Christian and Jewish (Finchley was one of the places with a big Jewish population). The school had once been a private institution (for some reason we call these "public schools" in England) and as a state school was unwilling to let go of the rites and rituals of its past. My father had by then been entrapped by a fringe sect, the Jehovah's Witnesses, so I ended up in a small group of pupils, who attended neither the Jewish nor the Christian morning assemblies. Religious knowledge was not on the formal curriculum, but I was encouraged to take the examinations on my own, passing them without great effort. A benefit of this was that I compared multiple religions and rapidly concluded that they were all both fascinating – and nonsense. I had my first experience of expert mentoring during those school years and I retain a strong sense of gratitude for it.

I studied English Language and Literature at the University of London at a college that had just opened to men, so the ratio of women to men was six to one. It was a remarkable education in many ways! I thought I would become an academic and gained a place at the University of Southern California to study the origins of journalism. Lack of access to grants forced a rethink and I joined the UK Civil Service for a year until I found a role as a science journalist. From there I joined the magazine *New Scientist,* where my role was to make advances in one area of technology meaningful to engineers and others working in different areas. I learnt the skill of extracting the essence of a topic and recasting it to become more widely accessible.

Ten years as journalist, then editor, of *International Management,* travelling the world reporting on good practice and new ideas embedded me firmly into the sphere of management and leadership. My role remained one of making knowledge accessible. My first book was published during this period.

By my mid-thirties, I was ready to become an entrepreneur. With a colleague, I established a communications boutique called *Item.* We initiated a lot of original research into employee communication. In the late 1990s, a collapse of the sector caused most of our competitors to fold. We hung on and eventually I was able to sell the company to the staff. As a recognition for their efforts in keeping the business alive, the price was based on what they could raise, rather than the higher valuation of what the company was worth.

In parallel, I had established a consultancy built around freelance management journalism and research, plus some management consultancy and training based on concepts I had pioneered, such as 360 feedback. With the publication of *Everyone needs a mentor* in 1985, Clutterbuck Associates' emphasis shifted swiftly into mentoring and then coaching. I sold this company to a US consultancy in 2009.

Along the line, I picked up various honorary fellowships and doctorates and a traditional doctorate by research. When I supervise doctoral students now, I guide them towards limiting the scope of their research. Pity I didn't get that advice myself![1] I designed a programme of research that involved both the development and validation of measures for mentoring relationships *and* their application to mentoring pairs over time. It was a highly complicated and demanding exercise that took far too long – but which clearly established developmental mentoring as distinct from the mixture of mentoring and sponsorship dominating US literature.

In the early 1990s, I was fortunate to meet the late David Megginson at a mentoring conference. A lifelong friendship bloomed rapidly. Together, we formed the European Mentoring and Coaching Council and co-wrote or co-edited multiple books. It is a rare privilege to find such a perfect collaborator and foil – I am very grateful to have done so.

I've left my immediate family till last, because they are so important to me. My wife Polly is the sensible, detailed half of our more than five-decade partnership. My four sons are all people who I would choose as friends. The three eldest have accompanied me on numerous expeditions to the world's highest mountain ranges and they have given me six grandchildren, all of whom have learned how to poke fun at grandad. My youngest son, Jonathan, has Down's Syndrome and autism. He has been an immense source of learning for me and a continuing joy. The patience I have learned with him has made me a better person than I might have been.

Why, at 75, am I still writing, researching, and teaching? Because I have the energy and because it gives me energy. My life story is not a stand-alone tale – it is a footnote in the story of all those wonderful people I have been lucky enough to interact. I thank them all.

## Note

1  If I am brutally honest with myself, I let my ego tell me that, as a leader in the field, I had to do a seminal study!

# Conclusion

The late Maurice Chevalier and Hermione Gingold captured it well in their song *I Remember It Well*. The narratives we tell to and about ourselves are part reality, part fiction. Every time we recall a part of the story, our inventive brain edits it, adding and subtracting detail in unpredictable ways.

Writing a historical review from a personal perspective has been a challenge! How do I verify my own recollections? How do I ensure credit due to all the other people I have been lucky enough to interact with, or whose ideas inspired my own? Especially when I have outlived so many of them!

Google Scholar has been a great help in getting date order right. I'm grateful, too, to all my colleagues around the world, who have critiqued the manuscript and posed the difficult questions that needed to be asked.

The idea of writing an autobiography appalled me. I can't imagine why anyone would want to engage in such an egotistical pursuit unless they had a deep-seated need for self-justification. But the learning and self-discovery I have gained from this retrospective evaluation has been immense and humbling. If my learning journey over more than four decades is helpful to other coaches, mentors, and leaders in thinking about their open learning journeys, then it has been a worthwhile endeavour. And, if nobody cares, then at least I had fun putting all the pieces together!

David Clutterbuck

# Appendices

## Appendix 1: David's books, authored, co-authored, and co-edited

- *How to be a good corporate citizen*, (1981) McGraw-Hill, Maidenhead
- *The Remaking of Work*, (1981) with Roy Hill, Grant McIntyre, London
- *The Winning Streak*, (1983) with Walter Goldsmith, Weidenfeld/Penguin
- *The Winning Streak Workout Book* (1983) with Walter Goldsmith, Weidenfeld, London
- *The Winning Streak Check Book*, (1983) with Walter Goldsmith, Penguin, London
- *New Patterns of Work* (1985) Gower, Aldershot
- *Everyone needs a mentor* (1985, 1991, 2001, 2004, 2014) CIPD Wimbledon
- *Clore: The Man and his Millions* (1986) with Marion Devine, Weidenfeld, London
- *Businesswoman* (1987) with Marion Devine, Macmillan, London
- *The Marketing Edge*, with Tony McBurnie, Weidenfeld, London
- *Management Buyouts*, with Marion Devine, Hutchinson, London
- *Turnaround* (1988) with Rebecca Nelson, Mercury, London
- *The Decline & Rise of British Industry* (1988) with Stuart Crainer, Weidenfeld, London
- *Just-in-time: A global status report* (1989) with Chris Voss, IFS, London
- *Information 2000* (1990) Pitman, London
- *The Makers of Management* (1990) with Stuart Crainer, Macmillan
- *The Phoenix Factor: a study of corporate decline* (1990), with Sue Kernaghan, Weidenfeld, London
- *Making Customers Count* (1991) with Sue Kernaghan, Mercury, London
- *Working with the Community* (1991) with Deborah Snow, Weidenfeld, London
- *Going private* (1991) with Susan Kernaghan and Deborah Snow, Mercury, London
- *Actions speak louder* (1992) with Dez Dearlove and Deborah Snow, Kogan Page, London
- *Inspired Customer Service* (1993) with Graham Clark and Colin Armistead, Kogan Page, London

- *The independent board director* (1993) with Peter Waine, McGraw-Hill, Maidenhead
- *Raising the profile: marketing the HR function* (1993) with Desmond Dearlove, CIPD, Wimbledon
- *The power of empowerment* (1994) Kogan Page, London
- *Mentoring in Action* (1995) with David Megginson, Kogan Page, London
- *Consenting Adults: Making the most of mentoring*, Channel Four Publications, London,
- *The charity as a business* (1986) with Dez Dearlove, Directory of Social Change, London
- *Strategic management of internal communications*, (1996) with Linda Gatley, Business Intelligence, London
- *The Winning Streak, Mark II* (1997) with Walter Goldsmith, Orion, London
- *The Interim Manager* (1998) with Dez Dearlove, Pitman
- *Learning Alliances* (1998) CIPD, Wimbledon
- *Mentoring Diagnostic Kit* (1998) Clutterbuck Associates, Burnham, Bucks
- *Doing it different* (1999) Orion, London
- *Mentoring Executives and Directors* (1999) with David Megginson, Blackwell, Oxford
- *Making 360 degree appraisal work for you* (2000) with Bernard Wynne, Peter Honey Publications
- *Transforming Internal Communication* (2001) with Sue Kernaghan, Business Intelligence, London
- *Mentoring and Diversity: An international perspective* (2002) with Belle Rose Ragins, Butterworth/Heinemann, Oxford
- *Implementing mentoring schemes* (2002) with Nadine Klasen, Butterworth/ Heinemann, Oxford
- *Talking Business* (2002) with Sheila Hirst, Butterworth/Heinemann
- *The Situational Mentor* (2003) with Gill Lane, Gower, Aldershot
- *Managing Work-Life Balance* (2003) CIPD, Wimbledon
- *Techniques for Coaching and Mentoring* (20004) with David Megginson, Butterworth, Oxford
- *Making Coaching Work: Creating a coaching culture* (2005) with David Megginson, CIPD, Wimbledon
- *Mentoring in Action 2* (2005) with David Megginson, Bob Garvey, Paul Stokes and Ruth Garrett-Harris, Kogan Page, London
- *Coaching the Team at Work* (2007) Nicholas Brealey, London
- Thesis: A longitudinal study of the effectiveness of developmental mentoring, King's College London
- *Further Techniques for Coaching and Mentoring* (2009) with David Megginson
- *Complete Handbook of Coaching* (2010) Ed. With Elaine Cox and Tatiana Bachkirova), Sage, London
- *Virtual Coach, Virtual Mentor* (2010) with Zulfi Hussain, IAP Publishing, Charlotte, N

- *Developing Successful Diversity Mentoring Programmes* (2012) with Kirsten M. Poulsen and France Kochan, McGraw-Hill, Maidenhead
- *Coaching and Mentoring Supervision: Theory and Practice* (2012) Ed. With Tatiana Bachkirova & Peter Jackson) McGraw-Hill, Maidenhead
- *Writing your first book* (2012) David Clutterbuck Partnership, Maidenhead
- *The Talent Wave* (2012) Kogan Page, London
- *Beyond Goals: Effective Strategies for Coaching and Mentoring* (2013) with David Megginson and Susan David, Gower
- *Making the most of developmental mentoring* (2013) Coaching and Mentoring International, Maidenhead
- *Powerful questions for coaches and mentors* (2013) Coaching and Mentoring International, Maidenhead
- *The Leader's Guide to Being Coached* (2014) Coaching and Mentoring International, Maidenhead
- *Maintaining momentum of mentoring programmes* (e-book, 2014) Coaching and Mentoring International, Maidenhead
- *Techniques for Coaching and Mentoring vol 3* (2016) with David Megginson and Natalie Lancer, Routledge, Abingdon, Oxford
- *Coaching Supervision: A practical Guide for Supervisees* (2016) with Carol Whitaker and Michelle Lucas, Routledge, Oxford
- *Building and sustaining the coaching culture* (2016) with David Megginson and Agnieszka Bajer, CIPD, Wimbledon
- *Mentoring New Parents at Work* (2016) with Nicki Seignot, Routledge, Oxford
- *The Sage Handbook of Mentoring* (2016) with Frances Kochan, Laura Lunsford, Nora Dominguez, and Julie Haddock-Millar, Sage, London
- *Coaching & Mentoring in Asia-Pacific* (2017), with Anna Blackman and Derrick Kon
- *Cool Coaching and Mentoring for Kids* (2017) Coaching and Mentoring International, Maidenhead
- *Powerful questions for team coaches* (2017) Coaching and Mentoring International, Maidenhead
- *Practitioner's Handbook of Team Coaching* (2019) with Judie Gannon, Sandra Hayes, Ioanna Iordanou, Krister Lowe, and Doug McKie, Routledge, London
- *Coaching the Team at Work 2* (2020) Nicholas Brealey, London
- *How to be a great coachee,* (2020) Coaching and Mentoring International, Maidenhead
- *The team coaching casebook* (2022) with Tammy Turner and Colm Murphy, Open University Press, London

**Books in progress**

- *Handbook of Ethics in Coaching* (2022) Ed with Wendy-Ann Smith, Jonathan Passmore, Eve Turner and Yi-Ling Lai

- *The complete guide to team coaching: tools and techniques* (2023) with Colm Murphy and Dumisani Magadlela, Routledge, Oxford
- *The Coach's Guide to Reflective Practice* (2023) with Eve Turner, Routledge, Oxford
- *Coaching in a politicised environment* (2023) with Lise Lewis, Tim Bright, and Riddhika Khoosal), Routledge, Oxford

Plus books on

- Coach maturity (the becoming of a coach)
- Reciprocal mentoring
- Mentoring dads
- Neurodiversity in coaching

### Children's books

- *The Tales of Gribble the Goblin* (1983) Hodder & Stoughton, London
- *Pegleg the Pirate* (2014) David Clutterbuck Partnership, Maidenhead
- *My grandad's a dragon* (2015) David Clutterbuck Partnership, Maidenhead

## Appendix 2: The tradition of April Fools' blogs

The tradition of April Fool is hundreds of years old. For me, it's a valuable reminder of how susceptible even the wisest and most intelligence are to fake news. For some years now, I have every year produced a blog on an aspect of coaching. The aim is to poke fun at some aspect of the coaching profession, where there is hubris, pomposity, or gullibility (or all three). The items below are all from blogs in recent years. If you think "I'd never be caught by that!", ask yourself, what parts of what is written did you instinctively agree with? And what does that tell you about your own susceptibility to false information generally?

### A warm reception for hot stone coaching

Coaching works best when the client is relaxed and attentive to both the conversation and to themselves. Hot stone coaching has been proposed as a means of heightening the client's attention to their inner world and their general mindfulness. Unlike normal coaching, where the client and coach sit opposite to each other, in hot stone coaching the coach sits to the side of the client, while the client lies face down, or behind their head, if the client is lying face up, so there is no eye contact. This separation is claimed to enhance the purity of the coaching conversation and the feeling of trust between coach and client. The client may be fully clothed or with the top half of their body exposed.

Practitioners of hot stone coaching insist that the stones are an important part of the process. A typical set of stones will range from relatively large to quite small. Usually they are highly polished and contain fossils – it is claimed that the incorporation of former living creatures enhances the "connection" between coach and client, although no mechanism has been suggested as to how this might work. Stones are placed at strategic places, broadly equivalent to acupuncture points. The size of stone selected is in accordance with the importance of the organ it covers. Two stones of different *chakras* are usually used on the forehead, one to denote intellect, the other emotion. These again may vary in size, with the smallest stones commonly used for people from purchasing departments, bank managers, and Uber drivers.

Although this approach is relatively new, some empirical evidence has been gathered as to its efficacy. One case study has found that hot stone coaching has a statistically significant impact in curing stupidity. It should be noted that the stones in this case were heated to more than 90 degrees centigrade. Another study, in which the clients were all politicians, used a control group (eight clients, eight controls) and found no significant differences between the two groups. The researchers in this study suggest that dermatological density may have had a mediating effect here.

Enthusiasts for hot stone coaching maintain that there are eight key guiding principles to effective, client-centred practice. These are:

- Timelessness – it is important that the client feels you have all the time in the world for them and that they are released from the pressures of time
- Inquisitiveness – coach and client allow the conversation to find its own path, in the knowledge that this path will lead them back to the goal in its own time and manner
- Happiness – the coach promotes spiritual healing in the client through their own "inner smiles." In Thailand, from where hot stone coaching appears to derive, the language recognises 13 different types of smile.
- Stillness – the absence of movement promotes mental and physical relaxation
- Love – the coach communicates in both verbal and non-verbal ways the fact that they care about the client and their aspirations
- Life flow – the sense of communion between mind and body
- Unconditional positive regard – the essential Rogerian position
- Belief – in the process and in the client's ability to find their own way, if they can relax sufficiently

No doubt at some point someone will come up with a suitable acronym for these qualities.[1]

1 April 2017

### Be the first coach in space

Elon Musk put a car into space. We will put a coach into orbit!

The EMCC is proud to announce, in association with Richard Branson's Virgin Galactic, a competition to become **the first coach in space**. One lucky coach will have the opportunity to conduct a coaching session during a 45-minute flight orbiting the Earth in early 2021.

Richard Branson attributes much of his success to the great coaches and mentors in his life. This competition will literally take coaching to giddy new heights.

To be eligible for this competition, coaches must be in good general health, with no conditions that might be affected by high gravity or weightlessness, have coached for at least five years, and be formally nominated by five clients and their supervisor. Preference will be given to holders of EMCC EIA certification at Practitioner level or above; or an equivalent qualification from ICF or AC. Ten coaches will be selected for brief astronaut training – one will go through to the actual flight.

If you would like to take this opportunity to boost your coaching career, application forms are available through the address below. In addition to your coaching history and references, you will be asked to provide a short essay of between 1000 and 2000 words on the following topic: *How do you help your clients maintain a balance between keeping their feet on the ground and taking a strategic high-altitude perspective looking down on themselves, their work and their career?* Marks will be awarded for originality of concept, relationship to theory, and gravity of presentation.

Wherever you are in your career as a coach, you will never get an opportunity to aim higher than this! Plan to see your coaching practice lift off like a rocket next year!

For more information and application forms, contact headabovetheclouds @emccouncil.org

1 April 2020

### *Rethinking psychopathy in coaching?*

The past year has seen an unprecedented rise in voices questioning accepted wisdom about coaching. Amongst the most controversial is the announcement, in early March this year, of the formation of the *International Alliance of Sociopathic Coaches*, which claims over 300 members in North America, Europe, and Asia-Pacific. The official founding statement of this body explains that "The majority of leaders in business and politics are high on the narcissistic and sociopathic spectra. Yet coaches are typically trained to 'cure' these leaders. The IASC exists to give legitimacy to the traits that make these leaders successful and to match them with coaches, who understand and empathise with the sociopathic personality."

Membership of the IASC is limited to coaches and leaders, who score at least 16 on the 26 item Levenson Psychopathy Scale. A pilot Code of Conduct is being trialled under the sponsorship of the Trump Foundation for Truth and Reconciliation. For more details see the website iasc.com

1 April 2021

*Are coaches more gullible than most?*

A recent study suggests they might be. A paper in the Journal of Divergent Thinking Studies[2] reports on a research project that gathered survey responses from nearly 6000 people selected using Linked In profiles. The selection criteria were random except for job role and location. Twelve job roles were selected and these included engineer, other scientist, marketing and sales, human resources … and coach. Location was confined to the US and North America, to reduce the influence of cultural factors. The respondents all completed online the Conway Gullibility survey, a 24-item diagnostic that measures the level of critical ability people apply when faced with new information.

The most gullible occupations turn out – on the basis of this study – to be the creative arts and marketing and sales. This is in line with other recent research that suggest being more imaginative leads us to more easily create narratives that incorporate new information into our existing narratives. Then came Human Resources and third – coaches. The authors of the paper say that they are not able to distinguish between cause and effect (does level of gullibility influence people's choice of career, or does the job role influence how gullible they are?). They do not offer explanations for their findings, but suggest further research is needed.

If this study (which as the first of its kind has not been replicated) holds true, it raises some interesting questions for coaches and the coaching profession generally. The authors pose five questions they suggest everyone in a professional role should ask themselves frequently:

- What is the evidence for an approach or method I have incorporated into my professional practice?
- How can I separate out what I want to believe from what is objectively true?
- How can I expose my thinking to perspectives that challenge deeply held assumptions?
- When presented with new information, how can I be sure to question it rigorously?
- How gullible am I being right now?

1 April 2022

## Appendix 3: How fair is the psychological contract between you and your organisation?[3]

This questionnaire is designed to measure how you view three critical dimensions of how you relate to the organisation. These are:

1. The *worth* exchange – how fair you feel the exchange is between how the organisation rewards and invests in you, and what you contribute to the organisation
2. The *respect* exchange – the extent, to which you feel recognised and respected by the organisation, and to which you feel proud to be part of it

3.  The *belief* exchange – the extent, to which you feel you and the organisation share the same values

Please tick or circle one answer in each question and add up your scores at the end.

*The Worth Dimension*

- I believe I am
  - Well-paid for what I do
  - Fairly paid for what I do
  - Underpaid for what I do
- I believe that I have
  - Above average opportunities for developing my skills
  - Average opportunities for developing my skills
  - Below average opportunities for developing my skills
  - I believe that this organisation
  - Invests substantially in me
  - Invests somewhat in me
  - Invests little in me
- I believe that my market value (what I am worth on the open job market)
  - Increases every year I stay here
  - Remains constant every year I stay here
  - Reduces every year I stay here
- I feel the organisation has given me
  - A high level of security in my retirement
  - A reasonable level of security in my retirement
  - A poor level of security in my retirement
- I believe that
  - I contribute highly to the performance of the organisation
  - I contribute fairly to the performance of the organisation
  - I don't contribute a lot to the performance of the organisation
- I believe that the organisation
  - Rewards me very well for what I do
  - Rewards me reasonably well for what I do
  - Rewards me poorly for what I do
- I believe that
  - I have a lot to learn by staying with this organisation
  - A reasonable amount to learn by staying with this organisation
  - Not much to learn by staying with this organisation

*The Respect Dimension*

- I feel that I receive
  - High recognition for my efforts
  - Reasonable recognition for my efforts
  - Poor recognition for my efforts

- I feel that my opinions are
  - Are always listened to and valued
  - Are sometimes listened to and valued
  - Are rarely listened to and valued
- I feel I have
  - Immense pride in working for this organisation
  - Some pride in working for this organisation
  - Little or no pride in working for this organisation
- I believe that I am treated
  - With a great deal of respect by my seniors at work
  - With reasonable respect by my seniors at work
  - With little respect by my seniors at work
- I believe that I am treated
  - With a great deal of respect by my peers at work
  - With reasonable respect by my peers at work
  - With little respect by my peers at work
- I feel I am
  - Always treated as an individual
  - Usually treated as an individual
  - Rarely treated as an individual
- I feel
  - A high level of loyalty towards the company
  - Some loyalty towards the company
  - Very little loyalty towards the company
- I look forward to coming to work
  - All or most of the time
  - Some of the time
  - Rarely or never

*The Shared-Values Dimension*

- I believe that this organisation
  - Has very clear values
  - Has fairly clear values
  - Has very little clarity of values
- I believe that
  - Leaders in this organisation are good role models for the business values
  - Leaders in this organisation are reasonably good role models for the business values
  - Leaders in this organisation are poor role models for the business values
- I believe that leaders in this company
  - Care about people a great deal
  - Care about people sometimes
  - Don't care about people

- I feel that I and the company have
  - Very similar perceptions about what's important to employees
  - Reasonably similar perceptions about what's important to employees
  - Very different perceptions about what's important to employees
- I feel that I and the company have
  - Very similar perceptions about what's important in how we treat customers
  - Reasonably similar perceptions about what's important in how we treat customers
  - Very different perceptions about what's important in how we treat customers
- I feel that I and the company have
  - Very similar perceptions about what's important on environmental issues
  - Reasonably similar perceptions about what's important on environmental issues
  - Very different perceptions about what's important on environmental issues
- I feel I could
  - Always discuss ethical concerns openly with colleagues and superiors
  - Generally discuss ethical concerns openly with colleagues and superiors
  - Rarely or never discuss ethical concerns openly with colleagues and superiors
- I believe that
  - People here will always try to do the right thing, even when there are economic pressures to compromise on principles
  - People here will sometimes try to do the right thing, even when there are economic pressures to compromise on principles
  - People here tend to let economic pressures compromise their principles

|  | Number of a scores | Number of b scores | Number of c scores |
|---|---|---|---|
| **Worth** |  |  |  |
| **Respect** |  |  |  |
| **Beliefs** |  |  |  |

### Interpreting the scores

The fewer 'a' responses in any area, the weaker the *psychological contract* (how fair you perceive the exchange between you and the organisation) to be. If any of the three dimensions is weak, then the psychological contract as a whole is at risk. If all three are weak, then employee motivation and job commitment are likely to be low, employees are more open to moving elsewhere, and change resistance will be relatively high.

The three dimensions can also be used to compare with other stakeholders, such as customers, or shareholders.

## Appendix 4: The Coaching Culture Questionnaire[4]

*The coaching culture questionnaire*

| A Nascent | B Tactical | C Strategic | D Embedded |
|---|---|---|---|
| 11A Coaching happens without reference to strategy and process | 11B Coaching is referred to in strategy documents | 11C Managers are measured on the effects of their coaching | 11D Key organisation performance measures include coaching outputs |
| 12A Coaching is used to correct poor performers | 12B Coaching is used to contribute to performance of all | 12C Coaching is used as the main driver of performance | 12D Coaching is the way of performance managing individuals, teams, and the organisation |
| 13A A coach is seen as "nice to have" | 13B Coaching is compatible with core business drivers | 13C Core business driver articulated and coaching is the means of delivering it | 13D The more urgent/ important/ mission-critical a project, the more coaching is used |
| 14A Coaching is a specialist activity separate from normal managing | 14B Coaching is used by bosses one-on-one to improve performance | 14C Coaching is widely used as a way of working in teams and projects | 14D Coaching is used in all settings from shop floor to boardroom |
| 21A People are coached only if their boss is keen on it | 21B Coachees are coached as part of performance management processes | 21C From induction to retirement people expect to be coached | 21D Staff seek coaching internally and from customers/ suppliers/ outside benchmarks |
| 22A Staff accept it if their bosses can't or won't coach | 22B Staff frequently ask for coaching | 22C The right to be coached is accepted throughout the organisation | 22D Coachees will coach their coaches in coaching if they need it |
| 23A Learning to be coached comes from being lucky to have a coaching boss | 23B Training of coachees has as much attention as coach training | 23C The coachees' drive to learn and perform stimulates coaching | 23D Coaching seen as one of many alliances to be managed by coachees |

*(Continued)*

(*Continued*)

| *The coaching culture questionnaire* | | | |
|---|---|---|---|
| *A Nascent* | *B Tactical* | *C Strategic* | *D Embedded* |
| 24A External coaches used as the stage before outplacement | 24B External coaches widely available to support a range of development issues | 24C External coaches support supervision/ development of senior managers as coaches | 24D External coaches work with internal leaders to steer coachee-led development agenda |
| 31A Managers do a range of coach training or none at all | 31B Coach training is widely available | 31C Different coach training offerings are integrated | 31D Coach training pervades development opportunities and agenda |
| 32A Coaching is a private concern, not noticed or commented upon | 32B Coaches get feedback from staff on whether they coach | 32C Coaches get on-going feedback from coachees on how they coach | 32D All managers get 360 degree feedback on how they coach |
| 33A Once trained, coaches are left to their own devices | 33B Coaches get follow-up support from tutors after training | 33C Coaches get feedback between and after training workshops from peers, coaches, and tutors | 33D Coaches have on-going supervision of their practice from peers and tutors |
| 34A The organisation does not recognise or certificate coaches | 34B Coaches are recognised for their contribution to the performance of others | 34C Coaches have opportunities to deepen their learning through certification | 34D Accreditation widely used as part of CPD of coaches |
| 41A Knowledge is used as a source of power | 41B Knowledge sharing is common from experienced staff to new colleagues | 41C Knowledge sharing is used, recognised, and valued | 41D Knowledge sharing upward, downward, and between peers is a way of life |
| 42A Having a coach is seen as a fashion accessory | 42B Coaching helps to improve performance | 42C High performing team members coach one another | 42D Coaching is widely used to develop a high performing organisation |

(*Continued*)

(*Continued*)

*The coaching culture questionnaire*

| A Nascent | B Tactical | C Strategic | D Embedded |
|---|---|---|---|
| 43A Top team members who are coached don't talk about it | 43B Top team members talk about their coaching | 43C Top team talk about challenges in their coaching/ being coached | 43D Top team seek and use feedback on their coaching |
| 44A Coaches encourage coachees to take responsibility | 44B Coaching is led as an HR/ development project | 44C Line people take significant leadership of the move to coaching | 44D Dedicated line staff are committed to developing coaching |
| 51A Coaches focus on plugging skills gaps as seen by the coach | 51B Coaching begins from development goals of coachees | 51C Coaching is fuelled by learners' dreams or aspirations | 51D Coaching integrates individual dreams and shared organisational vision |
| 52A Coaching starts from individual needs | 52B Coaching involves shared learning and dialogue | 52C Networks of coaches develop together, using co-coaching | 52D Learning agendas and aspirations are widely shared throughout the organisation |
| 53A There are several different initiatives on coaching that are not connected | 53B Coaching initiatives have their own life and are linked to each other | 53C Coaching is used to develop an enquiring stance towards organisation agendas | 53D Autonomy and co-operation equally valued in widespread coaching between divisions/functions |
| 54A Coaches are often blunt and abrasive | 54B Coaches are often candid and forthright | 54C Mutual dialogue about tough issues – coach and coachee open to learning | 54D Organisation blind spots and weaknesses addressed in coaching relationships |
| 61A Coaching is an HR/ development initiative | 61B Senior group endorse the move to coaching | 61C Senior group demonstrate the use of coaching in achieving goals | 61D Senior group integrate development of organisation with use of coaching style |
| 62A Some individuals are enthusiastic about being a coach | 62B Line managers lead coaching initiatives in their own areas | 62C Line managers take responsibility for coaching throughout the organisation | 62D Coaching is used to manage projects and in a wide range of meetings |

(*Continued*)

(*Continued*)

| The coaching culture questionnaire | | | |
|---|---|---|---|
| *A Nascent* | *B Tactical* | *C Strategic* | *D Embedded* |
| 63A Coaches are conscious of the need for culture change | 63B Coaches use coaching to advocate culture change | 63C Coaches make the link between management style, coaching, and culture | 63D Coaches *live* the link between management style, coaching, and culture |
| 64A Coaches encourage coachees to take responsibility | 64B Coaches provide or create opportunities for coachees to perform | 64C Coachees and coaches actively manage mutual support and challenge between them | 64D Coachees take responsibility for their own performance accountably and in a no-blame way |

## Appendix 5: You and your six life-streams[5]

This self-completed questionnaire aims to help you gain a clearer picture of the balance you have between different aspects of your life and work, and of the balance you would like to have. The gaps between your "have" and "want" scores in each of the life-streams should help you plan and make changes in how you spend your time and energy.

You can add other elements, not in the list, which are important to you.

Use a scale of 1 (not like me) to 5 (very like me) for each item. Column 1 is for what you have/your current situation; Column 2 is for what you want/is important to you, either now or in the short/medium-term future. Column three is the difference between the scores in Columns 1 and 2, where 2 is higher than 1 (that is, you are not getting enough of what you want). Column 4 is for the scores (if any!) where you are getting more than you want.

When you have completed the questionnaire, look at the biggest gaps and consider:

- How important is it to me and those around me that I do something about this?
- Can I afford to put off doing something about this? (What are the likely consequences?)
- What specifically can I do and when?

## *You and your work (your current job)*

|  | 1 | 2 | 3 | 4 |
|---|---|---|---|---|
| Opportunities to be stretched and learn |  |  |  |  |
| High regular salary |  |  |  |  |
| Opportunities to earn substantial bonuses |  |  |  |  |
| Recognition from bosses |  |  |  |  |
| Recognition from peers |  |  |  |  |
| Independence – working on my own |  |  |  |  |
| Security |  |  |  |  |
| A great working relationship with my boss |  |  |  |  |
| Great working relationships with peers |  |  |  |  |
| Freedom to choose when and how I work |  |  |  |  |
| Feeling part of a team |  |  |  |  |
| Working with people |  |  |  |  |
| Good physical working conditions |  |  |  |  |
| Relatively free of stress |  |  |  |  |
| Being able to take initiative |  |  |  |  |
| Variety |  |  |  |  |
| Opportunities for travel |  |  |  |  |
| Opportunities for promotion |  |  |  |  |
| Other |  |  |  |  |

### *You and your career (your future work)*

| | 1 | 2 | 3 | 4 |
|---|---|---|---|---|
| Becoming financially independent | | | | |
| Achieving significantly greater responsibility | | | | |
| Becoming an expert in my field | | | | |
| Having a number of careers | | | | |
| Having a clear and predictable progression route | | | | |
| Have a flexible career plan that opens up lots of opportunities | | | | |
| Working in different cultures/regions | | | | |
| Being well-networked | | | | |
| Feeling in control of my career | | | | |
| Having a strong sense of purpose for my career | | | | |
| Doing work that aligns with my personal values | | | | |
| Other | | | | |

### *You and your close relationships*

| | 1 | 2 | 3 | 4 |
|---|---|---|---|---|
| The time you have to talk and relax with family | | | | |
| The time you have to talk and relax with friends | | | | |
| The energy you are able to put into your relationship with your family | | | | |
| The energy you are able to put into your relationship with friends | | | | |
| Having people around you who genuinely care about you | | | | |
| The quality of your relationships with family and friends | | | | |
| Having time for play | | | | |
| Other | | | | |

## You and your well-being

| | 1 | 2 | 3 | 4 |
|---|---|---|---|---|
| Keeping fit | | | | |
| Low levels of stress | | | | |
| Managing your weight | | | | |
| Your overall level of energy | | | | |
| Having a healthy diet | | | | |
| Your general sense of well-being | | | | |
| Other | | | | |

## Your intellectual growth

| | 1 | 2 | 3 | 4 |
|---|---|---|---|---|
| Pursuing a hobby or interest unconnected with your work | | | | |
| Achieving mental stimulation outside of work | | | | |
| Feeling that you are maturing as a person | | | | |
| Working towards a qualification | | | | |
| Having time to reflect upon experience | | | | |
| Reading widely | | | | |
| Other | | | | |

## You and your sense of wider belonging

| | 1 | 2 | 3 | 4 |
|---|---|---|---|---|
| Volunteering (putting something back) | | | | |
| Being part of a community outside of work (e.g., a church or mosque, an amateur drama group) | | | | |
| Contributing management skills (e.g., as a school governor, or charity trustee) | | | | |
| Asserting your cultural identity | | | | |
| Sense of spiritual well-being | | | | |
| Other | | | | |

## Notes

1  Hint: spell the first letter of each of the eight principles backwards…
2  Quick, PE and Doughty, CK (2022) *Journal of Divergent Thinking Studies* volume 3 pp 127–145.
3  ©This questionnaire is copyrighted by David Clutterbuck Partnership. Paper copies are free to use but a licence is required to upload the questionnaire electronically.
4  ©This questionnaire is copyrighted by David Clutterbuck Partnership. Paper copies are free to use but a licence is required to upload the questionnaire electronically.
5  ©This questionnaire is copyrighted by David Clutterbuck Partnership. Paper copies are free to use but a licence is required to upload the questionnaire electronically.

# Index